0060321

Into the Unknown

The Story of Exploration

Into the Unknown
The Story of Exploration

Published by
The National Geographic Society

Gilbert M. Grosvenor
*President and
Chairman of the Board*

Owen R. Anderson
Executive Vice President

Robert L. Breeden
*Senior Vice President,
Publications and
Educational Media*

Prepared by
National Geographic
Book Service

Charles O. Hyman
Director

Ross S. Bennett
Associate Director

Margaret Sedeen
Managing Editor

Susan C. Eckert
Director of Research

Staff for this book

Jonathan B. Tourtellot
Editor

Lynn Addison Yorke
Assistant Editor

Lise Swinson Sajewski
Chief Researcher

Mary B. Dickinson
Edward Lanouette
Elizabeth L. Newhouse
Robert M. Poole
David F. Robinson
Margaret Sedeen
Editor-Writers

Jennifer Gorham Ackerman
Paulette L. Claus
Susan C. Eckert
Lydia Howarth
Mary P. Luders
Melanie Patt-Corner
Jean Kaplan Teichroew
Penelope A. Timbers
Editorial Researchers

Kerry J. Kreiton
Brian L. McKean
Geography Interns

Leah Bendavid-Val
Illustrations Editor

David Ross
Illustrations Researcher

D. Samantha Johnston
Illustrations Assistant

Karen F. Edwards
Traffic Manager

Lydia Howarth
Jean Kaplan Teichroew
Map Coordinators

Maps by
John D. Garst, Jr.
Judith F. Bell
Donald L. Carrick
Marguerite S. Dunn
Hildegard B. Groves
Sharon J. Hongell
Gary M. Johnson
Joseph F. Ochlak
Susan Sanford
Nancy S. Stanford
Alexander M. Tait
Tibor G. Toth

R. Gary Colbert
Administrative Assistant

Teresita Cóquia Sison
Editorial Assistant

Teresa P. Barry
James B. Enzinna
Susan G. Zenel
Indexers

David M. Seager
Art Director

Charlotte Golin
Design Assistant

John T. Dunn
Technical Director

Richard S. Wain
Production Manager

Andrea Crosman
Production Coordinator

Leslie A. Adams
Production Assistant

David V. Evans
Engraving and Printing

Ratri Banerjee
Gretchen C. Bordelon
Cathryn P. Buchanan
Jean Shapiro Cantu
Michael Frost
Valerie Mattingley
Anne Meadows
Tom Melham
Jennifer Moseley
Suzanne Kane Poole
Shirley L. Scott
Anne E. Withers
Contributors

Color enhancement of
engravings and selected
photographs by
Michael A. Hampshire

Copyright © 1987, National
Geographic Society,
Washington, D. C. All rights
reserved. Reproduction of the
whole or any part of the contents
without written permission
is prohibited. Library of
Congress CIP data page 336.

First edition: 170,000 copies
336 pages, 266 illustrations,
plus 23 maps.

Page 2: A model of Henry Hudson's
17th-century ship, *Half Moon*, crests
the globe. The hourglass, compass,
calipers, and globe are all from
the 18th and early 19th centuries.
The map is a reproduction of an 18th-
century original. Photography by Kan.

Contents

Foreword

"Is there anything left on Earth to explore?" It's one of the questions people most often ask me. In the sense of finding unknown lands or oceans, as Columbus or Balboa did, the answer is no. But in another sense, the story of exploration has just begun.

Into the Unknown chronicles that story from the first explorers to push back the edge of the known world. Egyptians, Greeks, Arabs, and Chinese left records of their visits to new lands; sadly, others—Polynesians, native Americans, Malays—did not. The widest-ranging explorers were the Europeans and their progeny, who began to fan out over the globe in the 15th century. Great though these explorers were, theirs was often a parochial "unknown"; the lands they discovered had been long occupied by other people. Some explorers just followed local guides.

Today, explorers not only press on to realms beyond human habitation —ice caps, ocean deeps, and the reaches of space—they seek also to understand the world we have now encompassed, including its past and, in some ways, its future.

Sometimes present and past collide. In 1986 National Geographic writer Thomas Abercrombie, having used satellite images to pinpoint the source of the Indus River in a remote corner of China, obtained government permission to approach by land—only to find his expedition barred by a hazard of Marco Polo's era: warlords who did not acknowledge the authority of Beijing.

Explorers of both past and present ventured forth, ideally, to seek knowledge. James Cook perhaps epitomizes that "pure" explorer. But many went forth for other reasons— trade, fame, gold, God, conquest, safety from conquest. Missionaries went to convert; pioneers to colonize. Conquistadores set courses of greed, and left wakes of blood. Were they all explorers? This book counts them so if they fit its title, if they did go "into the unknown"—unknown as they saw it—however honorable or heinous we judge their motives.

They did share one thing—the discoverer's thrill. Can it still happen? In 1979 I joined a party that cut through the Arctic Ocean ice pack and dived beneath it. We were only a few miles from the North Pole, goal of famous explorers like Peary and Nansen, who struggled for months across jagged pressure ridges formed by this ice. From below, with the cold seeping into our insulated wet suits and the hollow whoosh of the breathing hoses in our ears, we could look up at those pressure ridges to see how the clear ice had been folded and twisted into fantastic structures—cathedrals of ice atop a darkling sea. "No one has ever seen this before," I thought, and in that moment knew, just a little, that thrill the great explorers knew.

What were these explorers like? After each chapter in *Into the Unknown* you will find a story about one or two of them. Some were famous,

Destination: the Pole. Struggling to heave a dogsled over cracked, jumbled Arctic Ocean ice, the Steger International Polar Expedition drives northward in 1986, much as Robert Peary's expedition did in 1909. Steger crossed nearly 500 miles of ice to reach the Pole, one of the few to succeed among the hopefuls who now make the attempt each year, by sled, ski, snowmobile, helicopter, even motorcycle.

some less so. To convey more vividly the nature of their adventures, our writers have sometimes used dramatic devices—an imaginary trial, some correspondence, a companion's viewpoint, a re-created scene. You'll find the stories enjoyable to read and, unlike many television docudramas, accurate; National Geographic's researchers have verified every event.

Some explorers you'll meet in this book—Peary, Beebe, Rock, Cousteau, Ballard, and others—received National Geographic support. That support continues today, for explorers you will read about tomorrow.

What's left to discover? In *Into the Unknown* you will learn how ocean floor exploration has revolutionized our ideas of geology and biology, how rain forest explorers find new medicines, and how space travel has changed our view of our own planet.

Today we explore our past, too. Archaeologist-divers in the Mediterranean seek traces of ancient civilizations—and perhaps of *their* explorers—in shipwrecks on the seafloor.

And we explore our future. Scientists in Antarctica have discovered remnants of forests that flourished about three million years ago; some of the wood can still burn. If Antarctica was that free of ice, that recently, what does today's global greenhouse effect portend for tomorrow?

The story is far from over.

Gilbert M. Grosvenor

7

Early Quests

By Ian Cameron

Monument to a monarch and her passion for exploration, the mortuary temple of Egypt's Queen Hatshepsut cascades from the Deir el Bahri cliffs near ancient Thebes. Relief carvings on the colonnades trace a reign crowned by a 15th-century B.C. sea expedition to the distant land of Punt on the east coast of Africa. These detailed pictures, which show African natives, reed houses on stilts, and long-tailed apes, are among the earliest known records of geographical discovery.

Two *Homo erectus* hunters stood before a fresh kill. It was their first for many days, and not enough to feed all 34 men, women, and children in their group. Hunting had been bad during the dry season and the group was desperate for food. They decided to move on—into the unknown. They climbed the mountains that rimmed the horizon, crossed a vast plain covered in shrub, then came to a slow-flowing river. Here at last they found water and an abundance of game. Here they would stay until food once again became scarce.

Human beings had discovered another part of their planet.

Such scenes were commonplace half a million to a million years ago, as our ancestors fanned out from Africa to populate the Earth. What journeys they must have made! Stone Age hunters gazed in wonder at lakes and mountains no human had set eyes on before. These were surely among the greatest moments in the exploration of our planet, for few people have ever journeyed into so vast an unknown.

Like their Stone Age ancestors, people of ancient civilizations around the globe no doubt traveled remarkable distances and made great discoveries. But scant records—or no records at all—remain to tell the tale of these fantastic voyages. Most of them are lost to us.

The Egyptians were the first peo-ple to make any records of their travels. From hieroglyphics and temple reliefs we can put together accounts of their voyages to a distant and mysterious land they called Punt.

The story began on the River Nile, around 3500 B.C. The Nile is an ideal river for waterborne traffic because it flows from south to north, while the prevailing wind blows up it from north to south. By 3500 B.C. the Egyptians were building long low ships they could row downstream with the current and sail upstream with the wind. These boats were excellent for river work but useless on the open sea, as they were built from papyrus—abundant in Egypt but unsuitable for oceangoing vessels. Before the Egyptians could leave the Nile or venture out of coastal waters they needed timber that could stand the pounding of waves. In 2600 B.C. King Snefru sent ships to Byblos, in Lebanon. From the Phoenicians who lived there on the shores of the Mediterranean, the Egyptians obtained cedar.

With the cedar the Egyptians built seaworthy ships, and around 2500 B.C. Pharaoh Sahure sent his new fleet to search for Punt, the legendary Land of the Gods—so called because Egyptians believed it was the home of their earliest ancestors, and because it was said to abound in all those treasures Egypt longed for: ebony and ivory, silver and gold, and incense to burn on its altars.

We cannot be certain exactly where Punt was, but we can make an

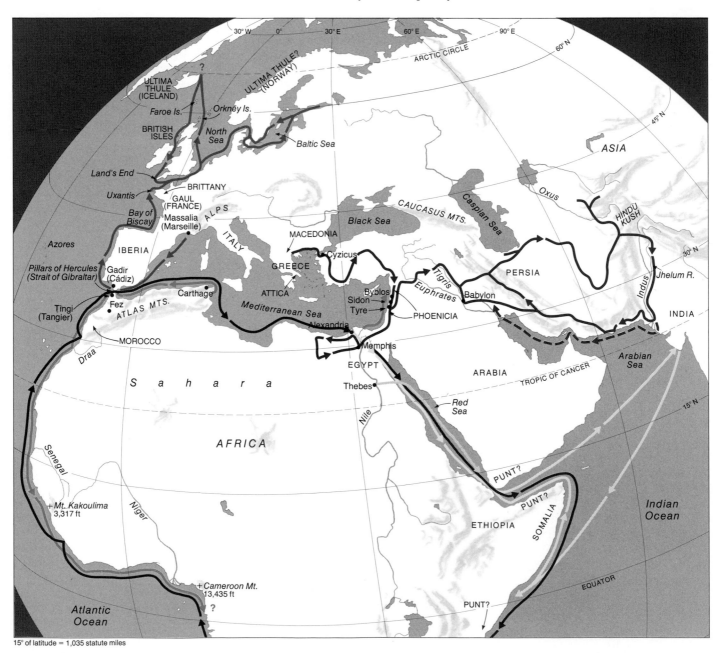

Long on legends and short on facts, the accounts of early explorers make guessing games of their exact routes and destinations. Egyptian mariners sailed many times to the place they called Punt, but forgot in the centuries between trips where they had gone; we still cannot be sure of its location on the map. Did a Phoenician crew hired by Egypt's King Necho II really circumnavigate Africa in 600 B.C. as Herodotus reports? No other ancient historian concurs—yet contemporary Greek maps correctly depicted Africa as an island joined to Asia. And what of the Greek astronomer Pytheas, who described voyaging beyond Britain to Ultima Thule—the edge of the Arctic? Although early chroniclers deride him as a charlatan, modern scholars consider his voyage real, and as remarkable as the better recorded campaigns that took Alexander the Great from the Mediterranean to the Indus River.

King Snefru 2600 B.C.
Egyptians:
  King Sahure 2500 B.C.
  Hennu 2000 B.C.
  Queen Hatshepsut 1493 B.C.
King Necho II 600 B.C.
Hanno 450 B.C.
Alexander the Great 334-323 B.C.
Nearchus 325-324 B.C.
Pytheas 325 B.C.
Eudoxus 120 B.C.

15° of latitude = 1,035 statute miles

informed guess. When Sahure's fleet returned, the ships were laden with 80,000 measures of myrrh; 6,000 bars of electrum, a gold-silver alloy; and 2,600 logs of wood—probably ebony. The state records that list this cargo contain no reference to Punt's whereabouts, but the freight suggests a distant location, possibly on the east coast of Africa.

Around 2000 B.C. Pharaoh Mentuhotep sent a court official named Hennu on another expedition to Punt. The words inscribed on Hennu's tomb record how Mentuhotep "sent me to dispatch a ship to Punt to bring him fresh myrrh. . . . I went with three thousand men. I made the road to be even as a river, and the desert even as a sown field. To each man I gave a leather bottle, a carrying pole, two jars of water, and twenty loaves of bread. . . . I dug two wells in the wasteland and three more in Idahet. I reached the Red Sea. I then built this ship. I dispatched it laden with everything. . . ."

The inference is that the ship was manhandled across the desert in sections—hence the large number of men, the water rationing, and the digging of wells—then assembled and launched on the Red Sea. Again the east coast of Africa seems a likely location for Punt.

The Egyptians' last recorded voyage to Punt is better documented. In 1493 B.C. Queen Hatshepsut sent five ships commanded by Nehsi to search again for the Land of the

Gods—it would seem that Punt was so far distant and sporadically visited that its whereabouts had either been forgotten or were still a matter of conjecture. Nehsi's ships were probably built on the shore of the Red Sea and then launched, heading south. After a couple of years they came back, bringing the "marvelous things of the land of Punt." Queen Hatshepsut had Punt's exports carved in relief and enumerated in hieroglyphic inscriptions on the walls of her mortuary temple at Deir el Bahri near Thebes. Incense trees in tubs, ebony, ivory, cinnamon, monkeys, dogs, panther skins— "Never was the like of this brought for any king since the beginning," declare the inscriptions.

The same carvings provide clues to the whereabouts of Punt. One bas-relief shows Nehsi's five ships with their small square sails and their 30 or so rowers setting out on the Red Sea, laden with merchandise for trading. We next see them anchored off a village of reed huts built on stilts. Finally we see Nehsi's crews carrying their precious burden up the ships' gangplanks. The animals and the village of huts suggest a location in southern Africa.

Another carving shows an Egyptian official receiving the king and queen of Punt with their retinue. Some people think that the sturdy limbs and buttocks of the queen suggest she was deformed. There is, however, a simpler explanation: She displayed a racial characteristic of

the Khoikhoi, or Hottentots—people who in prehistoric times inhabited much of the coast of southern Africa. If this was so, Punt might well have been in the neighborhood of present-day Mozambique.

We know, too, that Nehsi's cargo included antimony, an essential ingredient of the rouge found in cosmetic boxes in Egyptian tombs. One of the few antimony deposits known to have been mined in the ancient world lay in Mozambique.

So although the exact position of Punt cannot be pinpointed, it may well have been in southern Africa—a long way from the Nile. Egyptians who traveled there and back would have had to cover almost 8,000 miles: an amazing journey indeed.

Yet Egyptian voyages were far surpassed by those of the Phoenicians.

Around 3000 B.C. a dark-skinned Semitic people moved into the coastal region of what is now Israel and Lebanon. The territory these Phoenicians occupied, though small, was fertile. But it was soon overcrowded, for mountains and hostile neighbors kept the Phoenicians from expanding eastward. So the Phoenicians became sea traders, redistributing by ship the treasures that had reached them by caravan. Gradually they cornered the seaborne traffic of the Mediterranean Sea, and built up the world's first maritime empire.

It is difficult to generalize about the Phoenicians for they were a loosely knit network of self-governed trading posts. Determined to preserve their monopoly, they were also obsessively secretive. They falsified sailing orders in case they should fall into the wrong hands; destroyed cargo ledgers; and, to discourage competitors, disseminated fo'c'sle yarns of sea serpents that ate vessels and gales that blew ships off the rim of the world. The story goes that one Phoenician captain, rather than allow a foreign vessel to follow him on a trading expedition, deliberately ran his ship aground.

What we do know is that the Phoenicians built seaworthy ships, and that in these ships they could go virtually anywhere, trading with places as far apart as the British Isles and the coast of Africa.

Africa was the setting for two of the Phoenicians' greatest feats of exploration—the voyage of Hanno and an expedition sponsored by the Egyptian king Necho II.

Around 450 B.C. Hanno, a sailor from the Phoenician city of Carthage, traveled down the west coast of Africa with a fleet of 60 ships carrying settlers. He established colonies along the coast of present-day Morocco and Western Sahara, and some of the sites he described still exist. The place where he "founded a temple of Poseidon" was Cape Cantin; his "lagoon full of high and thick-grown cane . . . haunted by elephants and multitudes of other grazing beasts" was the mouth of the Tensift River; and his land of "the Troglodytes who . . . are said to run

The Phoenicians (opposite) were first to rove the entire Mediterranean—and first to navigate by the North Star. Commerce, not conquest, spurred their daring voyages, as they continually sought new markets and new sources of trade goods. Starting with Cyprus, Sicily, Carthage, and Malta, they had built by 800 B.C. a network of trading posts around the Mediterranean. As middlemen, the Phoenicians busily purveyed raw materials and finished goods: linen and papyrus from Egypt, ivory and gold from Nubia, grain and copper from Sardinia, olive oil and wine from Sicily, perfume and spice from the East.

Eventually these international traders, driven by insatiable curiosity, ventured beyond the Mediterranean. They reached England and perhaps the Azores, and possibly the stormy waters (below) around Africa's Cape of Good Hope—more than 2,000 years before Vasco da Gama dazzled Europe with the same feat.

A sleek pirate galley prepares to ram a merchant ship on a sixth-century B.C. Grecian vase. Epic tales mixing fact and fiction glorify the ancient Greeks who succeeded the Phoenicians as chief traders of the Mediterranean. The story of Jason (opposite), who leaves his ship Argo to overpower fire-breathing bulls, slay a sleepless dragon, and seize the golden fleece, may relate an actual voyage to the Black Sea. The Greek geographer Strabo believed Jason's saga showed that "the ancients made longer journeys, both by land and by sea, than have men of later time."

OVERLEAF: A 20th-century copy of a late Bronze Age pirate galley like Jason's stands off Attica's Cape Sounion, where temple ruins honor Poseidon. Navigational aids were limited then; even mythic heroes relied mainly on sun and stars—and the favor of the gods.

faster than horses" was part of the Atlas Mountains.

Hanno's southernmost colony was "an island we called Cerne." We do not know where Cerne was; but after leaving the last of his colonists there, Hanno headed south, exploring the unknown coast of Africa.

"We sailed away in fear, and in four days' journey saw the land ablaze by night. In the centre a leaping flame towered above the others and appeared to reach the stars. This was the highest mountain which we saw: it was called the Chariot of the Gods."

They came to an island that "was full of wild people. By far the greater number were women with hairy bodies. Our interpreters called them Gorillas. We gave chase to the men, but could not catch any, for they all scampered up steep rocks and pelted us with stones."

Where was this "Chariot of the Gods"? Obviously it was a volcano. Some say it was the 3,317-foot Mount Kakoulima in the Republic of Guinea, and that Hanno's "gorillas" were really chimpanzees. Others claim that Hanno sailed almost as far as the Equator, and sighted the great volcanic peak of Mount Cameroon. Today this mountain is one of the last strongholds of the gorilla and, at 13,435 feet, could easily have been the highest any of his crew had seen. Not for another 2,000 years were Europeans to penetrate so far south along the coast of Africa.

The Phoenician voyage sponsored

by King Necho II took place about 150 years before Hanno sailed, and in some ways was even more remarkable. The only account we have of it is by the Greek historian Herodotus, who writes: "Libya [Africa] shows that it has sea all round except the part that borders on Asia, Necho a king of Egypt being the first within our knowledge to show this fact. . . . He sent forth Phoenician men in ships, ordering them to sail back between the Pillars of Heracles [the Strait of Gibraltar] until they came to the Northern [Mediterranean] Sea and thus to Egypt. The Phoenicians therefore setting forth from the Red Sea sailed in the Southern Sea [Indian Ocean] and whenever autumn came, they each time put ashore and sowed the land wherever they might be in Libya. . . . After the passing of two years they doubled the Pillars of Heracles in the third year and came to Egypt. And they told things believable perhaps for others but unbelievable for me, namely that in sailing round Libya they had the sun on the right hand."

Herodotus' story is creditable on many counts. He describes the voyage as being made from east to west, which is the route by which winds and currents are most favorable. His words about the sun ring true because, incredible as it must have seemed to the ancients, when Necho's ships rounded the Cape of Good Hope the crews, being in the Southern Hemisphere, would indeed have seen the midday sun on their right. Also, Greek maps drawn between 450 B.C and A.D. 43 all show Africa surrounded by sea, and how could the Greeks have known that the continent was a virtual island

After defeating Persian king Darius III, Alexander the Great confronts his archenemy's family, fancifully shown in 16th-century Italian brocades before a neoclassic facade. An enlightened ruler, Alexander aimed to unite West with East rather than to subjugate the vanquished. He encouraged his soldiers to marry into conquered tribes; Alexander himself wed Stateira, one of Darius's daughters.

unless someone had sailed round it?

Herodotus was a historian, not an explorer. But he was Greek, and he shared with other Greeks a lust for knowing the unknown. Greeks like Pytheas of Massalia, who voyaged north to the edge of the known world and kept copious records that have, unfortunately, been lost to us. Greeks like Eudoxus of Cyzicus, who disappeared trying to circumnavigate Africa. Or Greeks like Alexander of Macedonia—Alexander the Great—who was an explorer truly worthy of that name.

More than a warlord, Alexander was a seeker of truth. He took with him on his campaigns geographers, engineers, architects, botanists, historians, and "steppers" to count their paces as they traveled, and thus judge the distances of their journeys.

In 334 B.C. Alexander, in pursuit of the Persians, led his troops into the unknown regions of Asia. Two of his many momentous achievements were crossing the Hindu Kush and navigating the Indus River.

The bleakly beautiful mountains of the Hindu Kush, along with the Himalayas and the Pamirs, create a formidable barrier between the subcontinent of India and the rest of Asia. Alexander, eager to mount a surprise spring offensive against the Persians in Afghanistan, led his army through the mountains on a 1,700-mile march. Autumn passed; the winter brought bitter winds, ice, and snow. The men struggled on until snow blocked their passage, then

19

camped until the spring of 329 B.C., when they made their way through an 11,000-foot pass to cross the Hindu Kush. Reaching the Oxus River, swollen with spring's melting snow, they filled their leather tents with straw and used them as rafts to float across. It had never occurred to the Persians that a scouting party, let alone an entire army, would attempt to cross the Kush in early spring. They fled, but were soon captured.

Lured now by the unknown regions of India, Alexander and his troops in 327 B.C. marched east to the upper Indus River. Here they found crocodiles, and since the only others he had seen were in the Nile, Alexander wrote to his mother that he had discovered its source—a mistake he subsequently admitted.

Halfway to the sea the Rivers Indus and Jhelum converge. "Here," the Roman historian Arrian tells us, were "swift currents through a narrows and terrific whirlpools where the water surges and boils. So great was the roar of the rapids that the oarsmen . . . were struck dumb with amazement. . . .Many ships were in trouble, and two actually collided and were wrecked, with the loss of many of their crews."

Near the mouth of the Indus lay even greater peril. "There ensued the ebbing of the tide," writes Arrian, "with the result that the entire fleet was left stranded. Now this was something of which Alexander's company had no previous knowledge, so that it caused them great be-wilderment. But they were yet more surprised when after the normal interval the sea advanced again and the ships were floated. As the tide rushed in all at once . . . the ships . . . were knocked together or hurled against the land and staved in." But nothing could stop Alexander. He rebuilt his fleet, explored the Indus Delta, then sent his officer Nearchus to the Persian Gulf while he marched back to Babylon.

It was not the least of Alexander's achievements that he brought to his travels an inquisitive mind and a desire to record and disseminate the knowledge he gained. His are among the first truly detailed accounts of exploration.

Europe's Great Age of Discovery had yet to dawn when the Egyptians, Phoenicians, and Greeks struck out into the unknown. And even as these ancient civilizations explored their worlds, other journeys of discovery were underway. In the Pacific the Polynesians sailed thousands of miles through unknown seas to build their island kingdoms. Chinese merchants trekked thousands of miles across China and Tibet to establish a trade route for silk. Arab traders in their sailing ships voyaged thousands of miles across the Indian Ocean to trade in India and China.

The Earth's first people were true discoverers, but detailed stories of only a few survive. We see the ancient explorers as "through a glass, darkly," and in the end can only guess at their greatness.

21

APOLLO

POSEIDON

PYTHEAS

Pytheas

By Ian Cameron

Sailors loading wine and figs as the Mediterranean astronomer Pytheas asks protection from the gods for a voyage in search of tin and amber. In this modern painting, his fourth-century B.C. expedition reaches the land of the midnight sun, but the Greek's claim to have rounded "the farthest of all known islands"—probably Iceland— was not credited until the 20th century.

Imagine, if you will, a trial, with you the jury. Imagine that what is on trial is a man's historical reputation: Was he or was he not a charlatan and a liar?

The judge of our imagined court has been able to reach back across the ages to classical times, to summon the defendant and witnesses. These witnesses—eminent historians and geographers of the ancient world—have testified, and they have branded the man in the dock "an arch-falsifier," "that charlatan Pytheas," "the greatest of liars." For it is obvious, these learned men say, that the stories Pytheas of Massalia brought back of his travels in the Atlantic around 325 B.C. are tall tales, the sort of yarns that seamen indulge in when their tongues are loosened by wine.

The judge now asks Pytheas if he can produce evidence to refute his critics, and the Massalian steps into the witness-box. "My books vindicate me," he cries. "In *On the Ocean* and *Description of the Earth* you will find all the evidence you need."

"But not a page of these books has survived," the judge says. "All that has come down to us are a few fragments quoted by later writers."

Pytheas is indignant: "Must I be judged by those fragments alone? What of my scientific background? My astronomical discoveries? I invented a calibrated sundial which enabled me to determine latitude accurately. I discovered the exact direction of true north. I discovered—"

The judge cuts him short. "We have no doubt you were a bona fide scientist. The question is, were you also a bona fide explorer? Did you or did you not tell the truth about your expedition into the North Atlantic, and in particular about a land you claim to have discovered on the rim of the world, next to a 'jellyfish' sea? Suppose you take us with you on this expedition, step by step. And at each step prove—if you can— that it is you and not your critics who speak the truth. But remember, this investigation is for history, so you must limit yourself to evidence from the written record."

The court becomes suddenly silent. What hope, all are thinking, has this solitary man of refuting his many eminent accusers?

"The Greek geographer Strabo," the judge is saying, "quotes you as

Druida Britannus. *Britannus Vetus.* *Britannus pictus.* *Britannus pictis vicinus.*
Druida Inglese. *Antico Inglese.* *Inglese dipinto. Inglese vicino' à dipinti.*

Ancient Britons as Pytheas may have seen them. The engravings are based on Caesar's Commentaries.

claiming that after passing through the Pillars of Hercules, you took 'five days to sail from Gadir'—that's Cádiz—'to the Sacred Cape,' Cape St. Vincent. But Strabo points out that five days is a ridiculously long time to cover the hundred or so miles in question. Others have claimed that the Carthaginian warships patrolling the Strait of Gibraltar would never have allowed you, a Massalian, to pass through; that their blockade was intended to keep Greeks like yourself from finding out about their lucrative Atlantic trade."

"This is easily answered. To avoid the Carthaginian warships I sailed close inshore, and by night, as later historians have conjectured. For this reason the voyage took much longer than it should have."

The judge makes a note. "Next, the Greek geographer Artemidorus quoted you as observing that northern Iberia 'is more readily accessible by way of the Celtic land'—France—'than in sailing by way of the Atlantic'; and this, he says, is another instance of your falsehoods."

Pytheas smiles. "Look at a modern map, and you will see who deals in falsehood. It is more than 2,000 miles from Massalia to the Bay of Biscay by sea and less than 500 by land."

"Then consider your description of France," responds the judge. "You describe that great 'bulge of Europe . . . opposite Iberia and projecting toward the west for more than 3,000 stades'—almost 400 miles—'likewise the various headlands . . . and islands there along, the last of which is Uxantis.' Yet maps of Strabo's time show the coast of France running not west but north, and he says that 'all these places . . . in the north . . . are mere inventions of Pytheas.'"

"When I returned to Massalia," the explorer explains, "my description of France was at first believed, and the maps of Europe were drawn correctly. It was only later, after my death, when cartographers listened to the jibes of men like Strabo—who wrote 300 years after my voyage!—that the maps of Europe were redrawn. And redrawn incorrectly,

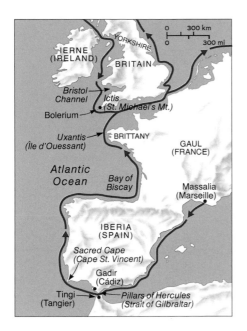

with the coast of France running due north. Yet later geographers found that the French coast does indeed curve to the northwest, exactly as I described, to Brittany and the Île d'Ouessant—my Uxantis."

The judge acknowledges the point. "But," he adds, "it is now as we leave the world known to the Mediterranean that you stretch credulity too far. Can you *prove* that you visited Bolerium—Land's End?"

"Why, surely! I wrote a description of it that is quoted by the Sicilian Diodorus: 'The natives of Britain by the headland of Bolerium . . . extract the tin from its bed by a cunning process. The bed is of rock, but contains earthy interstices along which they cut a gallery. Having smelted the tin and refined it, they hammer it into knuckle-bone shape and convey it to an adjacent island named Ictis'—St. Michael's Mount. 'They wait till the ebb-tide has drained the intervening frith, and then transport whole loads of tin on wagons.' For confirmation you need no written record, for even after 2,000 years, you can still see the remains of a smelting pit and the refuse of smelted ores."

The judge looks at Pytheas with new interest. Could it be that the man has been misjudged by the ancient scholars, that he is *not* a charlatan?

"Even if we accept that you *did* land in Bolerium," the judge presses on, "what of your stories of Britain? You claim to have seen tides north of Britain swell to 120 feet."

"I kept detailed accounts of what I saw there," says Pytheas, growing annoyed. "I wrote: 'Britain is triangular in shape, like Sicily, but its sides are not equal; It stretches out along Europe slantwise.'" Pytheas cites some detailed measurements, and continues. "Since the size and shape of Britain were previously unknown, my detailed description is surely evidence that I sailed around it. I landed in several places, and over a period of 3 years I observed that the longest day was exactly 18 hours near Inverness, and 17 hours in Yorkshire. And I observed the inhabitants of this island. I described their habits: 'They do not drink wine, but a fermented liquor made from barley.'

"I did indeed report great tide ebbs and waves, and to the people of our almost tideless Mediterranean this must have seemed incredible. Yet modern British observers have recorded an ebb of over 50 feet in the Bristol Channel, occasional waves of 60 feet between Scotland and the Orkneys, and one remarkable wave that climbed the 200-foot cliffs of Stroma and swept clean over the island. So you see once again I reported nothing but the truth."

The judge ponders all he has heard. "In the opinion of this court," he says, "you have gone far toward salvaging your reputation. But what of this amazing island on the rim of the world where the sun never sets and where your ship and crew were brought up short by a strange 'jellyfish' sea, where land and sea and air merge?"

"I first heard of Ultima Thule," Pytheas tells us, "when I was in northern Britain. It was said to be an island, six days' sail to the north of Britain. When we arrived, we found the sun was above the horizon

Any man who has told such great falsehoods about the known regions would hardly, I imagine, be able to tell the truth about places that are not known to anybody.
STRABO

25

for 20 hours out of 24, and that even at midnight there was sufficient light to read by. We would have sailed farther, but a day to the north of Thule our ship was stopped by a strange metamorphosis of the sea. It seemed to combine with the air to form a mass like jellyfish, which could be crossed neither on foot nor by boat. The fishermen told us that this was the end of the world, and no man could go farther. We therefore returned home via the Baltic Sea, visiting an island where each spring the waves wash amber up onto the shore."

"We know of Baltic amber, but a sun that gives light at midnight," the judge says, "sounds almost past belief to people of the ancient Mediterranean—though astronomers might concede it possible. But sea and

A modern artist's vision: Pytheas trading spear blades and wine for amber beads scooped from the sea by natives of an island in northeast Europe. Greek myth held the prized beads to be the hardened tears of the Heliades, sisters turned to poplar trees by Zeus. Returning home, Pytheas orders a bull sacrificed to the sea god, Poseidon, in thanksgiving for his successful voyage.

air combining into a mass like jellyfish! How can anyone credit this?"

"Yet explorers of later centuries have seen this phenomenon. Scientists and scholars. Will you believe *their* evidence?"

"Let us hear who these men are, and what they say."

"The first man I would have as my witness is Fridtjof Nansen, Norwegian explorer at the turn of the 20th century. He has written: 'What Pytheas himself saw may have been the ice-sludge . . . which is formed . . . along the edge of the drift ice, when this has been ground to a pulp by the action of waves. The expression "can neither be traversed on foot nor by boat" is exactly applicable to this ice-sludge. If we add to this the thick fog, which is often found near drift ice, then the description that the air is also involved . . . and that land and sea and everything is merged in it, will appear very graphic.'

"My second witness is Frank Debenham, polar explorer and Emeritus Professor of Geography at the University of Cambridge. The professor has written: 'When ice forms on sea water it forms a thin flexible skin and is immediately broken up by the wave motion into small cakes of ice, the edges jostled into a thicker rim so that we call it pancake ice.

'It is a curious thought that if Pytheas had used the pancake . . . simile instead of . . . jelly-fish he might have been believed and his narrative might have been preserved to posterity.' My third witness—"

The judge raises his hand. "Enough. You have said enough to convince this court that what once seemed unbelievable can be accepted as fact. One question only remains. Why did you do it? Why did you spend so many years exploring these regions on the edge of the world?"

"We Greeks of Massalia were of course interested in learning whence came the Carthaginian wealth from beyond the Pillars of Hercules. But I, a scientist, had other goals. Before we left, I spent many hours with

my calibrated sundial calculating Massalia's exact latitude on the Earth's surface. In the countries we visited I again worked out our position. This enabled me—albeit imperfectly—to map our route, to define and to learn what lay beyond our Mediterranean horizon." Pytheas pauses, then says thoughtfully, "After our return, the Carthaginian hold on the Strait of Gibraltar tightened. No further Greek expeditions ever penetrated the blockade to confirm my reports. Perhaps that is why so many scholars thereafter questioned my veracity."

Pytheas of Massalia, one of the world's least known explorers, stands down. Was he also one of the least appreciated? You, the jury, decide.

Today scholars continue trying to reconstruct Pytheas's route from such fragments of evidence as those cited in our imaginary trial. Modern geography has vindicated many of Pytheas's claims, but the location of Ultima Thule remains uncertain—some say Iceland, others Norway or the Faroe Islands. For more on Pytheas and other ancient explorers, see Beyond The Pillars of Heracles *by Rhys Carpenter.*

To Cross the Seven Seas

By David F. Robinson

Billowing sails recall exploration's golden age—the 15th and 16th centuries—when bold mariners probed beyond the limits of the known world. Here a recreation of Sir Francis Drake's Golden Hind completes a trial run off England's coast after its launching in 1973. In 1580, half a century after Ferdinand Magellan circled the globe, Drake plundered Spanish treasures in South America and reconnoitered western North America from California to Oregon and perhaps beyond.

It was but a puny glimmer, like the light of a wax candle moving up and down. But the admiral says he saw it earlier this evening, far across the jostling waves. And now he promises a silken jacket to him who first spies the land on which the light must have burned.

Ah, but this sea captain from Genoa, this Christopher Columbus, has told his Spanish seamen many things to lure them on toward his vision of Cathay just over the rim of the horizon. That seabird, this floating weed, those clouds, all tell of land out here in the empty waters. So he says. More than a month at sea, and this square-rigged nao and its two companion caravels will nose into a snug harbor on the morrow. So he says. So he has said for weeks.

Still, what is there to do but hope? Eyes bleary from the midnight watch peer anxiously from the ship's fo'c'sle at the empty seam where sea meets sky. Hands raw from wrestling with the lurching rudder keep a straight wake by the feel of the tiller. Great squares of canvas bulge with the wind like hide over muscle. Spars groan, planks creak, halyards whack the masts, grains crawl through the *ampolleta,* the sandglass that binds a weary man to his duty station until the last grain falls. Eight times the grains must run through until a four-hour watch is done. It is 2 a.m.; one dreary hour to go. How great the temptation to hang the infernal ampolleta above the lantern so the heat will expand the glass and the grains will hurry through faster!

Listen—from the *Pinta,* the lead ship of this little fleet of three, a cry splits the night, a cry that soon will awaken Europe to a New World.

"Tierra! Tierra!" bellows the lookout. "Land! Land!"

Spanish words. But they could have been Chinese.

Why weren't they? China had the ships, the men, the money for such an expedition long before Columbus was born. And so did other nations, for that matter; some had explored far and wide by the time he set sail. So why didn't China or one of these other nations discover America?

Europe in the 15th century had awakened from a millennium of feudalism, stretched, and found its arms spanning not just a Mediterranean world but a whole globe. In the blink of a lifetime, daring sea captains would round the tip of Africa and fetch home the riches of the Orient . . . breast the uncharted Atlantic and butt into land . . . traverse the land and glimpse another ocean beyond . . . struggle down the endless coast of South America, find its end at last, and limp across the Pacific, leaving a wake around a globe whose surface is but two-sevenths dry land. Their names are firmly anchored in the history of this Great Age of Discovery: da Gama, Cabral, Columbus, Dias, Magellan, names known to any schoolchild. But who ever heard of Cheng Ho?

Half a century before Columbus

From a realm of fantasy to a world of reality—such was the leap of the Great Age of Discovery. Beginning with Portuguese voyages down the west coast of Africa, the century-long outburst of exploration erased medieval notions of a flat Earth populated by monsters and mythical beings. Columbus himself reckoned the distance between Europe and Cathay at 4,000 miles—about 9,000 short. By the 1500s, explorers had added to their charts Earth's largest feature: the Pacific Ocean.

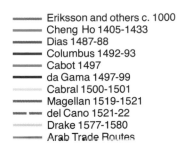

———	Eriksson and others c. 1000
———	Cheng Ho 1405-1433
———	Dias 1487-88
———	Columbus 1492-93
———	Cabot 1497
———	da Gama 1497-99
———	Cabral 1500-1501
———	Magellan 1519-1521
– – –	del Cano 1521-22
———	Drake 1577-1580
———	Arab Trade Routes

was born, a new emperor seized the throne of China. This haughty demigod had little use for the rude wares of barbarians beyond his Great Wall. He wanted only their profound respect. And so in 1405 began a series of sea voyages like none before. The emperor's trusted admiral, the eunuch Cheng Ho, coursed the seas from Japan to Zanzibar with flotillas numbering up to 317 ships.

On one mighty vessel a forest of 9 masts sprouted from a hull 444 feet long by 180 feet wide. This was the treasure ship, from whose hold poured gifts to dazzle petty potentates at every port of call. Smaller vessels schooled about this great whale: horse ships, supply ships, billet ships, and the little combat ships.

Little? At 180 feet end to end, with 68-foot beam and 5 masts, they dwarfed anything Europe would launch for the next 100 years. Surely Cheng Ho could have captained even the smallest of his ships across an ocean, financed by the wealth of his emperor and guided by a magnetic compass that Europe's mariners disdained as a tool of fortune-tellers.

But the Chinese were too advanced to go grubbing for commerce. Their fleets sailed to neighbor nations seven times, not to trade or conquer, but to impress. Having done that, the ships sailed home to rot as the lotus of China slowly closed back into itself.

Tierra! Electrified by the realization that they have sailed into the unknown and made it to the other

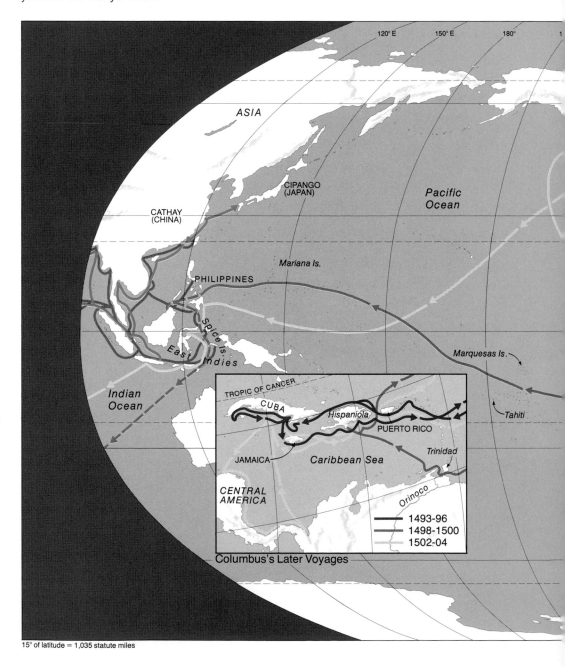

Columbus's Later Voyages

———	1493-96
———	1498-1500
———	1502-04

15° of latitude = 1,035 statute miles

A slithering sea serpent snatches a hapless seaman from the deck of his ship in this 1555 woodcut by Swedish map maker Olaus Magnus. Fear of such terrors kept most mariners sailing close to shore until the era of Columbus.

OVERLEAF: Summer ice clots the harbor of a fishing village in southern Greenland. Along these shores slumber the ruins of Viking colonies that defied such seas and coastlines and served as stepping-stones to the New World.

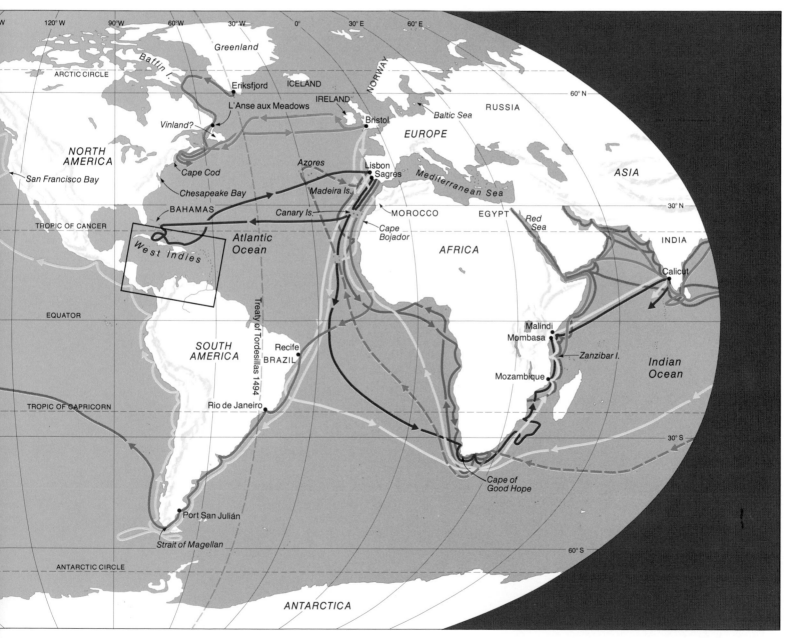

Relics of a Nordic past evoke daring sea voyages across the North Atlantic to the New World. The finely wrought warrior's helmet, found in a ship burial near Stockholm, dates from the seventh century. A tenth-century Anglo-Saxon drawing caricatures the dreaded dragon ships of Viking sea rovers who raided and traded throughout Europe from the Baltic to the Mediterranean. Such vessels, built of overlapping planks, were among the most seaworthy ever built. Lithe and supple longships probed the brawling reaches of the northern seas as early as the ninth century A.D., bringing raiders and settlers to outposts from Ireland to Russia. A bulkier, beamier ship known as a knarr carried settlers to Iceland and Greenland—and may have coasted North America's shores as early as A.D. 986.

side, the crewmen of Columbus's nao scramble to the deck. Columbus speaks an order, and the helmsman below decks hauls the long tiller arm hard alee. The deep, narrow rudder swings like a cathedral door, and the wind spills from the sails. Now they thrash and flap, and the sheets and clew lines bound to their corners crack like whips as deckhands lunge for the flailing lines.

Square sails let a ship run before the wind, but the new, triangular lateen sail on the mizzenmast makes a ship more maneuverable and helps her beat into the wind. Thus could Columbus's ships, the *Santa Clara* (*Niña* was only her nickname), the *Pinta*, and the *Santa María* win the confidence of these sailors who have driven them down the wind into oblivion: They held the promise of bringing their sailors back home.

Spanish sailors. But they could have been Arab.

It was, after all, the Arab traders who most likely invented that lateen sail. Under its bellying triangle they had sailed the Indian Ocean for generations. In the marts of India and the Spice Islands they filled their holds with silks, medicines, jewels, and spices—especially pepper for the taste buds of Europe.

Not that Europeans were such gourmets; the spice trade sprang from much humbler roots. By a quirk of geography, Europe had little that it could use for fodder to feed its cattle over the winter. Thus stockmen had to butcher many of their animals

in the fall and salt the meat so it would keep. If it didn't, well, it would likely be eaten anyway. In either case, pepper made it palatable.

And made the Venetians rich. Venice's merchants had cornered the market on the spice trade from the islands of the Indian Ocean. A hundredweight of pepper was worth 3 ducats in Calicut—but by the time it crossed the Indian Ocean under lateen sails, jounced by camel caravan through the deserts of Egypt, and thudded onto the warehouse floors of Venice, the price had zoomed to 80 ducats. Egypt's sultans restricted the annual tonnage, keeping pepper precious by keeping it rare.

In the lucrative spice trade, the Arab sailors were the deliverymen, riding the northeast monsoons to Africa and the Red Sea in the fall and the southwest monsoons back to India in the summer. It was a trade route; why struggle off into nothingness when there was commerce

Under a cloud of canvas, a full-scale re-creation of Lord Baltimore's Dove *furrows the waters of Chesapeake Bay. Square-riggers such as this pinnace ran well with the wind, but to make good headway against the wind on a return voyage took another sail—the triangular lateen used by Arab seamen. Navigators of the time used a sandglass and "log" line (below) to measure speed and a compass to gauge direction.*

aplenty right here? Father, son, and grandson commuted across the Indian Ocean under a sail that could have taken them around the world.

As spices reached the Mediterranean, so too did the sail that brought them. Medieval knights from western Europe had seen tricornered sails dotting the harbors and seaways as they journeyed along the eastern Mediterranean on their Crusades. They called the rigs lateen after the Latin countries whose sailors hoisted them aloft on long spars held by stout, raked masts.

The wonder is not only in the cleverness of the fore-and-aft rig but in the slowness of western Europe to adopt it. Not until the 1400s did the Portuguese develop a ship with full lateen rig—the oceangoing caravel, fast, nimble, able to tack well upwind. The caravel was the high-tech space shuttle of its day, a capsule fit for crossing the seven seas. Yet Columbus, pausing in the Canary Islands on his first voyage of discovery, stripped down the two-masted caravel *Niña*, gave her a lateen mizzen, and rerigged main and fore with the old reliable square sails for better downwind speed in the open sea.

Tierra! But which land? Columbus is certain it's the Orient, so the Orient it must be. An offshore island, surely. A dot off the coast of Cipango, the island realm told of by Marco Polo. The Indies, at last.

In his stuffy little cabin aft, the admiral thumbs his logbook. October 12, 1492. Thirty-three days out of the Canary Islands. A crude magnetic compass has guided him westward. Mariners to come will speak of him as a consummate dead-reckoning navigator, for he can watch the water hiss past his hull and estimate his speed within a tenth of a knot.

Each day he tells his men how far they have sailed. And they believe him. But he lies. When they make 59 leagues he tells them 44, lest they despair at sailing so far into the void.

A liar, but a pious one. In gratitude for safe passage, the devout Columbus names his landfall after his Holy Savior. San Salvador.

A Spanish name. But it could have been Norse.

It probably *was* through the eyes of Norsemen that Europe first beheld

Embarking on his grand adventure from Palos, Spain, Christopher Columbus bids farewell to King Ferdinand and Queen Isabella. A 19th-century artist has romanticized the scene; the royal pair did not attend the pre-dawn sailing on August 3, 1492. Columbus's three ships made landfall in the Bahamas early on October 12. Historians ever since have debated which island he sighted. Aided by computers, a National Geographic study in 1986 traced his wake to tiny Samana Cay.

At a banquet following his first voyage of discovery, Columbus stands an egg on end—by crushing its base. His companions, who had scorned the uniqueness of his sea exploit, take the point: After a deed is done, everybody knows how to do it. The pleasant fable shows the value of unorthodoxy—in Columbus's case, sailing west to arrive in the East. Not so pleasant for Columbus was his return to Spain in chains in 1500, after his third voyage (right), in disgrace for hanging rebellious settlers.

OVERLEAF: *The island of Dominica remains much as Columbus found it on November 3, 1493, during the second of his four voyages to the New World. Its name in Spanish means "sabbath," for he sighted it on a Sunday. The island, wrote one adventurer, "is notable for the beauty of its mountains and the charm of its verdure."*

North America. Half a millennium before that lookout's cry, graceful ships with single square sails and a bristle of oars were pouring out of the rock-walled fjords of Scandinavia. Neighboring peoples saw little grace in those slender warships with their dragon figureheads, for they brought warriors to pillage and burn.

What plunder could be richer, what victims easier, than the gentle monks of Ireland in their monasteries filled with gold chalices and bejeweled reliquaries? The fearsome dragon ships became a plague upon the shores. And when the Vikings prowled westward to Iceland, they found Irish monks there too—mostly hermits with little to steal. But the brothers knew only too well what "viking" meant; the Norseman's word for "raiding" had become the name for all his kind. The panicky monks had but two choices: stand fast and die, or flee.

And so the Irish monk became an unlikely seafarer in an even more unlikely ship of skin—the curragh, a sailing skiff made of leather stretched over a wicker frame. Through the treacherous northern seas the brothers plowed a path to Greenland with the dreaded longships almost in their wake. Did Irish monks make it even farther—to mainland North America, or even to the same Caribbean islands that Columbus knelt upon and named? The chronicles of a sixth-century saint named Brendan speak vaguely of a 40-day voyage westward, of a flat and treeless island like those of the Bahamas, of grapes as big as apples on a perfumed isle some say might be Jamaica. We can only read the chronicles and wonder.

But the Vikings surely beached their admirable *knarrs* in the New World. Like stepping-stones, the remains of their colonies cross the North Atlantic: Iceland . . . Greenland . . . and finally L'Anse aux Meadows in Newfoundland. There we see their imprints today—here a longhouse foundation, there a cookhouse with a slate-lined cooking pit.

In their sagas we read of another place, an evanescent paradise, a Vinland the Good with wonderful berries for making wine. Surely this was not rocky, cold Newfoundland. Where then? Cape Cod? Again, we

can only read the sagas and wonder.

In time the *skraelings*—native Americans whom Columbus will stubbornly call Indians; after all, this *is* the Indies!—turned the Norsemen back toward Greenland and Iceland. A spindle whorl, a posthole, a bronze pin—the Norse saga is written in the dirt of a New World that, to them, was just another settlement that didn't work out.

Tierra! By morning light Columbus and his captains clamber over the ships' gunwales into a boat, prudently armed, and soon the oarsmen crunch its prow onto the sandy shore. Feet that staggered on pitching decks for more than a month must now learn again the feel of firm ground. And so must stomachs that now turn landsick on a footing that seems to roll but does not.

The men seek fresh water to replace the rancid broth now stinking in the water casks. They seek fruits and meats and vegetables for crews weary of leathery salt beef and beans turned to cannon shot and biscuits like bricks. They seek human contact, for a ship is small and a voyage long and a gang of seamen rounded up on a sordid waterfront not the most enchanting of societies. But above all, Columbus seeks the Great Khan of Cathay.

In his zeal to make this place fit into the world where it ought to, Columbus identifies plants and birds and animals as species found in Asia. Humans dwell here too—naked, copper skinned, shy at first, then gleeful over the red cloth caps and glass beads the strangers give them.

But no Great Khan. Columbus will voyage to these waters three times more before his death, yet never will he heed a rising chorus of scoffers nor know that the Great Khan sits 9,000 miles farther west.

Columbus steps from the boat, clutching the royal standard. Two captains each carry a banner of the green cross bearing the initials of the king and queen, the sovereigns who dithered six years before agreeing to fund what Columbus so grandly called his Enterprise of the Indies. Ferdinand and Isabella.

Spanish sovereigns. But they might have been Portuguese.

It took Columbus more than a decade of lobbying, wheedling, and string pulling before he finally found a sponsor. Much of that time he cajoled the royal councils not of Spain but of Portugal. And what better choice? It was Portugal's Prince Henry the Navigator who had set up a kind of Renaissance Cape Canaveral at Sagres and sent ship after ship down the fearsome coast of Africa.

There at Sagres the prince who never went to sea prodded his captains to sail farther south while his naval architects perfected the nimble caravel. They had to. There were no steady tail winds to blow a square-rigger around the western shoulder of Africa, down the long coastline, around the southern tip, and up across the Indian Ocean. Only a lateener could make good headway

Seabirds crowd a ragged rock on New-foundland's brooding shore. Perhaps to such a forbidding landfall came John Cabot, a Venetian sent by England's Henry VII to search the "eastern, western and northern sea" for "islands, countries, regions or provinces . . . unknown to all Christians." In this painting (below), the black-robed monarch sees him off on the 50-ton Matthew at Bristol on May 2, 1497. Scholars agree he reached North America, but little is known of his voyage.

against that mishmash of winds.

League by league, voyage by voyage, Henry's captains groped down the continent's interminable flank, planting stone pillars called *padrões* on shore to mark their progress and reassure the ships that followed. In 1434 Gil Eannes rounded the dreaded Cape Bojador, once considered impassable. He dodged its shallows by sailing many days out to sea and around the long, lurking shoal. His breakthrough heartened others to sail in his wake. Farther and farther south the padrões marched.

Then in 1488 Bartholomeu Dias, exasperated by weeks of ornery head winds far down the coast, turned south-southwestward and ran out into the South Atlantic for 13 days in search of better breezes. When he found them he rode them eastward—and rounded the continent's rock-toothed tip at long last. To Portugal's sovereign, John II, Dias brought back tales of a tempestuous promontory. One account says he called it the Cape of Storms, but John had another name: the Cape of Good Hope. And the hope would be fulfilled, for Portugal had made an end run around the empire of Islam and the Venetian spice cartel.

The Portuguese crown in 1497 sent the steel-willed nobleman Vasco da Gama to inaugurate trade on the route blazed by Dias. Da Gama sailed from Portugal with two square-riggers, a caravel, and a fat storeship heavy with trade goods and provi-

Amerigo Vespucci drops in on America, an allegorical figure who stares from her hammock at the overdressed visitor as natives roast a human leg nearby. Her guest holds an astrolabe, used to navigate by star sights. He was first to call this a "new world," but a 1507 pamphlet gave it his name: "Let it be named America." Two continents now bear the name—but where or how often he landed, no one knows.

sions for a three-year expedition.

All boded well as the fleet sailed across the Indian Ocean in a mere 22 days. But a rude reception awaited them on the Malabar coast. Sultans and merchants used to trafficking in gems by the handful guffawed at the newcomers' chintzy beads and caps.

After weeks of dickering the fleet slunk away, ill prepared for bucking the Indian Ocean's head winds. The crossing now took three months—and many lives, as scurvy and malnutrition wrought their full horror.

Two years after leaving Portugal a remnant of the fleet staggered home. Da Gama could present his king with only a few gems and a sprinkle of spice—a modest profit to show for a voyage of 27,000 miles, but reason enough for joyous celebration. Portuguese merchant seamen soon were swarming around the cape, well provisioned for trading in the sumptuous bazaars of the Indies.

The princes of Portugal had spent heavily for half a century to pioneer this hard-won path to profit. Why bankroll a Genoese dreamer to sail in the opposite direction for another route to the same place?

The dreamer had sailed anyway, financed by Spanish monarchs seeking their own end run around both Venice's monopoly on land trade and Portugal's hammerlock on the sea route around Africa. How the scoffing Portuguese monarch must have squirmed on his throne when Columbus sailed back to Europe with news that he had fetched the Indies

46

in a single voyage! And how Columbus must have squirmed when, clawing his way homeward through a murderous tempest, he found himself limping into a Portuguese port only four miles from Lisbon!

Two rival Catholic powers had apparently reached the same lands by opposite tracks. Which had the right to colonize where? Pope Alexander VI finally drew a line down the middle of the Atlantic; westward was Spain's domain, eastward was the rest of Europe's. Portugal objected—and, by the Treaty of Tordesillas in 1494, moved the line nearly a thousand miles west and claimed any new lands to the east of it, ignoring the rest of Europe entirely. It was a momentous coup, for it enabled the courtly Pedro Álvares Cabral to take his fleet of 13 ships far to the west on his voyage to India in 1500—so far west that he sighted land, a shore that was now his right to claim for Portugal. A shore we call Brazil.

Down that shoreline 19 years later Ferdinand Magellan would sail. By then most of the learned world would know that this was not the Indies but a barrier of land. Magellan came to take the measure of that barrier and find a chink in it, if chink there be. Through a storm-lashed strait he would grope at last, only to find another trackless ocean—and a berth in history as the first to lead an expedition that circled the globe.

Tierra! Shouted in triumph, the cry now hangs like a curse as Columbus leans on the rail and scans the

"They are a people of a tractable, free, and loving nature, without guile or treachery," wrote Francis Drake of the natives he met along the California coast in the summer of 1579. Drake and his men put into a "convenient and fit harborough"—probably in the San Francisco Bay area—for ship repairs after seven months of sailing and raiding along the western coasts of the Americas. He claimed the land for his queen and named it Nova Albion because of "the white bancks and cliffes,

which lie toward the sea." On July 23, after more than a month ashore, Drake set out across the broad Pacific—the first Englishman to circle the globe.

Young sailors still take to the sea under square sails. Argentine cadets lay aloft on the training ship Libertad (opposite)—at first fearfully, then with confidence. So the sailors of centuries past dared the empty oceans and found them filled with discovery.

boy should ever steer, "come wind, come calm"? Yet, while he slept below—minus his bed canopy, which he had given to a minor nabob on one of those interminable islands—a weary helmsman gave the tiller to a cabin boy, and the ship struck a reef and was lost. A cabin boy!

The admiral squints ahead at the empty Atlantic. No more will he pass this way, returning to skeptical sovereigns with reports of the Indies while they listen instead to wild theories about a whole New World. Someone else will command the armies that plunder these lands of their gold and skew Europe's economy into disarray. The English corsair Francis Drake will grow rich on the gold and silver of this vast new realm, then scout its sunset coast on his way around the world. And other sea captains will plant lasting settlements on the continent north of the Indies, from which a mighty nation will spring.

English settlements. But they might have been Spanish. For the saga of discovery by sea is a story not only of what was but of what might have been. Columbus's voyage was the first sponsored attempt to cross the Ocean Sea to the Orient, but instead it ran into a wall of land. Later explorers would round that wall and sail another ocean that few Europeans knew was even there. In a single generation the sea explorers jarred the mind of Europe out of its Mediterranean mind-set and put it to pondering a whole stupendous sphere.

heaving sea. It is 1504. His bows aim homeward after his fourth voyage to lands he still calls the Indies. But where are those accursed bazaars?

The fourth voyage has borne no more fruit than his first three. Still no bustling marketplaces, no dazzling cities, no steely-eyed merchants proffering baskets of pearls. Mostly he has met only naked inhabitants who sleep in nets of string and drink the smoke from a rolled-up leaf they call *tabaco*. But they can fight. Pitting their wooden spears against his thundering bombards and swivel guns, they have sometimes attacked

the colonies he has tried to plant and slain his shipmates.

Other times it has been his shipmates who have turned against him, disobeying his orders, fomenting mutiny—and even costing him his old flagship, the *Santa María*, on Christmas Day of the first voyage.

How that big, beamy nao would wallow in following seas like these, he recalls. She'd slide down each hill of water, then fishtail until the next roller buoyed her stern again. But the *Santa María* was his flagship, and there was no excuse for her loss. Did he not make it clear that no cabin

Leif Eriksson and Clan

By Edwards Park

A Viking raid, depicted in a medieval manuscript. Such fleets drove monks of western Europe to their knees in a common prayer: "From the fury of the Northmen deliver us, O Lord!"

The Viking flame barely flickered in Bjarni Herjolfsson. A good sailor? Of course. Look at how he prospered, trading between Iceland and Norway. But where was the lust to conquer and explore? Where was the good old berserker spirit that had driven Svein Forkbeard to skip along the oar shafts, yelling murderous oaths as his crew rowed to the attack? Bjarni never shrieked bloody threats at cowering abbots, or sprang at French castles with flashing battle-ax. His passions ran to the mundane: like getting to port at the right time with the right cargo.

Bjarni was master of a sturdy *knarr*, beamier and more seaworthy than the longships of his Viking forebears. And in the 986th year of the Christian Lord, he sailed her straight toward glory. Then, at the last minute, this stolid captain came about and sailed her straight away again, taking with him only a tale of strange shores and a voyage gone awry.

But what a tale to stir a Viking lad! It begins with Bjarni sailing to his Iceland home with cargo in the hold. Before he could unload, he heard that his father, Herjolf, had sailed with the notorious Erik the Red to a western land that Erik had found and was touting as a "green land."

What in the world, thought Bjarni, was a nice old man like his father doing with a rascal like Erik? Beard as fiery as the great god Thor's, Erik had been in trouble all his life. Ousted from Norway for murder, then from Iceland for killing again, he had sailed off into the sunset. Many in Iceland had sighed with relief that this was probably the last of him.

Incredibly, he had returned, bragging of making a landfall, of following a bleak coast west below mountains of ice, of finding deep fjords cut into lush green hills. In one he built his hall and dubbed himself a jarl, second only to a king. With him settled a brawling brood: his formidable daughter Freydis . . . his wife Thjodhild, daughter of that obviously splendid woman, Thorbjorg Ship-bosom . . . a youngster thirsty for

51

adventure—his eldest son Leif. But family was not enough; Erik wanted settlers for Greenland. He got them, too, for Iceland was overcrowded.

"Insanity!" snorted Bjarni at the idea of 25 ships and 300 or 400 people, including Herjolf, sailing for Greenland. He nodded wisely when told that many had hastily returned, weary of steep seas that even oceangoing knarrs couldn't weather. Some settlers may have gotten through, but was Herjolf among them? Bjarni had to find out.

Bjarni took a bearing on an Icelandic mountain and sailed west. When the land slid below the horizon he checked his latitude by the sun's shadow at midday. At night he used his outstretched palms to gauge the height of the North Star. When a brisk breeze filled the single sail, the big vessel slid along at a good seven knots. She was built the old way, her lower strakes lashed to the oaken ribs and keel with vines. This allowed the planking to work, the hull to writhe and twist. That flexing, Bjarni knew, gave knarrs their durability in the open sea.

Bjarni's simple navigation forsook him when, as the old Norse sagas say, "the fair wind failed and northerly winds and fog set in, and for many days they had no idea what their course was." One thing was certain: They had fallen too far south and missed Greenland altogether.

They were groping northwestward when they sighted a low shore with forested hills. The crew grinned at the land and cracked each other on the back for having beaten the odds. Not Bjarni. He had never seen Greenland, but he'd been told what to expect—and this wasn't it.

"Leaving the land on their larboard with their sail swung over toward it, they sailed for two days before they sighted another land." It was flat and wooded, no more like Greenland than the first landfall. No matter; the crew wanted to land, refresh the water supply, and collect firewood. Bringing buckets on deck, they eyed the captain anxiously: "Well, sir?"

But Bjarni had not completed his passage. He growled something to his helmsman and waved his disgusted crew back to work. And the knarr, slapping through light waves, headed purposefully away.

Still too far south. He sailed northward, and a third time the lookout yelled, and the crew poured on deck, and they all craned at wild, ice-clad hills above a barren shore. This time the men grumbled little when Bjarni gestured to the helm to swing the bow toward the open sea.

Now they ran east with the wind, and in four days made land again, high mountains with a flash of distant ice, but with lush green fringing the sea. Here at last was the jarldom of Erik the Red. Now the skipper smiled, not for sighting a new world but for finally making port.

Bjarni's story stirred the Greenlanders. All that land for the taking! All those forests! All that adventure! They scoffed at good old Bjarni for ignoring it. And the sagas wrote him a bit part and forgot him, a dependable, coolheaded sea captain, but not much of a Viking.

Erik's sons, Leif, Thorvald, and Thorstein, grew up on Viking tales. Bjarni's story set Leif to daydreaming. Someday he would explore and

Blood feud: Erik the Red slays a rival settler in Iceland, circa 980.

conquer Bjarni's mysterious lands, and the sagas would laud him forever. And so, at about 25, "a big, strapping fellow, handsome to look at, thoughtful and temperate in all things," Leif Eriksson went to see old Bjarni, bought his ship, and hired a crew of 35. He was off to see what Bjarni had found.

Leif offered his sire a leading role in the expedition. But as Erik rode to the ship, the horse stumbled and he fell off. An evil omen. Said Erik, "I am not meant to discover more countries than this one we now live in. This is as far as we go together." Leif boarded without him, eased the knarr down the long stretch of Eriksfjord, and headed for the unknown.

Blessed with decent weather, Leif sailed to Bjarni's last landfall. As his shipmates clambered onto the layered rock of the coast, Leif crowed of outdoing Bjarni in this new country: "We at least have set foot on it." They named it Helluland ("flat-stone land"), and shoved off.

Coasting southward, they reached a stretch of low forest which Leif named Markland ("forest land"). White beaches rimmed the coast, and the men strode along the sand, found no sign of humans, and sailed away, huddled in their warm, hooded robes against a chilly nor'easter.

Landfall again; an island under a fair sky. The men climbed to its high point for a look around. And here the oft-embroidered sagas preserve one exquisitely real moment. "There was dew on the grass, and the first thing they did was to get some of it on their hands and put it to their lips, and to them it seemed the sweetest thing they had ever tasted." Here stand Leif Eriksson and his crew—real people with sweet dew on their lips—on the coast of North America a millennium ago.

The land to the south looked inviting, so they sailed to it. Rounding a cape, the ship headed close to shore. The men rowed a boat up a stream to a lake. At high tide they towed the knarr in and unloaded their sleeping bags of hide. Being Norse and fond of baths, they likely swam in the river, then dried out in the sun, lolling naked on the warm grass. "There was no lack of salmon in the river or the lake. . . . The country seemed to them so kind that no winter fodder would be needed for livestock." Leif decided to build shelters and stay the winter.

They explored all winter, and on one foray an old German in the group found grapes that he swore would yield wine. "Is that true, foster father?" Leif asked. "Where I was born there were plenty of vines and grapes," he answered. "And Leif named the country after its natural qualities," adds the saga, "and called it Vinland."

At last, with a sou'westerly astern, they sailed for home. Just off Greenland they rescued some shipwrecked mariners clinging to a reef. A woman was among them, the captain's wife, Gudrid. Leif's men eyed her hungrily, for even wet and bedraggled, she was a Norse beauty.

Reaching home, Leif told of Vinland to eager listeners. Old Erik soon died, and, as oldest son and heir, Leif the Lucky settled down to run the farm. But Leif's brother Thorvald was not so lucky. He set out for Vinland with a crew of 30, found Leif's houses, and moved right in. From

Leif Eriksson sighting America, circa 1000.

there on the venture was a disaster. One day Thorvald and his men saw three skin boats overturned on a beach. Under each, three men slept—small, fierce men with coarse hair and broad cheekbones. Thorvald's men dubbed them *skraelings* (wretches) and quickly slew eight of them. But the one that got away returned with a war party, shrieking and brandishing wooden bows. Thorvald died when an arrow struck home.

Now it was Leif's brother Thorstein who saw good luck turn bad. He won the fair widow Gudrid, and set out with her for Vinland to fetch Thorvald's body. But storms blew him about the ocean all summer, and his battered knarr finally staggered to Greenland a week before winter began. There he and many of his crew fell sick with fever and died.

Widowed again, Gudrid soon wed Thorfinn Karlsefni, a Norwegian seafarer. And when adventure beckoned, they sailed to Vinland with crews of Greenlanders and "all kinds of livestock."

But Leif's Vinland wasn't easy to find. At the first landfall, scouts found some grapes. That boded well. The passengers chattered happily as the two ships continued along the coast. In a series of bays and inlets the explorers found good land and deep water, and they eased the ships right into shore where they could at last off-load the livestock. The grass was tall, and the cattle grazed at will. And the people cleaned themselves, and the reeking ships, and set up camp.

They saw no sign of Leif's shelters, but the spot seemed hospitable enough for wintering over. In the fall Gudrid bore a son, Snorri—if the sagas be true, the first child of European lineage born in the New World. But a savage winter followed, and food ran short. When Thorhall the Hunter found a dead whale, he bragged that his incantations to Thor had washed it up. Most of the people refused to eat it, for they were Christians and wanted no favors from a pagan god. Perhaps a whiff of its putrid flesh stiffened their righteous resolve.

Things looked better by winter's end. One day Thorfinn and his explorers met with many skraelings, and began to trade peacefully. Then a bull from the Viking herd charged out of the woods. The skraelings fled. Three weeks later they replied with a howling attack of their own.

The Vikings fell back. Suddenly from their midst rang a woman's strident yell. "Why do you flee from such pitiful wretches, brave men like you?" bellowed Leif's sister, Freydis. Her blood ran rich with that old berserker fire: She seized a sword and faced the foe. Did she know that, in battle, skraelings never smote a woman? Or was it to make a splendid Viking gesture that she tore open her clothes and slapped the blade on her bared breast? They fled her shrieking charge, and no wonder.

Yet in the end, the skraelings won. Eventually, the harried Norse pulled out—but not before the doughty Freydis all but took over the expedition and carved out one more blazing episode for the sagas.

A group from Iceland had a larger boat than hers, and she wanted it. So she told her husband that they had maltreated her. "But you, spineless man that you are, will not avenge my shame or your own!"

Now we have done better than Bjarni where this country is concerned—we at least have set foot on it.
LEIF ERIKSSON

The henpecked husband "could endure her upbraidings no longer." He and his men slew the boatmen from Iceland. But no one would kill their women. No one? Seizing an ax, Freydis charged upon the five women and hacked them apart herself.

Freydis warned her crew that she would kill any man who peeped a word of her "damnable deed." But when the Norse abandoned Vinland and returned to Greenland, the story leaked out. Leif, like a true Viking, "took three men who had been with Freydis and tortured them to confess the whole affair."

But he couldn't bring himself to punish her. After all, she was family.

The Norse sagas blend history with storytelling, a mix that entertains but also distorts. The Grænlendinga Saga *and the less accurate* Eirik's Saga, *written in Iceland in the 12th and 13th centuries respectively, chronicle the Norse discovery of North America long after the fact. From their vague and sometimes conflicting details, this story has been woven. Some scholars place Helluland in Baffin Island. Most think Vinland was Newfoundland, where the ruins of a Norse settlement dot the grass at L'Anse aux Meadows.*

Ferdinand Magellan

By James A. Cox

Ferdinand Magellan. *"So valiant and noble a captain,"* wrote chronicler Antonio Pigafetta. *"No other had so much natural wit, boldness, or knowledge to sail . . . round the world."*

I do not deny that I plotted to kill my master's Spanish captains. Why should I not want to kill them? I was his slave, not theirs. He, the Captain-General Fernão de Magalhães, whom you know as Ferdinand Magellan, wrote in his will that when he died I would be free. He often told me about it. But when he died, in that calamitous battle on Mactan Island in the Philippines, his captains refused to free me. But that is not the only reason I decided to kill them.

I was with Magellan when he died. I fought by his side against Chief Lapulapu's 3,000 warriors, and fled only when they gathered around my fallen master like flies on a lump of sugar, plunging their bamboo spears into his body. Where were the Spanish captains then? Safe on their ships, licking their mustaches and winking at each other. Even when Humabon, the Filipino raja whom Magellan had converted to Christianity, went from ship to ship with tears in his eyes, pleading with them to save his blood brother and their leader, they did nothing. Nothing until Humabon, in desperation, sent two canoes to snatch the survivors to safety. Then Carvalho of the *Concepción* loaded his carronades and sank Humabon's canoes. You cannot believe that? Believe it. I was with my beloved master from the beginning of the expedition, and I saw how they schemed to get rid of him.

I am Enrique de Malacca, sometimes called Black Henry. Magellan named me when I was 13 and a miserable slave in the Malay city of Malacca. That was in the year 1511. The Portuguese sacked the city, and Magellan, captain of a caravel, purchased me. I was fortunate. He was a good master, firm but considerate. I loved him like a father, and he taught me many things.

I sailed with him everywhere—eastward from Malacca until we stumbled on islands we took to be the Philippines . . . to Morocco and battles with the Moors, where a lance thrust behind the knee gave him a limp for life . . . back to Portugal, where his king insulted him, humiliated him, and cast him aside like an old shoe . . . to Seville, in Spain, where he married Beatriz Barbosa and fathered his son, Rodrigo . . . and on to Valladolid, where we entered the service of Spain's King

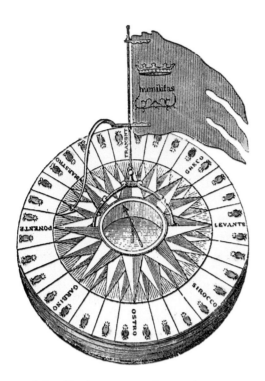

Magellan's compass, from a drawing by Pigafetta.

Charles. For a score of years and more, Portugal had owned the eastward sea route around Africa to the Moluccas, the Spice Islands. My master now would seek a route for Spain by sailing west and finding *el paso,* the passage through the wall of land that blocked and deluded the great Christopher Columbus. So began that terrible voyage that the gods frowned on from the start.

I was Magellan's servant, his loyal and faithful friend, and his interpreter when we reached the islands. And always the ears that listened when he was angry or overflowing with excitement about some new chance at fame and riches.

Never was his excitement greater than in the spring of 1518. With the backing of influential men, he had gained approval for the expedition. As captain-general, he was assigned five rotting old naos—*Trinidad,* his flagship, *San Antonio, Concepción, Victoria,* and *Santiago.*

Soon the smiling men of influence became predators. Most powerful was Bishop Juan Rodríguez de Fonseca. While Magellan was at the docks, refitting his ships and poring over nautical charts, Fonseca was busy replacing good Portuguese seamen with incompetent Spanish dandies. Juan de Cartagena, the bishop's natural son—though referred to as his nephew—was named second-in-command and captain of *San Antonio.* Luís de Mendoza and Gaspar de Quesada were given *Victoria* and *Concepción.* Only João Serrão, Magellan's cousin, kept his command—*Santiago,* smallest in the fleet.

On August 10, 1519, the crewmen—all 270 or so—assembled at dawn for a solemn Mass of farewell. Magellan received the silken royal standard and vowed to claim any lands he discovered in the name of King Charles. Then his captains, pilots, and masters knelt before him and swore to obey him in all things. Antonio Pigafetta, a young Venetian nobleman who was keeping a diary of all that befell us, whispered, "It seems these captains hate your master exceedingly. Can it be merely because he is Portuguese and they are Spanish?" I held my tongue.

Our sorrows began only six days out of Spain. As we anchored off the Canary Islands to take aboard fresh vegetables, a fast caravel arrived from Spain with a secret message for my master: The Spanish captains and two treacherous Portuguese pilots, Estevão Gomes and João Carvalho, were planning to kill the captain-general and replace him with Cartagena.

Magellan called a meeting in his cabin. The conspirators arrived, biting their lips nervously. My master let them insult him, and even gave in when they demanded that he change his sailing plans. His meekness made them bolder—but gave them no excuse to strike.

Weeks at sea went by. Terrible gales hurled us about among towering breakers. Then we drifted becalmed near the Equator while the sun roasted our flesh and gagging stenches boiled up from the bilges. We had been at sea twice as long as Columbus on his first crossing, and tempers began to flare. The captains complained about every decision the

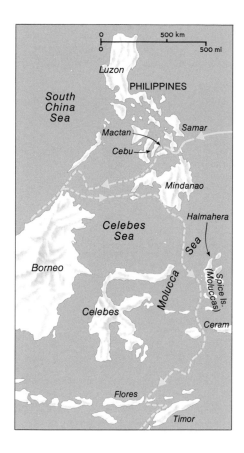

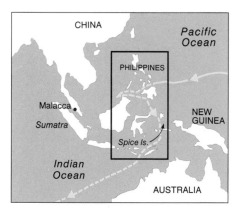

Site of Magellan's death on Mactan Island; subsequent route of the Victoria *under a minor Spanish mutineer, Juan Sebastián del Cano, who completed the voyage of circumnavigation.*

captain-general made. Even the seamen began to doubt his wisdom.

At a meeting aboard the flagship in November, the captains once again tried to provoke a quarrel. As before, my master accepted their taunts meekly, even when Cartagena, strutting about the cabin like an overweening cockerel, lectured him on navigation and accused him of endangering the fleet. Then the Spaniard went too far. "No longer am I prepared," he blurted, "to follow a hazardous course set by a fool!"

It was the moment Magellan had been waiting for. He seized Cartagena's doublet, roaring, "This is mutiny! You are my prisoner!"

"Stab him!" Cartagena screamed. But his henchmen dared not move, for the cabin was suddenly filled with *Trinidad*'s marines.

Magellan could have beheaded Cartagena on the spot. Instead, he sent him to *Victoria* as Mendoza's prisoner and gave the captaincy of *San Antonio* to Antonio de Coca, another "nephew" of the all-powerful bishop, instead of to one he could trust.

We sailed on. In December we raised the coast of Brazil. This was Portuguese territory, but no fleet guarded its shore. So we turned past a cone-shaped mountain into a beautiful, secluded bay; you know it as Rio de Janeiro. The natives were joyous at seeing us. They had been suffering a drought, and we arrived on the wings of thunderstorms—strange gods bearing the precious gift of rain. We stayed for 13 days, trading combs and little bells and playing cards for chickens, suckling pigs, and more fish than we could eat, and knives and hatchets for young women, who were comely and wore nothing but their hair.

This distressed my honorable master. He arrested his own brother-in-law, Duarte Barbosa, for carousing, and ordered the fleet to sail. Coca heard the crew grumble about leaving this paradise, so he released Cartagena, and the two illegitimate Fonsecas tried to stir up a mutiny. My master merely demoted Coca, put Cartagena back in irons, and named his own cousin, Alvaro de Mesquita, captain of *San Antonio*.

We could not linger in the realms of Spain's rival. Southward we drove, probing every inlet. The days grew shorter and the weather became bitter cold. Icy winds raged along a bleak, treeless coast. We were past latitude 40°, farther south than any explorer had ever been. We saw strange black-and-white geese that waddled upright and dived beneath the waves but could not fly. Who knew what terrors lay ahead?

Magellan sent the fleet into winter quarters in a bay he named Port San Julián. He had us build huts on the sandy shore, and reduced our daily rations. Again the air reeked of mutiny.

On Easter Sunday, Quesada of *Concepción* and 30 men stole aboard *San Antonio* and overpowered bumbling old Mesquita. When an officer yelled "Treason!" Quesada frantically stabbed him, then proclaimed himself captain of *San Antonio*. Mendoza of *Victoria* released the arrogant Cartagena, who took over *Concepción*. Next day, Quesada demanded the captain-general join him and the other captains on *San Antonio* to decide the expedition's future. An invitation to death.

Muffled in fog, Gonzalo Gómez de Espinosa, the fleet's master-at-arms, clambered aboard *Victoria* at dusk and handed Mendoza a letter

Magellan in the strait that bears his name, ushered by gods, demons, and nymphs.

from Magellan ordering him to the flagship. Mendoza laughed scornfully and crumpled the letter. Espinosa seized him by the beard and plunged a dagger into his throat. Before *Victoria*'s crew could react, Barbosa and a squad of armed men swarmed over the gunwale from a boat alongside. Barbosa weighed anchor, ranging *Victoria* near *Trinidad* and *Santiago*. Now the advantage was Magellan's, in numbers and position; his ships blocked the harbor. The mutineers laid down their arms.

This time there was a court-martial. Quesada paid with his head. Cartagena and Pedro Sanchez de Reina, the bawdy priest who was his advisor, would be marooned in that desolate land when we sailed in the spring. So it was done. I can but hope they were heard from no more.

But our troubles were by no means over. We left winter quarters in October, spring in that clime, in four ships, *Santiago* having been wrecked on a scouting mission. In a forbidding inlet only a few hundred miles south we at last found el paso—a series of deepwater channels and bays as far as the eye could see. My master was ecstatic, and so were the officers and crew at first. But they had been on short rations all winter. We were suffering the plague that afflicts sailors, swelling the gums and wasting the body. They looked at the harsh cliffs and snowcapped peaks and feared what lay ahead. Gomes, pilot of *San Antonio*, argued sourly that we should chart el paso and return home. Even Barbosa and Mesquita agreed. But Magellan did not. "Though we have nothing to eat but the leather wrappings from our masts," he cried, "we shall go on!"

We felt our way through the strait. One day *San Antonio* sailed behind an island and never rejoined us. Gomes had persuaded Mesquita—or overpowered him—and sailed for Spain.

The rest is short in the telling, though desperately long in the doing. We left el paso on November 28, 1520, on the bosom of a sea so calm Magellan named it Pacifico—"peaceful," in hopes it would always be so. We expected to anchor off the Spice Islands in a few days. All the chart makers in Europe agreed that this new sea was no wider than the Mediterranean was long. But the world was much bigger than they knew, and this endless ocean was the biggest thing on it.

One cloudless day followed another. Days became weeks. The sun burned hotter as we moved steadily north and west, but no sign of land did we see. Meat putrefied in the holds. Green scum fouled the water casks. We ate the last of our worm-filled biscuits, and hunting parties scoured the bilges for rats. Sharks circled the ships, growing fat on the bodies of our dead. And still there was no end to the emptiness.

Twice the gods pitied us, guiding us to islands where we found food and water. Over three months from el paso, more hollow-eyed skeletons than men, we finally reached the isles known as the Philippines. Somewhere in these isles, my master thought, he and I had made landfall many years before. If so, he and I became the first men to circle the globe completely, although not on a single voyage. It was a sweet triumph for the captain-general, for after some 550 days of hard sailing over thousands of miles of unknown seas, he had led us to the portals of our goal—the Spice Islands lay only a few days to the south.

But the gods of misfortune were not finished with Ferdinand Magellan. Our men had recovered from the terrible ordeal and were chafing to move on to the Spiceries and to fame and fortune in Spain. But the pious captain-general was obsessed with moving from island to island, persuading the natives to burn their idols and kiss the Cross of Christ. On Cebu he and the Filipino raja Humabon performed the native blood-mingling rite, and thousands eagerly embraced the new faith. My master came to see himself as an invincible instrument of his God.

So it was that, when Lapulapu scorned Humabon and Christ, Magellan, though never a bloodthirsty man, vowed to make an example of him. His officers pleaded to stay out of the matter and urged him to sail. But the captain-general would not be swayed. Since they were all against him and God's work, he said, he would lead the raid himself, taking only 60 volunteers from the crew. Humabon was appalled and offered a thousand trained warriors, but my master refused, saying that God would lead the soldiers of Christ to victory.

The outcome of that sad battle you know. Pigafetta, that man of words, spoke for those who grieved: "They slew our mirror, our light, our comfort, and our true guide." But I, who was like a son to him, was not allowed to mourn. The captains kicked and beat me when I told them I was a free man, and sent me ashore to collect provisions.

I sought out the disillusioned Humabon. I did not have to tell him how valuable the three ships would be in helping him subdue his rivals, or how valuable the trade goods in their holds. Back to the ships I went with Humabon's invitation for the Spanish officers to come to a farewell banquet and receive gifts of jewels and gold nuggets that the chief had promised to his lamented blood brother.

Like greedy, foolish sheep, 29 officers came ashore to gorge themselves with food and wine and the favors of Humabon's women. Something must have alerted Carvalho and Espinosa, for they slipped away to their ships. Otherwise, my vengeance would have been complete in the massacre that followed.

I watched the ships weigh anchor, pour a broadside into the native huts, and sail away for the Spiceries, leaving their officers for dead. I neither know nor care what befell them under their new leaders. I do miss Pigafetta and a few of the others, but I am serene in the knowledge that I have properly honored the memory of my beloved master, the Captain-General Ferdinand Magellan.

The facts of Black Henry's story are true, as best we can reconstruct it from the journals of Antonio Pigafetta and the various pilots' logs (Magellan's own were destroyed). Black Henry himself was never heard from after the ambush of the Spanish captains, and, so far as we know, he wrote no chronicle. But history should not forget him, for if one of Magellan's early, unrecorded voyages did go far enough east of Malacca, then Fernão de Magalhães and Enrique de Malacca were indeed the first men to circle the world.

I believe that nevermore will any man undertake to make such a voyage.
ANTONIO PIGAFETTA

April 27, 1521: Magellan falls in a skirmish on Mactan Island.

The Golden Americas

By Loren McIntyre

Grim warriors of basalt guard the ruins of Tula, capital of a pre-Aztec empire that flourished in Mexico from about A.D. 900 to 1200. From Tula sprang the legend of Quetzalcoatl, a bearded, light-skinned god banished by a rival. Sailing eastward on a giant raft, Quetzalcoatl vowed to return. His prophecy, and others like it, helped set the stage for the conquest of Mexico and Peru five centuries later, when ships brought bearded, fair-skinned strangers—the Spanish conquistadores.

Christopher Columbus *did* reach an outpost of China—in a way.

On that morning in 1492 when the admiral supposed that he had landed on an outer island of the Celestial Empire and asked the naked inhabitants if they were subjects of the Great Khan, he was not altogether mistaken.

Some 20 millennia earlier, when oceans were lower and ice lay thick upon the land, wanderers from northern China began to spread across a thousand-mile-wide isthmus into Alaska. They and their descendants explored all the way to Cape Horn. Then the ice melted, the oceans rose, and the first Americans had two continents to themselves.

Before Europeans had learned to tack against the wind, those Americans had created great cities and civilizations. They adorned their temples and themselves with gold, and fashioned fountains and figures of the metal. Since its value was largely aesthetic, they never imagined that gold would bring alien armies crashing into their realms.

For a quarter century after Columbus's first voyage, Spanish explorers saw little more than the West Indies and failed to realize a new world lay beyond. The early colonists never got far enough inland to encounter the empires of Aztec and Inca.

Travelers returned to Spain with monkeys, slaves, and trinkets. But it was their talk of treasure that aroused the aspirations of unemployed swordsmen who had drifted to the seaports after driving the Moors from Spain in 1492. For almost eight centuries this breed had fought a holy war against the Muslims. These Spanish soldiers were quick to anger and quicker to attack. They hungered to become *hidalgos*, "somebodies" by means of force or wealth—and, if the Virgin smiled, in the New World one begot the other.

The promise of pearls drew one of them, Vasco Núñez de Balboa, to the West Indian colonies in 1501. Settling in Hispaniola, he found no treasure and got deeply into debt. To escape, he stowed away in a ship's cask, emerged in a settlement near the Gulf of Urabá, between Colombia and Panama, and tried to make a new life. The settlement failed. Its colonists—with stomachs empty and poison arrows whistling around them—left for safer ground, led by Balboa and Francisco Pizarro, an Indies veteran since 1502. Balboa then founded Darién, the first stable colony on the American mainland.

With astonishing energy, considering the depressing humidity, Balboa spent years exploring both rain-lashed sides of the Gulf of Urabá. On one campaign with Francisco Pizarro, Balboa sighted the Pacific Ocean and took possession of the "South Sea" for his Spanish sovereigns.

A picture of the New World was emerging. Maps now showed a continuous coastline from the mouth of the Rio Grande to beyond the mouth

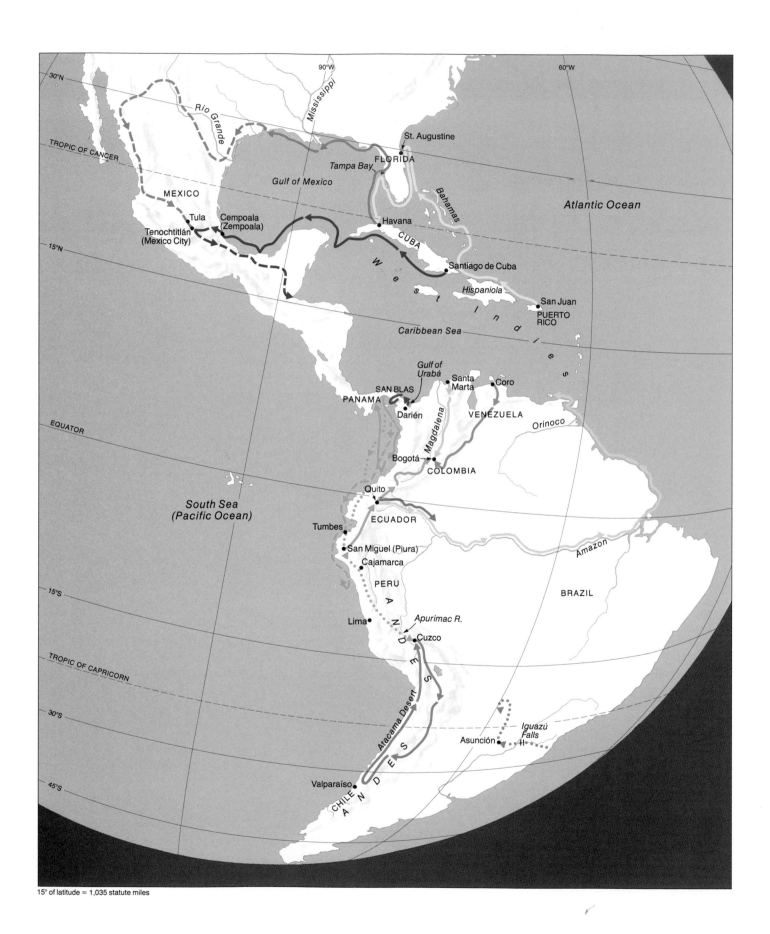

30°N

90°W

Mississippi

Río Grande

TROPIC OF CANCER

MEXICO

Tula

Cempoala (Zempoala)

Tenochtitlán (Mexico City)

St. Augustine

FLORIDA

Tampa Bay

Gulf of Mexico

Havana

CUBA

15°N

Santiago de Cuba

Hispaniola

Bahamas

60°W

Atlantic Ocean

San Juan

PUERTO RICO

West Indies

Caribbean Sea

Gulf of Urabá

Santa Marta

Coro

SAN BLAS

PANAMA

Darién

VENEZUELA

Orinoco

EQUATOR

Bogotá

Magdalena

COLOMBIA

Quito

ECUADOR

Tumbes

San Miguel (Piura)

Cajamarca

South Sea (Pacific Ocean)

PERU

15°S

Lima

Apurímac R.

Cuzco

Amazon

BRAZIL

TROPIC OF CAPRICORN

Atacama Desert

A N D E S

30°S

Iguazú Falls

Asunción

45°S

Valparaíso

CHILE

A N D E S

15° of latitude = 1,035 statute miles

68

Sixteenth-century dreams of gold and glory fueled one of the greatest outbursts of exploration, conquest, and colonization the world had yet seen. In less than half a century, Spaniards had reconnoitered and conquered vast regions of the New World. The widely heralded successes of Hernán Cortés in Mexico and Francisco Pizarro in Peru lent credence to tales of fabulous riches. Both men found gold treasures, like those shaped by Colombia's Tairona Indians (lower), but Cortés's luck eventually ran out. Restless for new riches, he left Tenochtitlán three years after conquering the Aztec capital, and struck southward on a fruitless two-year campaign through the jungles, where he found only illness and despair. Many others came in search of El Dorado, the fabled gilded man, said to be a chieftain whose subjects anointed him from head to toe with gold dust on ceremonial occasions (below).

of the Amazon River. And probes into Mexico in 1517 and 1518 suggested that it was not an island, as originally thought, but part of a mainland. The Indians living there were better dressed and housed than natives in Cuba. The Cuban governor could not authorize conquest and settlement, but he sent Hernán Cortés, a 33-year-old farmer, to "engage in discovery and trade" while scouting the Mexican shore for lost ships and sailors.

Cortés had something more in mind. He fitted out a force of 11 ships and 600 men, and put to sea before the governor could move to restrain him. The conquest of Mexico was underway.

Tales reaching Spain of his successful invasion—the smoking volcanoes, the plumed priests, the Indian mistress, the victims' screams—struck the European imagination like an Amadís exploit come true.

Amadís de Gaula was "the one knight errant above all others," a fictitious superman of chivalric romances. Spawned by medieval holy wars, the Amadís stories were perhaps the most popular printed matter in Spain. To gain gold and glory or rapturous love, Amadís fought pagan kings against astounding odds—just as Cortés attacked armies of real heathens in distant Mexico.

Cortés's success set off a rush to find more Mexicos. The king commissioned Pánfilo de Narváez to conquer and settle Florida. As with so many expeditions in the decade to

With sword and buckler raised to the heavens, Vasco Núñez de Balboa lays claim to the Pacific Ocean "for the royal Crown of Castile" on the evening of September 29, 1513. His dog, Leoncico—Little Lion—was one of a specially trained pack that tore Indians to pieces; Leoncico frolics on the beach in this 17th-century engraving. Two days earlier, from "a peak in Darién," Balboa had gazed upon the broad waters of the "South Sea"—the first European to do so. Friendly Indians, promising the riches that lay beyond, guided him across the narrow Isthmus of Panama on a 22-day march through the jungle. Today their descendants, the Cuna Indians of San Blas, inhabit villages (opposite) much like those visited by the explorer. Balboa did not long survive his triumph. A few years later he was arrested, tried, and beheaded on trumped-up treason charges brought by the governor of Panama.

Vasco Nuñez del Sur

come, Narváez's plans were scuttled by desertions, storms, starvation, Indian attack, and death. The expedition set out with hundreds of men, but only four survived. One of those four, Álvar Núñez Cabeza de Vaca, proved to be an explorer's explorer, working on two continents.

Shipwrecked off the Texas coast, Cabeza de Vaca wandered through southwestern North America, where Indians enslaved him. In 1536, eight years after his journey began, Cabeza de Vaca and his companions reappeared in Mexico, describing how they had seen bison and repeating rumors about rich Indian pueblos. The rumors became legend: the Seven Golden Cities of a land called Cíbola. Eager listeners went to search for them. Cabeza de Vaca turned to South America and there discovered the world's widest waterfall, Iguazú.

An explosive decade of discovery in South America was dominated by Francisco Pizarro, Balboa's companion at the discovery of the South Sea. Hearing of a rich realm to the south, Pizarro in 1524 began to probe the Pacific coast from Panama, sailing farther each time. Unlike Cortés, he returned to Spain for royal approval of his plans—and for a coat of arms displaying a llama and a title: governor and captain-general of Peru—wherever that might be. He sailed back to America with his four half brothers from Extremadura, the harsh frontier of west-central Spain where many conquistadores were born.

Early in 1531 Pizarro, then in his fifties, sailed on a final voyage from Panama. He landed inside the Inca Empire, near the Equator, and fought his way down the coast with a ridiculously small force of less than 200 soldiers. They were a thousand miles from Panama—and even farther from Cuzco, the Inca capital in the Andes. "The daring of the Spaniards is so great that nothing in the world can daunt them," wrote Pedro de Cieza de León, a soldier who came later with paper and ink in his saddlebags. "No other race," he wrote, "can penetrate through such rugged lands . . . solely by the valor of their persons . . . without bringing with them wagons of provisions, nor great store of baggage, nor tents in which to rest." But they always brought along a few firearms, and the cherished horses that vastly extended each rider's mobility and power.

Luckily for Pizarro the Inca realm was too disrupted by plague and civil war to pay him much heed. He recruited a force of dissident Indians to help him. The Indians, in turn, felt that *they* had enlisted Pizarro to fight their hated Inca overlords, who plucked whole populations from their homelands and exchanged them with others in distant parts of the empire—a device that restrained rebellion. Local tribes were often willing to collaborate with the Spaniards. When Pizarro heard that Atahuallpa, the ruling Inca, was camped

with his army at Cajamarca, he led his Indian allies, 62 cavalrymen, 105 foot soldiers, and a priest into the high Andes of Peru. His daring act abruptly changed the lives of the six million people who dwelt there.

Atahuallpa, protected by 30,000 to 80,000 Inca warriors, was bemused by the approach of the band of bearded strangers, their beasts, and their magic staves that spoke thunder. He withdrew his people from Cajamarca and let Pizarro's army occupy the town.

On the next day, November 16, 1532, Atahuallpa, surrounded by thousands of chanting courtiers, swept royally into Cajamarca to dine with the crafty Pizarro. At the sight of all these heathens, "many Spaniards wet their pants from terror," wrote an eyewitness. But then the conquistadores sprang their trap, charging out of the shadows of Cajamarca's doorways. Guns thundered. Horses' hooves clattered. Lances and swords thrust and slashed at feathered warriors who cowered as if attacked by supernatural forces. Thousands of Indians died, while Pizarro captured Atahuallpa without losing a single Spaniard.

For ransom, the Inca chief agreed to fill a 17-by-22-foot room once with gold and twice with silver as high as he could reach. Francisco Pizarro's half brother Hernando rode south with 20 horsemen to speed the flow of treasure. For three months Hernando gathered loot along a thousand miles of Inca highway,

An Inca-style footbridge made of twisted grasses sways above the gorge of the Apurímac River in Peru. At the time Francisco Pizarro was putting an end to the Inca Empire, hundreds of such spans linked more than 14,000 miles of roadways that reached from Chile to Ecuador. To cross the Huaca-chaca, or Holy Bridge, over the raging Apurímac was, in the words of one conquistador, "no small terror."

beneath lofty cordilleras heavy with ice and along deserts where rain falls once a generation. He paused in 40 towns, where time stood still: While Atahuallpa was captive, no Indian dared lift a weapon. By mid-1533 more than 24 tons of exquisite treasure had been melted down. Each common soldier got 45 pounds of gold and 90 of silver.

Hernando took the royal fifth of the booty to Spain, pausing long enough in the Indies to tell his story. Such was the ensuing gold rush to Peru that the governor of Puerto Rico cut off some settlers' feet to deter others and slow the exodus.

Meanwhile, Francisco's partner, Diego de Almagro, brought reinforcements to Cajamarca too late to share the ransom. The Spaniards executed Atahuallpa and set out for Cuzco. Pizarro sacked and occupied the Inca capital late in 1533.

In 1535 Almagro left Cuzco with 570 Spaniards and 12,000 Indians to explore lands to the south, awarded him by the king of Spain. On a year-and-a-half march into Chile, Almagro left a horrifying trail of dead and mutilated Indians. He found no golden cities, only terrain so arid that even 20,000-foot volcanoes held no snow. His "Men of Chile," disillusioned by their barren journey, later murdered Francisco Pizarro.

Sebastián de Benalcázar, who captured Quito for Pizarro in 1534, turned his attention northward to the gold-rich tribes of Colombia. Many adventurers had heard of such wealthy Indians, which led to the most astonishing coincidence in South American exploration: When Benalcázar finally reached the gold-smithing Muisca Indian homeland around present-day Bogotá, he found it already occupied—by Spaniards dressed like Muiscas, their European clothes long since rotted away. They were the remnants of a large expedition from the Caribbean led up the Magdalena River by a lawyer, Gonzalo Jiménez de Quesada. Within weeks of the wary meeting of conquistadores from north and south on the Muisca plain, yet a third group of explorers in sorry state appeared from the east, led by Nikolaus Federmann, a German whom the Spanish king had authorized to explore Venezuela. Federmann was hollow eyed from a fruitless two-year search for gold in the llanos—a grassland the size of California.

Other adventurers were drawn to the mountains near Bogotá, where a huge lake had been formed by a meteorite. Tribal memory held that a chieftain used to be ritually dusted with gold, rafted out, and rinsed in the lake to send a golden rain to the bottom—perhaps to propitiate a fiery god who had fallen to the Earth.

The mystique of El Dorado, The Gilded Man, had caught on in Quito by 1541. The first to search for him was the governor, Gonzalo Pizarro, Francisco's youngest brother. With 220 Spaniards, 4,000 Indians, and thousands of hogs, llamas, and dogs, Gonzalo marched into the steaming

"Santiago, and at them!" cry Francisco Pizarro's soldiers, invoking the aid of St. James in their fight for the Inca capital of Cuzco (below). The war whoop, used when Spaniards drove the Moors from their homeland, inspired the slaughter of countless American infidels as well. In just one year, Pizarro brought the mighty Inca Empire to its knees. The Incas' hand axes and clubs proved but a crude match for the sword-swinging horsemen of Spain and their Indian allies. When Pizarro's weary army finally captured Cuzco on November 15, 1533, a proud soldier described the prize in a letter to King Charles V: "We can assure Your Majesty that it is so beautiful and has such fine buildings that it would be remarkable even in Spain."

The conquistadores' bold campaign left a trail of carnage in the New World, recalled in a plundered burial site near Lima, Peru (opposite).

jungle east of the snowcapped Andes to claim the Land of Cinnamon and the Lake of El Dorado, as he called it. "Passing through great marshes and crossing many streams," he ran short of food, and was forced to eat his priceless horses.

Gonzalo sent a foraging party downriver under Francisco de Orellana, but the gathering waters swept Orellana's ship east into a huge river where skirted warriors fired arrows from the banks. "There was one woman among them who shot an arrow a span deep into one of the brigantines," wrote a chronicler, "and others less deep, so that our brigantines looked like porcupines." Orellana survived the 2,800-mile odyssey down the Amazon. He had explored Earth's largest river—so extensive that its ultimate source was unknown until the 20th century.

Meanwhile, Gonzalo Pizarro had slogged home to find Francisco murdered. He later met his own death on the block, for making himself dictator of Peru without royal approval.

Soon the tale of El Dorado grew into a legend that lured expeditions into humid undergrowth and frigid heights, and speeded the conquest of both continents. Retelling by chroniclers transformed The Gilded Man into a rich city "resplendent in the beaming sun" that passed into European literature and found its way onto maps of the Orinoco, the Amazon, and the Andes. In time, El Dorado came to symbolize splendors forever sought yet unattainable.

Hernán Cortés

By Elizabeth L. Newhouse

History notes that Marina, also called Malinche, was born near Aztec lands and sold into slavery as a child. We do not know if she ever sent Charles V a letter such as this, but we do know what it might have said—

Most High Mighty and Catholic Prince, Invincible Emperor and Sovereign:

Most humbly I write on behalf of my lord and master, Hernán Cortés, Marquess of the Valley of Oaxaca, Captain-General of New Spain, in support of his petition to be reinstated as governor of that same great dominion, which through constancy and valor he delivered unto your realm some ten years past. To his heroic service and unswerving loyalty I can attest, for from his arrival in this land until its conquest, I rarely left his side.

In the Year of Our Lord 1519, I was residing in a coastal town in the region of Tabasco, the slave of a Maya chief. One day 11 ships arrived; "temples in the sea," the people said. Thousands of our warriors shot arrows and hurled javelins and stones at the bearded white men. Over several days they furiously fought; the Spaniards' cannon and musket fire cut down hundreds but could not drive them off. Then from behind us came a terrifying surprise, snorting, racing creatures never before seen by our people. Our warriors, believing each horse and rider to be one animal, turned and fled, and the battle was lost.

In homage to the white lords, our Indian chieftains brought gifts of fowl and maize cakes, gold ornaments and cloth. And 20 women, including your most humble servant, myself. The Spaniards called us pagan idolaters and would not cohabit with us until we had been baptized into the True Faith, and so we were among the first native Christians of New Spain. I was christened Marina and given to Alonso Hernández Puertocarrero. Later the great Cortés would take me for his own, and I would bear him a son. But first I had a greater service to perform.

Allies against Moctezuma: A Tlaxcalan chief agrees to aid Hernán Cortés. Between them Marina, Cortés's Indian mistress, waits to translate. "Beautiful as a goddess," the chronicles said.

My understanding of both Maya and Aztec languages allowed me to interpret for Cortés through a Maya-speaking Spaniard he had found shipwrecked down the coast. The captain treated me kindly for he was well pleased; his ambitions on behalf of Your Sacred Majesty required communication with my countrymen. No other man has shown such zeal in Your Majesty's service. Fie on those rivals and enemies who now slur Cortés's name by falsely accusing him of squandering treasure and seeking the independent sovereignty of New Spain!

No hardship, no obstacle would divert him from his glorious cause: securing Moctezuma's empire for Your Majesty's Crown.

We met Moctezuma's emissaries on Good Friday, some leagues up

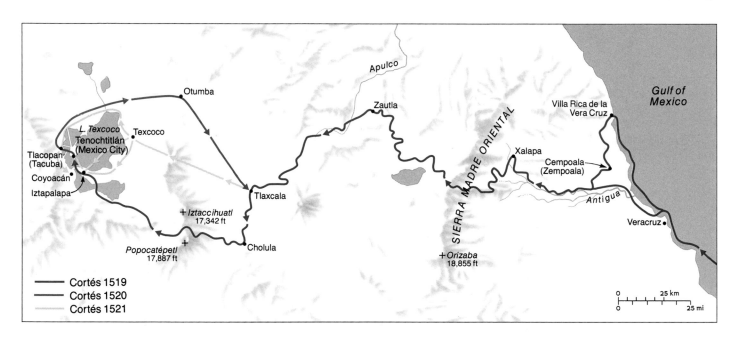

the coast from Tabasco. Cortés gave them blue beads and told them we were vassals of the greatest Emperor on Earth and that we had come in friendship to meet their prince. Artists made pictures of the Spaniards and their ships to send by runners to Moctezuma. The messengers described the horses as "deer" and showed him thundering cannon that could pulverize a tree, and dogs with "blazing eyes," an Aztec later said. "And when Moctezuma so heard, he was much terrified."

The emissaries returned with gifts astonishing to the Spaniards: a turquoise mask, gold ornaments in the shapes of animals, and two disks representing the sun and moon, one of gold, one of silver. They also brought food soaked in human blood, which nauseated the Spaniards on beholding. All this, Moctezuma's message said, for the *teules*—gods—who have come in fulfillment of a prophecy. But, he implored, venture no farther toward my capital, Tenochtitlán. Later he ordered his magicians to "cast a spell over them . . . cast stones at them . . . utter an incantation over them, so that they might take sick, might die, or else because of it turn back."

Cortés the conqueror in 1530, as captain-general of New Spain.

The gifts of gold made my brave captain ever more determined to proceed inland. "It is probable that this land contains as many riches as that from which Solomon is said to have obtained the gold for the temple," he exclaimed. But first there was a political matter to attend to.

The governor of Cuba had sent Cortés to trade and explore the coast of New Spain. Now the governor's officers accused my master of exceeding instructions and demanded his return to Cuba. Abandon Your Majesty's holy work? Not Cortés! He established a settlement, Villa Rica de la Vera Cruz, in Your Majesty's name and made himself captain-general, thus to renounce the governor's authority and serve directly Your Sovereign Majesty. Later he destroyed all his ships, lest they tempt the weakhearted into rebellion. An audacious move, but audacity came easily to Cortés in pursuit of Your Majesty's sacred interests.

Cortés had learned that Moctezuma had enemies too, important ones like the Totonacs, who would aid Your Majesty's cause. At Cempoala, their admirable capital, the fat chieftain told us how cruelly Moctezuma had subjugated and oppressed his people. Every year the prince demanded their sons and daughters for servitude or sacrifice. And his tax collectors kidnapped and ravished whatever women struck their fancy.

To prove his helpfulness, my captain ordered five of Moctezuma's tax collectors imprisoned. He told the quaking Totonacs: You and your allies should pay Moctezuma no more tribute or obedience. While saying these things, Cortés secretly arranged for the tax collectors to escape to Moctezuma with messages of friendship. Ah, the intrigues we concocted in Your Majesty's royal service!

The service of the Almighty Father was also on my pious master's mind. "How can we ever accomplish anything worth doing if for the honor of God we do not first abolish these sacrifices made to idols?" Cortés demanded. Every day at Cempoala he saw priests tear throbbing hearts from the chests of human victims and offer them to idols. When the Totonacs made clear they would not destroy the evil images, Cortés sent his soldiers to do it for them. Then he ordered lime to cleanse the temple of blood and had an altar built to the Virgin.

In August we sallied forth again, with 200 Totonac bearers and 40 chieftains to guide us. Our route led through the land of Moctezuma's bitter enemies, the Tlaxcalans, fierce warriors whom Cortés hoped to enlist as allies. From the tropical coast we crossed mountains and a high plateau, with cold, rain, and hunger our constant companions.

In the plaza of one town, we found more than 100,000 human skulls in piles. "Desist from your sacrifices, and no longer eat the flesh of your own relations, and the other evil customs which you practice," demanded staunch Cortés of the chieftains. He set about raising a cross when a priest stayed his hand: "It seems to me, sir, that the time has not yet come to leave crosses in the charge of these people for they are somewhat shameless and without fear."

Soon after we crossed into Tlaxcala Province the full force of an army, 40,000 Indians in feathery dress, came down upon our meager company of 400 soldiers and several hundred Indian allies. With bows

The meeting of Cortés and Moctezuma: November 8, 1519.

and arrows, clubs, and obsidian-pointed javelins the Tlaxcalans struck. Four times they charged. Four times our cannon, crossbows, and armored horsemen sent them fleeing. Finally, as God was on our side, they yielded. But the damage to our force and spirit was great. Cortés later wrote: "There was not one amongst us who was not heartily afraid at finding himself so far in the interior of the country among so many and such warlike people." But turn back? Many suggested it, but our captain exhorted them onward, reminding them of their opportunity to gain for Your Majesty the greatest dominions in the world.

And this is the man whom foes now call disloyal!

Forty-five Spaniards died in battle here. While others tended their vicious wounds, my valiant master commanded me to send messengers to the Tlaxcalans, saying if you do not come and make peace within two days, we will destroy you. Finally a large group of chieftains arrived and offered themselves as vassals of Your Majesty. We accepted entreaties to come to their capital, even while receiving emissaries from Moctezuma, who implored us not to go there, fearing an alliance. "I continued to treat with both one and the other," wrote the shrewd captain, "thanking each in secret for the advice . . . and professing to regard each with greater friendship than the other."

In Tlaxcala Cortés found much to praise. "The city is indeed so great and marvelous . . . much larger than Granada and much better fortified." We concluded a most excellent alliance with the Tlaxcalans and left for Cholula. Our new allies had warned us that the Cholulans were vassals of Moctezuma. But by now the Aztec prince, desperate to separate us from Tlaxcala, had invited us to his capital by this swift route. A thousand Tlaxcalan warriors accompanied us to Cholula's outskirts.

There, we were told, 20,000 of Moctezuma's warriors lay in ambush, and already pots with salt and peppers and tomatoes had been prepared to cook our flesh in. But bold Cortés moved first. "We fell upon the Indians in such fashion that within two hours more than three thousand of them lay dead," my captain wrote. He sent word to Moctezuma: Though the Cholulans blame you for the provocation, I do not believe so great a prince, a professed friend, could be capable of such treachery.

Ah, pity Moctezuma; surely he saw his match in Your Majesty's steadfast servant. The prince's emissaries brought gifts of gold to the Spaniards, who "lusted for it like pigs," an Aztec remarked. But pleas to advance no farther could not stay our captain.

We climbed over a high pass close by a smoking mountain—the first the awestruck Spaniards had ever seen. We proceeded through a valley and soon reached the shores of a vast lake. A league farther on, a causeway led us to an island city called Iztapalapa with fine stone houses, floating flower gardens, and pools of fresh water.

About two leagues down the causeway, we saw the glistening temples and palaces of the great Aztec capital, Tenochtitlán, rising like a vision in the lake's center. Thousands of people, many paddling canoes, came out to look at us; never had they seen horses or such as Spaniards. Though the day was hot, our foot soldiers walked in close formation. "As we are but human and feared death, we never ceased thinking about it. . . . we made short marches, and commended ourselves to God and to Our Lady. . . ." one said later, for they knew not what to expect.

Most Sovereign Lord, the rest of the story you know well: How Moctezuma, richly attired and borne on a litter, came to welcome Cortés and bow down in greeting; how he lodged us in great apartments, fed us sumptuously, and gave us splendid gifts of featherwork, embroidered cloth, and gold. How Moctezuma and Cortés exchanged all manner of flattery, and how Moctezuma pledged obedience, repeating the prophecy that a great lord would come and conquer this land. And how Your Majesty's servants discovered the city's awesome wealth—the fine buildings, the system of canals, the sweet gardens, the market where thousands traded foods, gold ornaments, and other manner of finery. And the stink and horror of the blood-encrusted temples.

When rumors started that the Aztecs schemed to cut the bridges and trap us, Cortés took Moctezuma hostage to ensure our safety. Unable by plea and reason to turn Moctezuma from his gods, our leader then had the prince's favored idols thrown from the temples and replaced them with our holy Christian images. Moctezuma, emboldened by this effrontery, warned us to leave before his people killed us.

Cortés did have to leave the capital, to battle a force under Pánfilo de Narváez that the Cuban governor sent to relieve Cortés of power, and it sorely cost Your Majesty's cause. The impetuous captain left in charge attacked a group of Aztec holidaymakers, provoking a general uprising against us. Although Cortés marched back and tried to make peace, the Aztecs fought on. Among the casualties was the great Moctezuma, stoned by his own people because they felt he had betrayed them.

We fled the city under darkness, but as we struggled down the causeway, the Aztecs caught part of our rear guard, dragged them to the temple, and slashed open their chests and offered their pulsing hearts to the gods. Hundreds of Spaniards and thousands of Tlaxcalans died on this sad night, *la noche triste*, June 30, 1520. But, Most Sovereign Lord, take pride, for as a survivor averred: "All the Spaniards who that day saw Hernán Cortés in action swear that never did a man fight as he did, or lead his troops, and that he alone in his own person saved them all."

Bowed, yes, but abandon the holy cause? Not Cortés. Six months later, his army reinforced by artillery, Spanish troops, and thousands of Tlaxcalans and other allies, he set out from Tlaxcala to reconquer Tenochtitlán. Bearers brought 13 brigantines in pieces across the mountains and began to assemble them by the lake. Your Majesty's shrewd captain laid siege to the city and cut off its fresh water. By May he sent assault parties down the causeways from Tlacopan, Coyoacán, and Iztapalapa, and he himself set sail across the lake. After almost 80 days, the capital lay in ruins, and the dead bodies of tens of thousands of Indians clogged the city. On the 13th of August in Our Lord's Year 1521, Spaniards seized the new ruler, Cuauhtémoc, and the Aztecs surrendered.

In the name of Your Most Excellent Prince, Cortés had secured Moctezuma's empire; now he would go on to rebuild the city and conquer more lands for Your realm. The deeds I have recounted here, Most Catholic Lord, bear witness to his invincible courage and steadfast loyalty. I close now in the humble expectation that Your Royal Person will see fit, in all justice, to restore the favors and honors so richly due Your Majesty's servant, the greatest of your conquistadores, Hernán Cortés.

On the 6th of December in the year of Our Lord 1530, Your Sacred Majesty's very humble slave and vassal who kisses the royal hands and feet of Your Highness,

Marina

The chronicles of Bernal Díaz del Castillo, one of Cortés's soldiers, document the events we have put in Marina's letter, as well as her devotion to her master and lover; Friar Bernardino de Sahagún recorded the Aztec side of the story. Perhaps a plea like this would have helped Cortés, for despite his own best efforts, he was never reinstated and died in Spain a bitter man.

CONQVISTA DE MEXICO POR CORTES. N.7

Cortés and his troops storming the Aztec capital: May 1521.

By Trail and Stream

By Ernest B. Furgurson

Cypress stumps in Louisiana's Atchafalaya swamp exemplify the forbidding terrain Hernando de Soto explored on his gold hunt through southeastern North America. The successes of Pizarro and Cortés brought on a rampaging gold fever that sent would-be conquistadores hacking and battling their way into North America's wilds. De Soto's extensive 1539-1542 expedition discovered the Mississippi River, but left him dead on its banks 50 miles from the Atchafalaya's northern end.

Some Americans have it all wrong.

It would be understandable for a visitor brainwashed in the many-layered historyland of the East Coast to arrive in Washington, focal point of American history, and stand beside the Potomac River and imagine out there one of our fabled explorers. Instead of monuments and jets and busy bridges, he might see brave Capt. John Smith of Virginia heading upstream nearly 400 years ago into the rich interior of the continent.

But it didn't happen that way.

We tend to forget that the continent was not seen first by Virginia cavaliers or Massachusetts Pilgrims, nor opened by hunters in raccoon caps and pioneers in covered wagons pressing west. In time they did move across the land and people our folklore, but long before Smith was born or the idea of Virginia conceived, the Spaniards and French were making bold flanking movements that left the English far behind on the Atlantic shore for most of the 1600s.

In western New Mexico you can still see reminders of that bygone Spanish presence. Here, where cloud shadows race across the juniper and rabbitbrush, the land is so big and empty it absorbs the modern marks of man just as it has enfolded the old.

The most poignant of those may be at Kyakima, easternmost of the Zuni pueblos, which rises against the towering, red and pale ocher Dowa Yalanne mesa. Ravens and sometimes golden eagles soar on thermals up the face of the mesa. At its base, above the ruins, are graffiti left by disrespectful visitors of modern times. And beneath those, worn but clear to anyone who knows where to look, are centuries-old Indian petroglyphs. One, crude and eloquent, is the angular outline of a man on a horse, carrying a lance. It has been there, facing the constant wind, for almost 450 years, since the first horsemen rode up with Francisco Vásquez de Coronado, a great conquistador who, like many others, came in pride and left in humility.

The Spanish lust for gold and empire was heightened by the account of explorer Álvar Núñez Cabeza de Vaca, who in 1536 began repeating Indian tales of rich cities, the seven cities of Cíbola, somewhere north of the Mexican mountains. To the Spaniards, eager to plunder another Peru, this was new evidence that their favorite legend was true.

The legend of seven golden cities was a prime motivator for the Spaniards in ripping open the New World. It originated back in the mists of Moorish occupation of Spain, in a tale of how a Christian archbishop and six bishops led their people to escape into the Atlantic Ocean, to an island where each of the prelates created a flourishing city. In retelling, the cities grew and turned to gold and shifted about with the flow of Spanish history, always

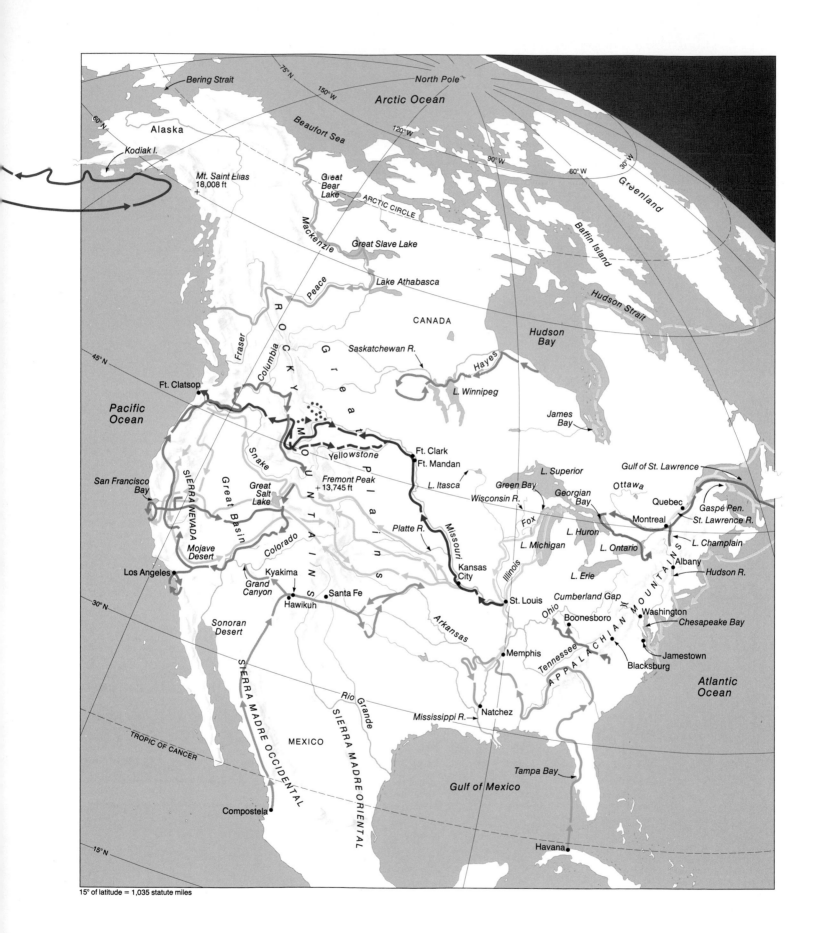

Bering Strait

Arctic Ocean

75° N

North Pole

150° W

120° W

90° W

60° W

30° W

60° N

Alaska

Beaufort Sea

Greenland

Kodiak I.

Mt. Saint Elias
18,008 ft

Great
Bear
Lake

ARCTIC CIRCLE

Baffin Island

Mackenzie

Great Slave Lake

Hudson Strait

Peace

Lake Athabasca

Hudson Bay

Fraser

CANADA

Saskatchewan R.

Hayes

Hudson
Bay

45° N

Columbia

R O C K Y

G
r
e
a
t

L. Winnipeg

James
Bay

Ft. Clatsop

Pacific
Ocean

Snake

M O U N T A I N S

Yellowstone

Ft. Clark
Ft. Mandan

Gulf of St. Lawrence

L. Itasca

L. Superior

San Francisco
Bay

SIERRA NEVADA

Great
Basin

Great
Salt
Lake

Fremont Peak
+ 13,745 ft

Green Bay

Wisconsin R.

Georgian
Bay

Ottawa

Quebec

Gaspé Pen.

Montreal

St. Lawrence R.

Platte R.

Missouri

Fox

L. Huron

L. Champlain

Colorado

L. Michigan

L. Ontario

Albany

Los Angeles

Mojave
Desert

Kyakima

Grand
Canyon

Santa Fe

Hawikuh

Arkansas

Kansas
City

Illinois

St. Louis

L. Erie

Cumberland Gap

Ohio

Boonesboro

APPALACHIAN MOUNTAINS

Washington

Hudson R.

Chesapeake Bay

30° N

Sonoran
Desert

SIERRA MADRE OCCIDENTAL

Rio Grande

SIERRA MADRE ORIENTAL

Memphis

Tennessee

Jamestown

Blacksburg

Atlantic
Ocean

TROPIC OF CANCER

Mississippi R.

Natchez

Tampa Bay

MEXICO

Gulf of Mexico

Compostela

15° N

Havana

15° of latitude = 1,035 statute miles

Lust for riches enticed the Europeans to penetrate deep into North America. Spanish conquistadores—de Soto and Coronado—sought gold in the South and West, as the French led by Cartier vainly sought a northwest route to China's treasures. But fur in the Great Lakes region proved a valuable consolation; for nearly 150 years the French competed with the British in northern Canada to explore and claim new fur-bearing lands. After American inde- *pendence, coastal settlers began to move inland and over the Appalachians. Lewis and Clark explored the Northwest, revealing the West's potential for trading and settlement and befriending Hidatsa warriors like the richly attired Pehriska-Ruhpa below. In Lewis and Clark's wake came land speculators, army surveyors, fur traders, and scientists—explorers all.*

just beyond the last conquest, pulling men on and on.

Cabeza de Vaca's stories made the legend glow anew. Would-be conquistadores begged for royal permission to lead expeditions north from New Spain into the unexplored continent. One of these, Hernando de Soto, was appointed governor of Florida. To Spaniards that included everything running north and west from the Florida peninsula. Earlier excursions had been mounted by Juan Ponce de León and others, but none were on the scale of de Soto's. He gathered 622 men, horses, a herd of pigs for food on the march, and landed at Tampa Bay in May 1539.

From there, he led a cruel, courageous, and desperate campaign up through the Florida jungle and westward. He attacked tribe after tribe, taking hostage their chiefs for provisions and safe passage. Choctaws, then Chickasaws cut down his force.

De Soto and his dwindling army pushed onward until May 1541, when just below today's Memphis they came to the Mississippi. They called it Rio Grande. Crossing it, they still followed rumors of gold, but increasingly their aim became escape. Then de Soto fell ill, and on the Mississippi's bank near Natchez, he died. His survivors, who eventually made it back half dead to Mexico, weighted his body to the river bottom. On the map de Soto's journey left impressive curls and loops, but in the king's coffers, nothing.

While de Soto marched around

94

the Southeast, the viceroy of Mexico sent Coronado, an ambitious young soldier, northward up Mexico's west coast. Coronado led 336 men with some 1,500 horses and mules, plus nearly 1,000 Indians as helpers.

In the summer of 1540 Coronado reached Hawikuh, a Zuni pueblo. Today Hawikuh is a mound of rubble, dotted with shards of painted pottery. Some rough Indian sheep camps beside cottonwood-lined gullies have TV dish antennas, and now and then a pickup truck coils dust behind as it heads toward town.

For Coronado the living pueblo looked almost as bleak. The uninspiring huddle of adobe and stone was nothing remotely like the fairytale cities of Cíbola. Could the gold be hidden inside? Coronado tried to move in peaceably. The Zunis responded with arrows. Coronado's men charged; he himself narrowly escaped death. When Hawikuh fell, he found only beans, maize, and squash. After he took Kyakima and the other Zuni pueblos, he had conquered the alleged cities of gold, and he was not a peso richer.

When Indians pointed him and his predecessors to fantastic riches, they were not necessarily lying. To them, the humble pueblos were grand cities; the plenteous food, riches. And besides, it would be unfriendly not to tell the Spaniards what they wanted to hear. From the Sonora River, Coronado sent out patrols, one of which discovered the Grand Canyon. Indians told him of a

wonderland to the east, named Quivira, where plates were made of gold.

Ever hopeful, Coronado set out
the next spring across the Texas Pan-
handle, wandered southeast and
back north. In Kansas he met the
Quivira Indians, but found no gold,
not even pueblos. The riches of Quivira were tallgrass and buffalo herds.
Coronado staked a claim to the land
for the king of Spain. Later the world
realized that de Soto and Coronado
had come within about 350 miles of
linking a belt of Spanish exploration
across the continent.

Even before the Spaniards beat
their way toward the center of what
is now the United States, a long arm
of French exploration reached inland from the North Atlantic. Navigator Jacques Cartier, on his 1535
voyage, found a breach west of Newfoundland that he hoped would lead
to the Pacific. But it was a river, not
a strait. Later named the St. Lawrence, it was the route by which the
French drove deep into America.

Cartier pressed upstream until he
struck rapids around a river island
almost a thousand miles from the
ocean. Indians led him up a high
hill, and he named the place Mount
Royal. From the peak they pointed
toward the west, where lay a series of
inland seas—the farthest of them
said to be on the world's edge. The
prospect was grandiose enough to
raise Cartier's hopes of the long-
sought passage to the Orient.

That was the way visionary explorers insisted on thinking: There

must be a water route westward to
Asia. The rich Americas could not
be seen as a goal in themselves, but
rather a barrier to greater wealth
beyond. Only slowly did the truth
dawn. As gold from Peru and Mexico
continued to pour back across the
Atlantic through the 1500s to fi-
nance Spain's century of dominance
in Europe, France began to see that a
different kind of gold might be at the
end of its New World route: fur. A
vogue for furs in Europe had created
such an intense demand that the
continent's supply of fur-bearing animals had nearly been depleted.

Some 70 years after Cartier, the
quest for furs brought Samuel de
Champlain to Mount Royal, today's
Montreal, and for decades he was the
driving force of French exploration.

Three things distinguished this
French push: It was motivated by
trade with the Indians, rather than
the search for gold. It developed Indian diplomacy to such a high state
that some northern tribes became
France's major allies in the struggle
for the continent. And finally, the
French, through luck at choosing
their main route of entry, stayed on
the water as they drove inland.

South past Mount Royal, Champlain in 1609 accompanied a war
party of Indians down a St. Lawrence
tributary he called the Iroquois, today's Richelieu. As he crossed the
future U. S.-Canadian border, he
entered a lake "of great extent, say
eighty or a hundred leagues long."

Lake Champlain, lying between

Quebec's Percé Rock thrusts sandstone bulwarks into the Gulf of St. Lawrence. The nearby cliffs of Bonaventure Island sheltered Jacques Cartier from heavy winds in July 1534, only days before he claimed Canada for France. Upon sailing into Gaspé Bay, Cartier rowed ashore and met Indians who "showed great joy, and the men all began to sing and to dance . . . exhibiting great pleasure in our coming." At Brion Island he encountered walruses, "great beasts, like large oxen, which have two tusks . . . and swim about in the water." Returning the following year, he explored the St. Lawrence River to the Indian village of Hochelaga, site of today's Montreal.

Some 70 years later, Samuel de Champlain established Quebec City—France's first permanent New World colony. Subsequently he explored the Great Lakes region, where he drew a hunt (below) in which Indians, imitating wolf sounds and beating shoulder blade bones, drove deer into a trap.

the Green Mountains of Vermont and New York's Adirondacks, is only 125 miles long, less than half his estimate. Its rocky shores are still green with pines and cottonwoods. From a ferry crossing between Port Kent and Burlington, it is easy now to imagine Champlain and the war party slipping silently down the western side, crossing the mouths of cove after cove, leaving no trace after the wakes of their canoes rippled away.

The birchbark canoe helped make the 1600s the French century, as horses made the 1500s the Spanish. The French and their Indian allies would glide into the continent across wind-chopped lakes and weed-choked shallows, portaging around rapids and over watershed ridges. Champlain pointed the way.

In 1673 Louis Jolliet and the Jesuit Jacques Marquette paddled canoes down the Fox and Wisconsin Rivers to the Mississippi and on south almost to the mouth of the Arkansas.

Jolliet, born in Canada, was the first white native North American to become a great inland explorer. Marquette, the zealous priest, was driven to spread the word to pagan Indians. Their expedition of almost 2,000 miles opened the way for France's claim to the Mississippi Valley. Nearly a decade later René-Robert Cavelier de La Salle would reach the Gulf of Mexico. Near the Mississippi's mouth he took possession in his king's name of the river and all the lands it drained, however far they might stretch.

From its Minnesota headwaters at Lake Itasca, the Mississippi River loops and winds on its 2,348-mile course to the Gulf of Mexico. Indians knew the river as the Father of Waters—Missi Sipi. French explorers Louis Jolliet and Jacques Marquette in 1673 traced its upper reaches from near Lake Superior to present-day Arkansas. Nine years later René-Robert Cavelier de La Salle journeyed to its mouth and claimed the Mississippi basin for France. But his haughty, hard-driving manner stirred ill will among disgruntled followers. On a subsequent expedition in 1687, they lured him into ambush along the Trinity River in Texas (below, right) and put a bullet through his head.

In 1687 La Salle was murdered by mutineers—not a unique fate for great explorers. Leading expeditions farther, ever farther demands a determination that followers, often sick, hungry, and demoralized, may consider madness. One of those who dared too long was Henry Hudson, who took the British flag deep into North America.

Hudson and other English navigators had tested the northern waters repeatedly in search of a sea passage to China, but they were turned back by ice. The Dutch, also eager to reach the magical East, hired Hudson to try again. He sought first to loop across the top of Europe, then reversed course and worked down the American coast from Maine to the Chesapeake Bay before testing the broad river that is named after him. Pushing past the stony island that now anchors the towers of Manhattan, Hudson sailed as far north as Albany before turning back. The following year, 1610, under the English flag, he set out northwestward, past Greenland. Through fog and ice, he drove his surly crew beyond Hudson Strait. When the shores fell away before them he was confident that he had found the far ocean at last.

Hudson was instead beating down the forbidding east coast of the immense inland sea that would be known as Hudson Bay. When he reached the southern tip of James Bay this truth dawned, but by the time he had tacked uncertainly back and forth it was late fall, and ice had locked in his ship *Discovery*. After wintering in James Bay, Hudson debated whether to press on but wavered once too often before his starving, mutinous crew, who set him and his son and a handful of sick men adrift in a small boat to die. Still, he had given England a new frontier on the edge of one of the world's greatest fur forests.

Other English captains sailed after Hudson for the Northwest Passage, but none could force his way through the ice. And so for the British, too, the immediate riches of the fur trade began to push aside the dream of the distant Orient.

English king Charles II sent two French brothers-in-law, Médard Chouart des Groseilliers and Pierre Esprit Radisson, to bypass the Dutch and French fur operations below the Great Lakes and open the vast Canadian wilderness to the northwest. Their first winter at James Bay was such a success that in 1670 "The Governor and Company of Adventurers of England trading into Hudson's Bay" were granted a charter for an enterprise called the Hudson's Bay Company. The extent of its lands was as vaguely comprehended as La Salle's claim to Louisiana and Coronado's claim in the Southwest.

By now the English, bogged down so long on the middle Atlantic coast, had at last gathered strength to pierce the mountains. Their first, earlier attempt had failed. John Smith had arrived with the Virginia colonists to settle at Jamestown in

1607, almost a quarter century after Sir Walter Raleigh's colony on the North Carolina shore had disappeared. Smith believed that somewhere tantalizingly close lay the passage to the Orient. Hardly had the Jamestown English settled when Smith started looking for that passage, poking up the Chesapeake Bay and its rivers. On one trip he reached the falls of the Potomac, but the 14 men in his shallop were exhausted, their bread sodden, their spirits unresponsive to his cajoling. They returned to Jamestown.

There malaria, dysentery, famine, and Indian massacres kept the Virginians clinging to life by their fingernails. Hundreds of miles southwest, west, north and northwest, other nations were striking into the heart of North America, but some 60 years would pass before the English made their first recorded expedition into the Blue Ridge Mountains.

In 1669 Virginia governor Sir William Berkeley sent a German physician, John Lederer, to find a way through the mountains. He became the first white person to see the Shenandoah Valley, from near Manassas Gap in the Blue Ridge.

Interstate 66 runs through that gap now. Travelers flashing past do not see the state marker that notes Lederer's accomplishment beside the old parallel road. They do see the ancient rounded mountains, many of them as thickly forested as they were in the 1600s. Beneath the Virginia pines, tulip poplars, and red oaks,

Highway to the interior, Canada's Mackenzie River mirrors the midnight sun on its 1,120-mile run to the Arctic Ocean. Alexander Mackenzie explored the river for Britain in 1789, opening extensive hinterlands to the fur trade—the region's economic mainstay into the 20th century.

A Hudson's Bay Company trader gripping his beaver hat runs the Fraser River (below). His birchbark canoe, a 25-foot canot du nord, could haul 1½ tons of pelts and trade goods.

"There wee found very loving people," wrote a crewman on Englishman Henry Hudson's *Half Moon* in the river now named for the navigator. But to the Dutch, who had sent him to find the Northwest Passage, the voyage was a failure. Later they could claim land in America based on Hudson's discovery. On his next voyage, he sailed into a northern bay and thought it was the passage; soon after, the crew mutinied, casting him and his son (below) and the ship's sick adrift to die.

undergrowth covers the slopes. Catbriers, poison ivy, and brambles clutch at passing legs, and the roller coaster ridges stretch one behind another toward the sunset horizon. Lederer, after his grueling trips through here, reported back with a perception few before him had had: "They are certainly in a great errour," he wrote, "who imagine that the Continent of North America is but eight or ten days over from the Atlantick to the Indian Ocean."

Not until a forceful frontier commander named Abraham Wood sent a horseback party up the north branch of the Roanoke in 1671 did Virginians cross the eastern divide. Near today's Blacksburg a rough ridge separates the uppermost fingers of the Roanoke and the creeks feeding the New River, which runs northwest into the Kanawha, thence to the Ohio, the Mississippi, and the Gulf. The explorers, Thomas Batts and Robert Fallam, dismounted to scramble over the ridge. They followed the New River three days and ran out of food. As they started to turn back, they saw beyond the mountains "a fog arise and a glimmering light as from water. We supposed there to be a great Bay."

There was not, of course, as James Needham, another explorer sent by Wood, found when he reached the Cherokee nation along the upper Tennessee River two years later. Those Cherokees had never seen a great bay, white man, or horse, but they did have Spanish trade goods.

107

Shipwrecked and ravaged by scurvy, Vitus Bering and his crew make a desperate push for a rocky island off Kamchatka, in this romanticized painting. Here Bering would die of the disease along with many of his men. On this voyage in 1741 the Danish navigator, commissioned by the Russian navy, had set off from Siberia with two ships to explore the North Pacific. The vessels sailed parallel to the Aleutian Islands and then separated. Bering went on to sight Alaska's Mount Saint Elias, thus discovering America from the west, and met his death returning home. The second ship had sailed home independently, contrary to what this painting shows.

The survivors among Bering's crew rebuilt their ship and returned to Siberia. The luxurious sea otter pelts they carried led to a fortune in fur trading for Tsar Peter the Great and, eventually, to a Russian settlement in Alaska.

So among the English on the coast, still bedazzled by the glimmering light of illusory seas beyond the mountains, awareness grew that the Spaniards down that way and the French up the other way were not stories, but real. These metal hatchets and glass beads said so. By 1689 the Virginians and their coastal countrymen were struggling with the French in an off-and-on frontier war that would last nearly 75 years longer. For many of those years, the French and Spaniards were also contending for the great spaces between the Mississippi and the still elusive western sea.

Farther north, the British were looking in the same direction. In 1690 the Hudson's Bay Company sent west a young man who had learned Indian ways. Henry Kelsey pushed across the head of Lake Winnipeg to the Great Plains. In the journal of his two-year trip he recorded seeing "a great sort of bear . . . neither white nor black but silver haired like our English rabbit"— the grizzly. He probably was the first European to see the musk-ox. He had blazed what would become Canada's historic route west.

A century later Britain's Alexander Mackenzie left the Great Slave

109

An outcrop now dubbed Rebel's Rock looms over the Kentucky region that Daniel Boone explored in 1769. Having heard tales of wondrous, game-rich lands beyond the Appalachians, Boone and a few companions crossed through the Cumberland Gap into the forests of eastern Kentucky. A path he cleared six years later became the Wilderness Road, which served pioneering settlers for many years as the gateway to the West. Seen here with dog and rifle in his later years, Daniel Boone lived to become a new nation's quintessential frontiersman—celebrated as much in folklore as in fact.

The hazards of frontier life—as dramatized below—included the abduction by Shawnee Indians and rescue of Boone's daughter Jemima and two of her friends in the summer of 1776, soon after the establishment of a permanent settlement at Boonesboro.

Lake to trace the river that has his name, expecting to reach the Pacific. Instead it curved north, and he followed it to where it spills into the Beaufort Sea and the Arctic Ocean. In 1793 he paddled up the Peace River into the Rocky Mountains, crossed them, and then ran down the Bella Coola to the Pacific. He thus became the first European to traverse the continent north of Mexico.

Back East, population pressure was building that would eventually explode in a broad movement across North America. In 1775 frontiersman Daniel Boone, born in Pennsylvania and brought up there and in the mountains of North Carolina, led the band that blazed the Wilderness Road. He took them through the mountains at Cumberland Gap to open the way into Kentucky. Land agent Thomas Walker had discovered that gap, an old Indian trail, a quarter century earlier while probing the Tennessee Valley.

Boone is well known in legend for fighting Indians, but his raptures over the land he opened inspired others to poetry on his behalf. At first, his ghostwriter penned, Boone might have been seized with melancholy without his family, but the land's beauty "expelled every gloomy thought." He did not return to his family till the next year, "with a determination to bring them as soon as possible to live in Kentucke, which I esteemed a second paradise."

Settlers poured through the gap into Boone's paradise, and looked

beyond it to the Mississippi River and French Louisiana. Americans were following Alexander Hamilton's advice: "Learn to think continentally." In 1803 President Thomas Jefferson bought that vast French domain and determined to make it American. He sent Virginians Meriwether Lewis and William Clark on an epic venture up the Missouri, across the Rockies, and down the Columbia River to the western sea.

Except for Alaska and the Arctic, the broad geography of North America was settled. But a large part of it still had to be filled in. The Great Basin, between the Rockies and the Sierra Nevada, was not explored until 1826 when an indomitable fur trader named Jedediah Smith set out to find a link between the Great Salt Lake and the Pacific—the legendary Rio Buenaventura. He found no river, but he crossed the Mojave Desert, becoming the first American to enter California from the east, and returned over the Sierra Nevada. He later traveled the California coast to Oregon. Smith's small parties of explorers were repeatedly attacked by Indians, but he kept going out again. Once he was half-scalped by a grizzly and calmly instructed his comrade how to sew his head back together.

Almost two decades after Smith's determined journeys, the flamboyant soldier-surveyor John Charles Frémont went on his first western expedition, to establish American claims in Oregon. On the way he met the famous Indian agent Kit Carson, who signed on as guide. Frémont's three major expeditions earned him the nickname The Pathfinder. A zealous expansionist, he mapped much of the land between the Mississippi Valley and the Pacific, methodically recording temperatures, geological structures, topography. His third journey in 1845 took him over the Sierra at the outset of the Mexican War, in which he aided in the conquest of California.

The westward sweep of settlers after the war left only a few places to be explored. The formidable valley of the Colorado River was one of them.

John Wesley Powell, who had lost his right arm at Shiloh but fought on through the Civil War, was a professor of geology when he and his nine assistants put four heavily laden boats into the water at Green River, Wyoming, on May 24, 1869. Propelled by a swift current, his boats plunged south, leaping like "herds of startled deer bounding through forests beset with fallen timber." That was only a suggestion of what lay ahead. The evening before tackling the Canyon of Lodore, Powell wrote of black shadows creeping downward, making the canyon "a dark portal to a region of gloom—the gateway through which we are to enter on our voyage of exploration tomorrow. What shall we find?" They found dangerous rapids that had to be portaged, but one of his boats missed his signal from shore and shot into the maelstrom, to be smashed into splinters. Other deadly chutes

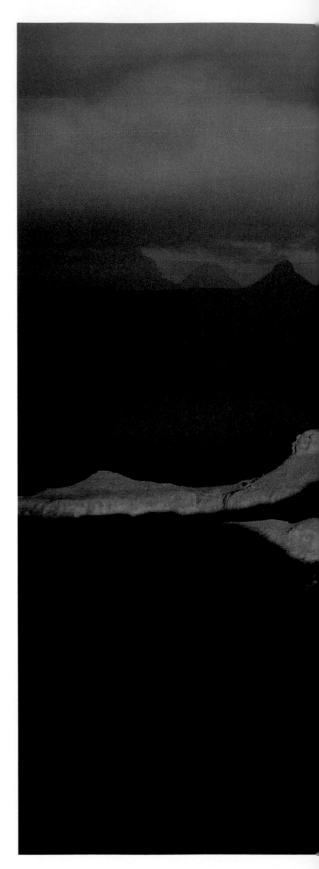

Tumbling rapids hurtle John Wesley Powell and his crew through the Grand Canyon in 1869. On this 1,000-mile journey down the Green and Colorado Rivers, the men suffered near starvation and arduous portages to explore the unknown region Coronado's men found more than 300 years before. Geologist Powell wrote: "All these canyons unite to form one grand canyon, the most sublime spectacle on earth."

roared downstream, day after day, with few stretches of calm.

Eleven weeks of this, and Powell was only then heading into the Grand Canyon itself. He wrote, "What falls there are, we know not; what rocks beset the channel, we know not; what walls rise over the river, we know not. . . . The men talk as cheerfully as ever; . . . but to me the cheer is sombre." Pressing on, they plunged over rapids where the canyon walls were so high there was no way to portage around. They made it, and another, and another, until a smooth run enabled Powell to write, "a few days like this, and we shall be out of prison."

He was too optimistic. There was more. To traverse the gorge where sightseeing planes and helicopters flash today, the expedition endured murderous portages, capsizings, near starvation. Three men deserted; after climbing up to the plateau, they were killed by Indians. Eventually Powell brought his surviving crewmen out of the Grand Canyon 98 days and some 1,000 miles below his entry. He became a national hero.

John Wesley Powell was one of the last of his premechanized kind. Through more than 300 years, these men risked their lives to slash across North America. Spaniards, French, English, and Americans, they opened the land of the Indians and buffalo. They died not knowing that their legacy to us—a land once considered a barrier to riches—would turn out to be the richest in history.

Meriwether Lewis
William Clark

By Margaret Sedeen

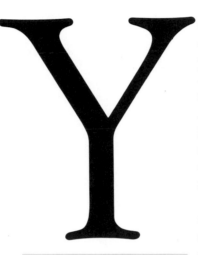

May 26, 1805: Capt. Meriwether Lewis, near the source of the Missouri River, feels "a secret pleasure" at his first view of the Rocky Mountains.

Y*our mission is to explore the Missouri river, & such principal stream of it, as*—today the ink on the yellowed paper is faint, the writing here and there almost illegible—*by it's course & communication with the waters of the Pacific Ocean, may offer the most direct & practicable water communication across this continent, for the purposes of commerce.* The date, *this 20th day of June 1803,* and the signature, *Th. Jefferson Pr. U. S. of America.*

A year later Jefferson's Corps of Discovery set out. The place they went, by pirogue and canoe, by horseback and bleeding, aching feet, was an unimaginable other world from the tidy frontier of coastal plain and round-shouldered Appalachians. For months they were given up for dead, long before they set their downstream oars in the mighty Missouri. They were Virginians and Kentuckians, Georgians and Pennsylvanians, Tarheels and Yankees. From St. Louis they paddled and poled, towed and rode, and walked 1,610 miles, to build themselves a log fortification surrounded by the earthen lodges of Mandans, Arikaras, and Hidatsas, in the midst of bleak Dakota hills, in a winter so cold the whiskey froze, on a bend along the north bank of the Missouri River.

Come spring, they would paddle and pole, ride and tow, and walk in the end 8,000 miles—almost a third of the way around the world—in hardscrabble pursuit of the destiny of the United States of America.

Meriwether Lewis and William Clark, wilderness soldiers and Virginia gentlemen, led the search for trade routes and trading partners among the Indian nations. Lewis, secretary to President Jefferson, was 29 years old. From the age of 18, he'd seen this mission as a "da[r]ling project." Others had almost gotten it, but now it was his.

And Clark's. William Clark, draftsman, geographer of genius, and cocaptain, was 33 years old. Among the corps Patrick Gass and Nathaniel Hale Pryor were carpenters; the smiths were John Shields (kin

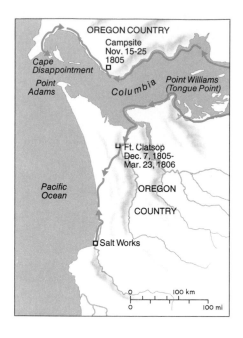

to Daniel Boone), William Bratton, and Alexander Hamilton Willard; Joseph Whitehouse was a hide curer and tailor; Pierre Cruzatte knew the hand signs that made a common language across the plains; several men were expert hunters whose game fed the explorers and multitudes of Indian friends. Lewis's Newfoundland, Scannon, pulled fowl out of the rivers. Clark's servant and companion since childhood, a large black man called York, delighted in the consternation of Indians who judged his mysterious color "big medicine."

They named their Dakota camp Fort Mandan and placed it at an ancient crossroads of Plains Indian traders. While men of the corps scouted for timber, hewed logs, and built the stockaded cabins, Indians milled about day and night. Along the riverbanks between villages, women in buckskin dresses, with vermilion-painted faces, filled their braided willow baskets with firewood, fish from the weirs, or corn harvested from the rich bottomlands. Some ferried their burdens across the river in coracles made of a buffalo skin with the tail still on, stretched on a willow frame. Men, women, and children dived into the river, bathing, swimming, and splashing. Haughty warriors, wrapped in painted buffalo robes and adorned with necklaces of three-inch, white-tipped grizzly claws, wheeled their spirited horses and galloped up and down flourishing muskets, bows, and battle-axes.

Captains Lewis and Clark planned a winter of diplomacy and accordingly had packed $669.50 worth of Indian presents, the largest item in their budget. They held official meetings with Indian leaders to remind any and all that by virtue of the Louisiana Purchase this was now American territory. Amidst much ritual handing around of medicine pipes, solemn puffing for the success of the councils, and speechifying on all sides, the captains "made chiefs." One was Black Moccasin, the Hidatsa who nicknamed Lewis "Long Knife," for his sword, and Clark "Red Hair," so strange was such a thing.

In deference to Indian protocol, they presented to first-rank chiefs hollow, silver medals imprinted with Jefferson's likeness; to less important chiefs medals with motifs of farm and home. All received American flags and clothing: cocked hats with red feathers, belts, garters, calico shirts, and especially, gaudy frock coats.

On one windy October day Lewis and Clark ratified 21 Indian chiefs, all of them chiefs already well made by feats of bravery, by largesse, by the acclaim of their own people, in a land where their culture had ripened over seven centuries. Probably Black Moccasin and his fellows thought they were joining a chiefdom of commerce, since the coats and other symbols were the same as they'd already received from British and French fur traders. Jefferson had supplied the captains with printed forms that declared in lawyers' English the confidence of the United States government in the friendship of the particular Indian leader. Each certificate had a dotted line where the chief's or the warrior's name was written in: *Sha-ha-ka* or *Min-nis-sur-ra-ree* or *Omp-se-ha-ra*

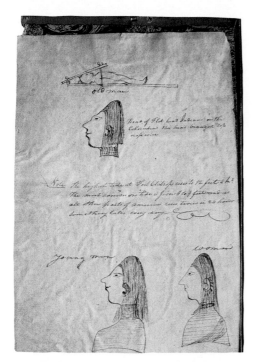

Clark's journal sketches: Clatsop Indians beautifying the skulls of their infants; a sage grouse, discovered by Lewis on the Marias River in northwest Montana.

(Black Moccasin). Then the two captains dated and signed each page.

The Indians reciprocated with social calls—"as usial Stay all Day," complained Clark—and gifts of food. Some brought dried pumpkin and pemmican. All winter of 1804 and 1805 they came with corn in payment for the labor of the corps' hardworking smiths, who fixed tools and guns and made iron battle-axes.

In March the river ice broke up. The water rose in the banks. Ducks and geese flew north, and the Indians began to set the prairie fires that would bring rich green grass for the buffalo. By the dim light of April dawns, Indians on the Missouri bluffs watched two pirogues and six canoes point their prows upstream, seeking the western ocean. The 31 corpsmen viewed their "little fleet" with as much pride as Columbus or Cook had theirs. Two thousand miles of unknown terrain lay ahead, and "the good or evil it had in store," Lewis somberly observed, "was for experiment yet to determine, and these little vessells contained every article by which we were to . . . subsist or defend ourselves."

In camp the captains shared their buffalo-skin tepee with the interpreters George Drouillard and Toussaint Charbonneau, and Charbonneau's 17-year-old wife and infant son. That the woman, Sacagawea, was Shoshoni was a happy accident, for it was the Shoshoni from whom captains Lewis and Clark hoped to buy horses to span the trail between navigable water at the head of the Missouri and the western river they sought to the Pacific. Sacagawea would be useful as an interpreter, they hoped, and as a sign of friendship to Indians they met, for no war party ever traveled with a woman and a baby.

With a good wind, the pirogues went under sail. In deep water the oarsmen rowed. In shallow, the men lined up on each side of the boat, poles in hand. One by one, each man at the head of the line thrust his pole into the riverbed, then walked aft. When he reached the stern, he pulled out the pole and took his place at the end of the line.

Early May was cold, with snow squalls and morning frosts, and ice on the oars. One of the captains usually walked on shore, often exploring miles into the countryside, hunting game and feeding a boundless curiosity about the stretches of the great continent where, they told themselves, "the foot of civilized man had never trodden." The river bluffs were high now, the current swift, and the bottom rocky. Sails, oars, and poles gave way to towropes—the best were of braided elk skin—man-handled by heaving crews sometimes up to their armpits in water, or barefoot on the slippery slopes. Not that moccasins lasted anyway. Two days was their lifespan, one day new, one day patched.

By the end of May, they'd made 2,500 miles upriver. Lewis thought the sandstone bluffs of the Missouri Breaks, "most romantic." They reminded him "of those large stone buildings in the U. States." But the perpendicular walls made the towing so painful that the captain called a halt one noon and gave a dram to his "faithful fellows."

Mindful of their duty, both Clark and Lewis recorded everything they saw, with an eye to its use to a young nation. What they took to be good coal was only lignite. The plains seemed fertile. And the game!

Clark and Lewis, with Sacagawea and Toussaint Charbonneau at Three Forks of the Missouri.

Elk, deer, antelope, buffalo by the thousand and tens of thousands, buffalo in "gangs." One bull, swimming the river in the middle of the night, clambered across a pirogue and charged up the riverbank, thundering inches from the heads of the sleeping men.

One day they came to an Indian buffalo jump, the stampeded carcasses in heaps at the foot of the cliff. Wolves prowled about so "verry gentle" that Clark killed one with his sword. Sergeant Ordway complained, "the Game is gitting so pleanty and tame in this country that Some of the party clubbed them out of their way."

Even so, the entire contingent of buckskinned hunters, pouring water down prairie dog holes, needed several hours to capture a single specimen of the intriguing species new to American science. The expedition also introduced to naturalists back East the pronghorn, mule deer, coyote, jack rabbit, and the grizzly, of which Lewis soon admitted that he'd rather fight two Indians than one of these "gentlemen."

A third of a ton, eight feet from nose to tail, and "so hard to die," the grizzly bear seemed an almost invincible spirit of the wilderness. The mountain men had a rule: Never fight a grizzly except in self-defense. But the animal held a fascination for the men of the corps that time and again almost cost them their lives. Grizzlies preyed among the swarms of game, and whenever Lewis or Clark or one of the men saw a bear, they shot. And usually had to flee from its rage, and shoot again and again—ten musket balls went into one—until the bear fell.

Early in June a critical question presented itself. The river split, one stream flowing from the north, another from the south. Which fork was the Missouri? Which the way to the Columbia? A mistake now would lose the rest of the season and jeopardize the enterprise. Men went investigating. All were asked an opinion; most voted for the north fork, with its muddy resemblance to the Missouri they knew. But it was on the south fork that Lewis found the magnificent Great Falls the Indians had told them about.

A nasty portage lay ahead. Clark surveyed it and found a 10-mile stretch where the river dropped 400 feet. In camp, Lewis supervised the construction of "four sets of truck wheels with couplings, toungs and bodies" for carrying baggage and canoes. In the whole neighborhood they found only one tree, a 22-inch cottonwood, large enough to make wheels. They'd left one pirogue behind long ago. Now they unloaded and cached the other. Clark staked out the best route he could find but it took the men 11 days and 18 miles of moccasin-piercing torture, cutting a riverside road as they went.

Stroke by stroke they were nearing the end of navigable water. Even now they spent more time dragging the boats through canyons than rowing. If they were to cross the Rocky Mountains before winter, they must find Shoshonis with horses. Sacagawea began to recognize the country. One August night they camped on the spot where she'd been captured by Hidatsa raiders five years before, to be carried off to the Dakotas and bought by Charbonneau for a horse or two, a gun or some blue beads, and maybe a gallon of whiskey.

Le Borgne, the fierce, one-eyed Hidatsa chief, baffled by a black man. A wet finger tries to rub away the "paint," as Le Borgne would stripe himself for war.

The captains split the group in order to widen the search. As bald eagles and ospreys soared overhead, and rattlesnakes and prickly pear lurked underfoot, both groups of explorers combed the countryside for nine days, hoping that from behind a clump of willows or out of a ravine would step the Indians they knew must be watching the approach of the strange people—obviously poor—who wore no blankets. When separated, the captains often left notes for each other on branches, white men's words fluttering in a wilderness that until now knew neither writing, nor paper, nor ink. When Lewis headed up a river fork, he posted the news on a green willow pole by the riverbank. Clark never found the message because a beaver appropriated the signpost.

But Sacagawea's message was clear. As they approached some Shoshoni horsemen, she began to skip and dance, joyously sucking on her fingers in sign language to Clark, "Here are the people who suckled me!" The Indian girl, by a small gift of grace, had come home.

Soon Indians were embracing the explorers in a bear-greasy, squeezing cheek-to-cheek. Lewis grew "heartily tired of the national hug." Before they could council, they must smoke a pipe, and as a sign of trust, remove the moccasins—Lewis, Clark, the braves, and the chief, Cameahwait, "a man of Influence Sence & easey & reserved manners," though hard times had made him lank jawed from hunger. Barefoot, the councils began, with Sacagawea interpreting. It was unusual enough to have a woman present, but this one broke all decorum by jumping up, bursting into tears, and throwing her blanket around Chief Cameahwait, whom she had suddenly recognized as her brother.

"We made [the Indians] sensible of their dependance on the will of our government," said Lewis and Clark through their sobbing interpreter, "for every species of merchandize as well as for their defence & comfort." They went on: "We also gave them as a reason why we wished to pe[ne]trate the country as far as the ocean to the west of them was to . . . find out a more direct way to bring merchandize to them." The captains distributed certificates, medals, coats, scarlet leggings, tobacco, knives, awls, beads, and looking glasses. With more presents they bought horses and guides.

Back in Virginia, early autumn meant cool mornings, hot sunny afternoons, red and gold leaves, and a dawdling summer. But to the men, and the Indian girl and her baby, who slogged along the Salmon and the Lehmi, high in the Bitterroot range of the Rockies, tracing the ridges of the Nez Perce buffalo road, September brought frost on their blankets, sleet, and eight inches of snow on the trail. Game was scarce and shy. Horses slipped and rolled down the mountainsides. Hungry, shivering in their brittle, heavy buckskins, the men stumbled over fallen timber, finding their way by the line of tree branches broken when the Indian horses packed buffalo meat back from the plains.

"High ruged mountains in every direction as far as I could see." On the sixth day of the climb, his feet freezing in thin moccasins, Clark forged ahead of the main party to get fires going and cook the "fine meat" of the second colt they'd eaten that week. Two days later, with a few men and no baggage, he descended rapidly toward the Nez Perce camp on the Clearwater, and food. The generosity of these Indians was a mixed blessing. Almost the entire corps fell ill with dysentery, probably from the dried salmon and camas root given them by the chief, Twisted Hair. But they wanted to press on. They had crossed the Rockies. The current that ran beside them now would lead to the Pacific.

They found some good stands of pine, and in eleven days the men who could work had made five dugouts. The swift flow of the Clearwater and the Snake led to the Columbia. They tackled rapids, shoals, rocks, cascades, portages, and a diet of rotting elk meat, dried salmon, dogmeat, acorns, and, with infrequent luck, "blue wing Teel," and Private Collins's delicious beer of camas root. Each day they met more Indians, people who had brass teakettles, scarlet and blue cloth, sailor jackets, and weapons—goods from traders on the coast. They also had fleas, as the explorers discovered in portaging by Indian campsites. "Every man of the party was obliged to Strip naked dureing the time of take-

Had I these white warriors in the upper plains, my young men would do for them as they would for so many wolves, for there are only two sensible men amongst them, the worker in iron and the mender of guns.
LE BORGNE, HIDATSA CHIEF

123

ing over the canoes, that they might have an oppertunity of brushing the flees of[f] their legs and bodies."

As the river widened and the fine-furred seals somersaulted among the rocks, the fare improved, and the corps ate deer, grouse, fish, and roots and vegetables gathered by Sacagawea. But they had learned to like dog, and bought it from the Indians when they could.

Early in a stormy November, they began riding the tide. At every flood, great swells dashed drift logs against the rocks. Flea-bitten and miserable, the men wore sodden, rotted clothes, and would have no better until they could hunt and dress skins, and sew during winter camp. But in their ears roared the breakers of the 20-mile-wide estuary.

"Ocian in view! O! the joy." Later a jubilant Clark led his men to a promontory above the Pacific, where they seemed "much Satisfied with their trip." Then they carved their names on the tree trunks.

Again the captains consulted their corps. Where to build the winter quarters? They explored the north bank of the river but chose the south, where they could make themselves salt from the seawater, and keep a watch for trading vessels that might call. None did. There were calls from Clatsops and Chinooks, including a chief and "six women of his nation which the old baud his wife had brought for market." During the five-months' winter they saw the sun only six days. In a windy, rainy spring, 1806, they turned their eyes to the east.

They would report to Thomas Jefferson that they had found a way: "Fur trade may be carried on . . . much cheaper than by any [other] rout by which it can be conveyed to the East indias." The Northwest Passage turned out to be the American frontier.

That they knew as they pulled their oars homeward. They prophesied that trading posts would rise at the mouth of the Yellowstone and the Marias; recommended that they be built on the Columbia. When Lewis and Clark rowed homeward past Fort Mandan, they might have guessed that their Hidatsa and Mandan friends would meet big medicine—the great thunder canoe—when steamboats came up the Missouri, and the biggest, when the smallpox that traveled with the white men killed the red men.

But they could never have known that by their success railroads would obliterate their footsteps along the Clearwater and the Columbia; that dams would drown their campsites; that the buffalo and the grizzly were not, after all, so hard to die. Going home in triumph, they made sometimes 70 downstream miles a day, in their wake the road now open. On the afternoon of September 20, 1806, just above St. Charles, Missouri, they rowed past a field of grazing cows, and raised a cheer.

To know Lewis and Clark is to know America, so well does their story embody our national icons. To know them best, read their journals in the original or in the classic one-volume edition by Bernard de Voto. The journals of George Catlin and Prince Maximilian of Wied, with the magnificent paintings of Catlin and Karl Bodmer, portray the Plains Indian life that Lewis and Clark knew on the eve of its demise.

The Corps of Discovery greeting Chinooks near the mouth of the Columbia, November 1805.

West Meets East

By Elisabeth B. Booz

The goatskin water bottles were dry. Camels, horses, and two score men plodded down the edge of the shimmering, wind-ridged Kyzyl Kum, one of west-central Asia's bleakest deserts. Anthony Jenkinson, the young English merchant-adventurer who had hired them, could only trust the word of his Muslim guides that a river, the Oxus, was near.

Bandits attacked the next morning, December 15, 1558. Shots from Jenkinson's four harquebuses held the intruders off until nightfall. Bales of woolen cloth made a fortress, but the bandits, encamped at arrow range, blocked the way to the river. Their price was the surrender of any Christians. A brave Muslim holy man from the caravan stepped out to vow that there were none. The bandits roughed him up and took a loaded camel as tribute, then vanished into the desert. That next evening the caravan reached the Oxus River and men and animals drank for the first time in three days.

One week later, Anthony Jenkinson sighted the great minaret of Bukhara on the horizon, a beacon to Cathay. If his luck held, an Englishman would at last find a shortcut to the wealth of the East.

That search had engrossed England since John Cabot failed to navigate a northwest passage through Canada's arctic seas in 1497. Cabot's son, Sebastian, sent mariners in 1553 to seek a northeast passage to the "backe side" of Cathay. They found Russia and forged a friendship. Young Ivan IV, the tsar, who had not yet earned his nickname, the Terrible, welcomed the English to his gaudy court in Moscow and agreed to trade with them through the White Sea. Anthony Jenkinson, captain-general of the new Muscovy Company, dreamed of taking England's trade to Cathay. He set out, with the tsar's blessing, to find a route through Russia.

Bukhara's twinkling turquoise domes, capped with lopsided storks' nests, greeted Jenkinson. The aroma of grilled mutton, yellow dust in the eyes, the babble of strange languages rose as he shoved his way through the city's massive gateway. Domed malls straddlèd intersections, enclosing a hubbub of bargaining for pungent cloves and cardamom, rugs, jewelry, a rare bolt of silk.

This small khanate was long past its 6th-century heyday on the Silk Road. Muslim invaders from Arabia had taken it in the 7th century; nomads from Mongolia under Genghis Khan did so again in the 13th. The Mongols welded Eurasia into the biggest empire the world has ever seen and stopped only after slaughtering all the way into Eastern Europe.

The Pope, much shaken, composed a letter in 1245 to the Great Khan protesting further invasions and suggesting he convert to Christianity. John of Plano Carpini and a companion friar carried the letter

Muslim Uygurs drive a traditional cart with donkey outriders past weathered mud-brick ruins of Turfan in the Gobi of northern China. Empires and religions swept across this region through many centuries. The hollows in a manmade hillside housed princes, merchants, scholars, and Buddhist monks when Turfan's wealthy oasis formed a vital link in Asia's fabled Silk Road. Mongol conquerors had occupied Turfan when the Polo brothers visited about 1265 en route to Cathay.

Hsuan-tsang, a Buddhist monk and one of Asia's first recorded explorers, returns to China in A.D. 645 carrying scriptures from India in his backpack. The advanced civilizations of China and India, separated by central Asia's formidable terrain, remained mysteries to one another. Europeans explored complex societies on the continent's periphery, and gradually penetrated interior deserts and mountains until Tibet, at the center, was opened to Western influences in the 20th century.

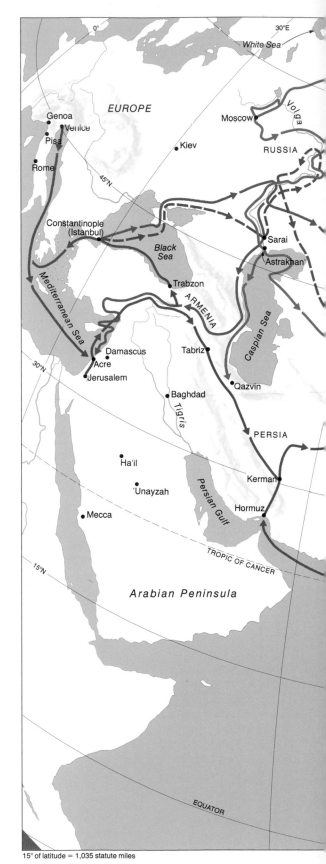

———— Rubrouck 1253-55
———— Marco Polo 1271-1295
– – – Elder Polos (where different from Marco Polo) 1254-1269
———— Xavier and other Jesuits 1540-1622
———— Ricci 1578-1610
———— Jenkinson 1557-1571
———— Yermak 1579-1585
———— Tavernier 1638-1668
———— Przhevalsky 1867-1888
———— Younghusband 1886-1904
———— David-Néel 1921-24

some 5,000 miles across deserts and mountains to Karakorum, a sprawling city of gold-embroidered tents glittering on Mongolia's grassy plain. Thus the friars became the first western Europeans to explore Mongolia and write about it. They marveled at the khan's elaborate throne, the silks and furs of his cosmopolitan courtiers. The khan, however, scoffed at the Pope's overture, offered without tribute.

Europe's scholars pored over the report the monks brought back, and the journal of William of Rubrouck, a friar who reached Karakorum a decade later. Like many who would venture into Asia, Rubrouck and Plano Carpini were not wilderness adventurers so much as social explorers, strangers in strange lands. When West met East, when European faced Asian, often the arena was religion, commerce, or military conquest, or a tangle of all three.

Europe had long gazed at Asia through a haze of fantasy that included a land of dogheaded humans. In 1298 a new account seized European imaginations, that of a young Venetian who accompanied his father and uncle, merchants Niccolò and Maffeo Polo, on their second trip to Cathay. Marco Polo's book amused readers, and in time was recognized as truth. In 1558 Anthony Jenkinson wanted to follow the Polos' footsteps to Cathay.

In Bukhara, Jenkinson's luck ran out. No traders had come from Cathay for years and he learned that the

15° of latitude = 1,035 statute miles

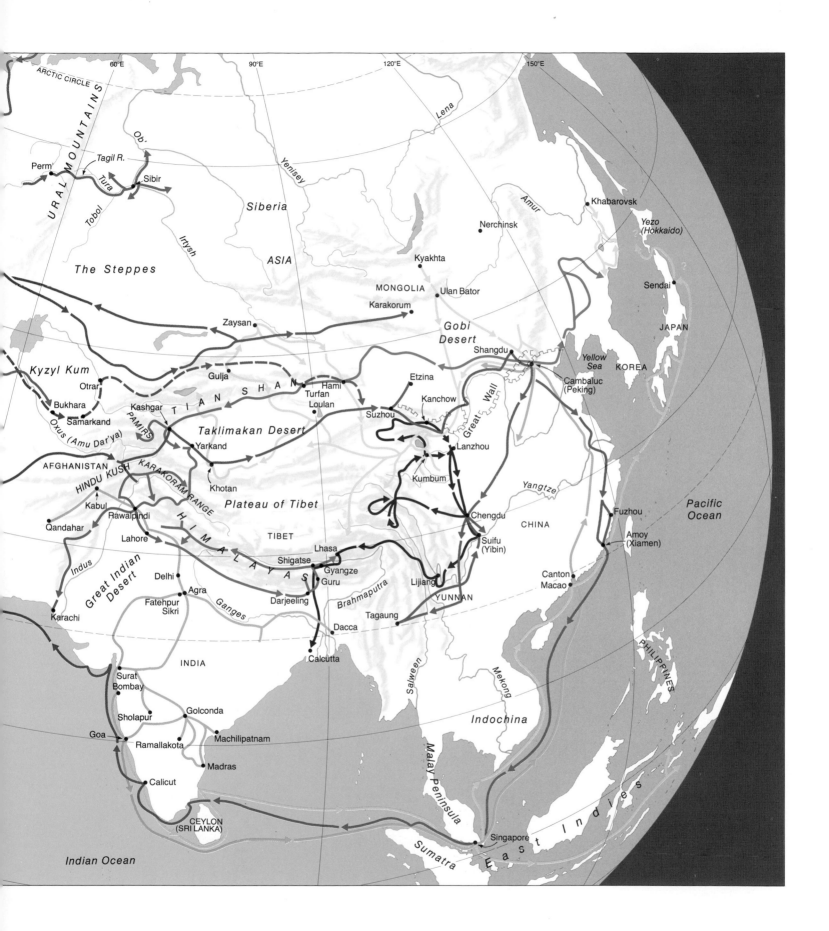

ARCTIC CIRCLE

60°E
90°E
120°E
150°E

URAL MOUNTAINS

Perm'
Tagil R.
Tura
Tobol
Sibir
Ob'
Irtysh
Yenisey
Lena
Siberia
ASIA

The Steppes

Zaysan

Amur
Khabarovsk
Yezo (Hokkaido)
Nerchinsk
Kyakhta
MONGOLIA
Ulan Bator
Karakorum
Gobi Desert

Sendai
JAPAN

Kyzyl Kum
Otrar
Bukhara
Samarkand
Oxus (Amu Dar'ya)
PAMIRS
Kashgar
TIAN SHAN
Gulja
Hami
Turfan
Loulan
Suzhou
Taklimakan Desert
Yarkand
Etzina
Kanchow
Great Wall
Shangdu
Yellow Sea
KOREA
Cambaluc (Peking)

Khotan
Lanzhou
Kumbum

AFGHANISTAN
HINDU KUSH
KARAKORAM RANGE
Kabul
Qandahar
Rawalpindi
Lahore
Indus
HIMALAYAS
Plateau of Tibet
TIBET
Chengdu
CHINA
Yangtze
Fuzhou
Pacific Ocean
Amoy (Xiamen)

Great Indian Desert
Delhi
Agra
Fatehpur Sikri
Ganges
Lhasa
Shigatse
Gyangze
Guru
Darjeeling
Brahmaputra
Suifu (Yibin)
Lijiang
YUNNAN
Canton
Macao

Karachi
Dacca
Tagaung
Salween

Surat
Bombay
INDIA
Calcutta

Sholapur
Golconda
Mekong
Indochina
PHILIPPINES

Goa
Ramallakota
Machilipatnam
Madras
Malay Peninsula

Calicut
CEYLON (SRI LANKA)

Indian Ocean
Sumatra
Singapore
East Indies

129

dangerous journey there took nine months; it was farther than anyone in England imagined. And the only customer for his cloth was Bukhara's crafty khan, who failed to pay.

Jenkinson retraced his way across the desert and the Caspian Sea, shepherding six Asian ambassadors to the tsar of Russia. His journey was not as fruitless as he believed. His observations provided a base for later European explorers. And by delivering the ambassadors to Tsar Ivan, he introduced the khanates of central Asia to modern Russia.

Ivan was to have another, less courtly Asian encounter. Near the Ural Mountains his vassals the Stroganovs ran a huge fur enterprise protected by Cossacks. Ivan depended on fur to pay his debts. So he shook with anger on hearing that the Stroganovs had left their lands unprotected. They had urged an outlaw Cossack named Yermak to cross the Urals and battle Kuchum Khan, a Tatar warlord who was terrorizing western Siberia.

It was 1581. Yermak Timofeyevich led into the mountains a Cossack army carrying muskets provided by the Stroganovs and banners embroidered with images of Russian saints. From there melting snow carried them in rough-hewn boats down the little Tagil River through silent, misty birch forests into Siberia. The silver treetops of winter dissolved into golden-green leaf as their stream joined the bigger Tura River and

flowed to the Tobol, the Irtysh, the Ob'. The Cossacks were entering one of the immense river systems that connect most of Siberia.

Kuchum Khan heard of their approach. He ordered an iron chain stretched across the lower Tura River and placed hundreds of bowmen out of sight on its overgrown banks. Yermak's boat, well ahead of the rest, met a hail of arrows but escaped upstream. When the hidden Tatars saw the main flotilla riding the swift current toward the chain, they realized too late that the "boatmen" were birch branches dressed in Cossack shirts. Yermak's men had sneaked ashore to attack them from the rear.

On the Irtysh a Tatar army waited to defend Kuchum Khan's log-built capital, Sibir—"sleeping land." Cossacks plunged into battle. When Kuchum's commander fell, the khan of Sibir retreated into the forest.

Winter assaulted the Cossack remnants. Kuchum Khan menaced, invisible. Yermak, the outlaw, took a bold gamble. He sent a ragged squad on snowshoes to Moscow, their sleds piled high with sable, black fox, beaver—tribute from Siberian tribes. Yermak was offering the conquered lands to the tsar in return for help.

A joyful Ivan embraced the exhausted messengers and set church bells pealing. He promised troops, and to Yermak himself he sent two suits of richly worked body armor and his own fur mantle.

133

A camphorwood torii gate rises above Japan's Hiroshima Bay, demarcating the holy space that extends from a Shinto shrine on shore. Japan's native religion espoused nationalistic values. Religious ceremonies were the foundation of the government. Shintoism would prove unfertile ground for some of the ideas imported by European traders and missionaries who arrived on Japan's shores in the 16th century.

A folding rice-paper screen painted around 1600 (below) shows a Portuguese ship embarking on a trading voyage to the Far East. The foreign port, possibly Goa, imagined by Japanese artist Kano Naizen teems with Europeans in exaggerated pantaloons.

Yermak held Sibir fast, but Kuchum Khan lurked in the forests. In late summer, 1585, out along the Irtysh, the Tatars attacked at night and butchered many Cossacks. Yermak made a run for his boat but the leap fell short. Dragged down by the tsar's splendid armor, he drowned.

Yermak's life and death lived on in legend. His feats had given Russia the foundation of its great Asian power. Explorers, followed by traders and soldiers, pressed on toward the Pacific. Eventually, Russians were confronting Chinese along the Amur River. In 1689 the two sides met at a small Siberian town.

They had no common tongue. To the Russians' amazement, western Europeans in Chinese clothing, speaking half a dozen languages, negotiated an agreement. The Treaty of Nerchinsk was written in three languages: Russian, Manchu, and Latin, the language of these indispensable Jesuit priests.

Jesuits had been in Asia for well over a century. Members of this quasi-military Society of Jesus fanned out to convert the heathen of newly discovered lands overseas. In 1542 Francis Xavier set up Asian headquarters at Goa, on India's west coast. Xavier went to Japan in 1549. The honesty and good manners of the Japanese people delighted him. In a letter to Goa he wrote, "We shall never find among heathens another race to equal the Japanese."

Xavier found that in Japan feudal lords, or daimyos, ruled fiefdoms as they pleased. Jesuits and other Christians who came after Xavier saw that if they could befriend and convert a daimyo, his retinue would follow. By 1614 there were 300,000

A Japanese Buddhist priest burns prayer sticks in a sacred ritual of the Tendai sect (opposite). Buddhism first flourished in India around 500 B.C. A thousand years later Koreans brought it to Japan, where it took root because it adapted to native customs and beliefs. Catholic missionaries from the militant Society of Jesus, called Jesuits, reached Japan in 1549, initiating what was called a Christian Century. But the European faith demanded obedience to a foreign God. This allegiance threat-ened a growing political unity in Japan, and rulers outlawed Christianity.

Expelled in 1614, Diogo Carvalho joined other Jesuits returning in disguise. Most were captured. A 17th-century engraving depicts Carvalho's slow execution by freezing in a river. The figure on the bank is the European artist's idea of a Japanese soldier.

Christians in Japan. European customs became fashionable. Daimyos wore imported hats and crucifixes, and sat sipping sherry from goblets.

The Jesuits became part of Japanese society. They made themselves indispensable to the daimyos as agents to the Portuguese merchants who for half a century had carried the lucrative silk trade from China. More than one daimyo may have embraced Christianity for the commercial opportunities it offered.

In 1600 a new ruler, Ieyasu, seized power in Japan, bringing the daimyos under his control. Wary of the growing Christian strength, Ieyasu banned Christianity in 1614.

Several Jesuits stayed, as outlaws. They traced clandestine Christian groups who had scattered northward into unknown regions. Girolamo de Angelis mapped part of Hokkaido, where he discovered Caucasoid aborigines known as Ainu. The men's stocky bodies were covered with thick hair, like the bears they sacrificed; the women wore tattooed moustaches. De Angelis began a glossary of their language.

Ieyasu's son captured de Angelis in 1622 and burned him at the stake. Other Jesuits, betrayed or discovered, also met death by torture. Japan snapped shut, to live in feudal isolation until American gunboats reopened the country in 1854.

Jesuits faced problems of a different kind with China's Ming emperors. The mandarins who ran China's bureaucracy on the principles of

China's Great Wall (opposite) winds from the Yellow Sea deep into central Asia. Conceived in the 3rd century B.C. as a barrier to fierce nomadic tribes, it came to represent China's voluntary isolation from the world. Haughty mandarins believed their land was the center of the Earth and all foreigners were barbarians.

When Jesuit Matteo Ricci showed mandarins a map of China's relationship to the rest of the world, they were so offended that he drew a new one, placing the Middle Kingdom closer to the center (below). "The Great Map of Ten Thousand Countries," produced in the 1580s, carried copious notes by Ricci in Chinese. A hand-painted copy, six feet by twelve on silk panels, was presented to the emperor in Peking. Woodblock copies sent to Europe gave scholars their first comprehensive view of the Far East. Ricci helped prove that the legendary Cathay—thought by some Europeans to be near India—was in fact China.

Confucian morality and filial piety were not unlike the Jesuits themselves—disciplined scholars, careful record keepers. Contemptuous of foreigners, they believed China was the center of the earth, the superior Middle Kingdom.

The Jesuits selected Matteo Ricci as their spearhead. Ricci was an Italian, skilled in mathematics, astronomy, literature, and languages, with a phenomenal memory and boundless patience. He, if anyone, could crack China's proud isolation.

Ricci slipped into China from Macao in 1583. At first he dressed as a Buddhist monk. In a mission house near Canton, he displayed European inventions—prisms, chiming clocks, oil paintings, astronomical instruments—to persuade visitors that foreigners were not barbarians.

He befriended mandarins, learned their etiquette, studied their literature, and found that classic Confucianism did not clash with Christianity. When he saw that intellectuals disdained his Buddhist guise he adopted a long silk gown and the cap of a Confucian scholar.

In Ricci's lifetime some 2,000 influential Chinese were converted, but the Jesuits' success in China depended far more on their skill as engineers, metallurgists, military technicians, and astronomers. When Manchus overthrew the Ming Dynasty in 1644, Jesuits served them as diplomats, too. In their most ambitious project they surveyed and mapped the whole of China—more

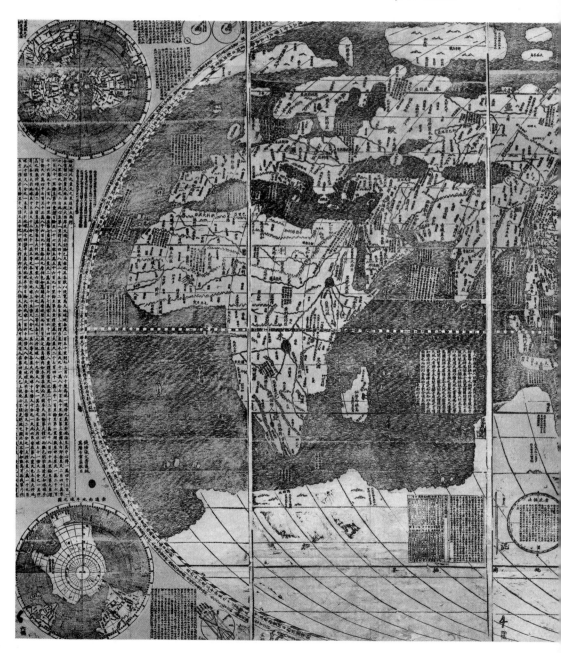

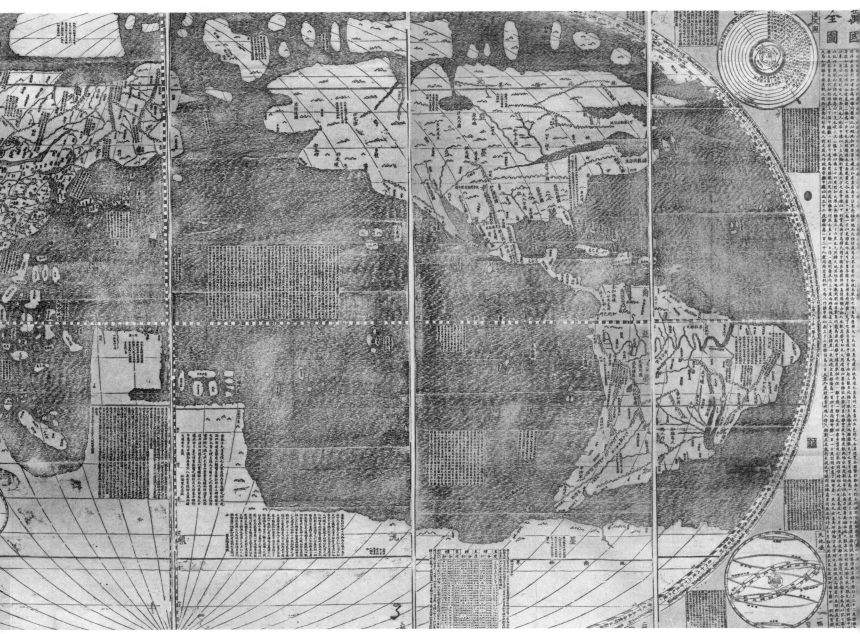

Francis Xavier (left) brought Roman Catholic zeal to Asia in 1542. He established Jesuit headquarters in the Portuguese enclave of Goa, on India's west coast. Jesuit priests spread through Asia hoping to convert its peoples by first converting their rulers. Emperor Akbar of India, a liberal Muslim, kept Jesuits like pets at his magnificent court in Fatehpur Sikri. Seated under a canopy, Akbar umpires a religious debate (opposite) pitting Father Ridolfo Aquaviva and a companion against Muslim mullahs. Though Jesuits failed to convert the emperor or his court, missions gained footholds in Delhi, Agra, and Lahore. Aquaviva and four fellow priests (below) were killed in 1583 by a mob near Goa, far from Akbar's personal protection.

than a million square miles, a task of over a decade. This Jesuit map of 1717 remained a standard for the world until the late 1800s.

But by the 18th century the Jesuits' time was ending. Jealousy inside China led to persecution, and their respect for Chinese customs drew fire from the Church in Europe, which condemned them for such practices as painting shoes on images of Christ to appease Chinese distaste for bare feet and, worse, for letting their converts perform ancient rites venerating ancestors. But their reports fueled a fascination with the East. European philosophers idealized the Jesuit picture of the rationally ordered government of China. Voltaire imagined that the Chinese had "perfected moral science."

Asia was curious about the West, too. In 1580, on the invitation of India's emperor, Akbar the Great, a group of Jesuits led by Ridolfo Aquaviva, a shy young Italian aristocrat, traveled to Fatehpur Sikri, Akbar's red stone city. The dazzled priests found themselves in debate with Hindus, Zoroastrians, Muslims, and Jews, while the emperor himself refereed, tossing gold coins to the winners. The Jesuits' letters about India's wealth and variety tempted a type of European traveler concerned not with Christianizing but with exploring to make money.

Jean-Baptiste Tavernier was a plump little Parisian gem merchant whose curiosity took him on five different trips to India between 1638 and 1668. Traveling like a gentleman, he often rode in a palanquin shaded by a parasol. Tavernier let jewels lead the way—from the diamond mines of Golconda, through caravansaries and village huts to the palaces of princes, where he found the nabobs would accept only "gold of the best sort" in trade for his gems.

Tavernier wrote a book about India's caste system, the tricks of money changers, and the wiles of fakirs, the itinerant Hindu ascetics. He described one fakir who "drags a heavy iron chain attached to one leg. . . . When he prays it is with a great noise . . . [and] an affected gravity which attracts the veneration of the people." Some fakirs summoned scores of disciples with drums and horns. "Vagabonds and idlers," judged Tavernier.

His book reinforced Europe's perception that Asia was too inviting to be left to freelancers. Nations followed their citizen explorers. England's East India Company took over India and parts of southeast Asia; Holland's turned the East Indies into a spice empire. France appropriated ore-rich Indochina, and by the mid-1800s Russia was thinking of a railway across Siberia.

Among the few regions still unmapped was the formidably inhospitable Arabian Peninsula, barred to all but Muslims. Unknown and forbidden, it lured Victorian romantics and scientists such as Charles Montagu Doughty. Unlike daredevils who courted death by penetrating

sacred Mecca disguised as Muslim pilgrims, Doughty lived openly as a Christian. Moving among Arabs of town, court, and caravan from 1876 to 1878, he often endured Muslim scorn and abuse but made friends with his medicinal skills. His landmark book *Travels in Arabia Deserta* presents, in prose as mannered and intricate as a Persian carpet, a panorama of life little known to the West: The nomad camp under "the blue night and clear hoary starlight," with the tethered camels who have "wandered all day upon the droughty face of the wilderness"; the supper of buttermilk and bread freshly baked on the campfire; the "sweet reek" of smoldering frankincense, passed beneath robes as live perfume; sandals made of "old camel sack-leather, moisty with the juice of the dates."

In the town of 'Unayzah, in central Arabia, Doughty watched the daily round of shopping in the souk, the calls to prayer, the endless talk among the idle, favored males of Arabian society—the "coffee-lords" —and the women as "veiled forms flitting to their gossips' houses," creeping home when the men go for late prayers to the mosque.

Doughty became legend in the desert. T. E. Lawrence—Lawrence of Arabia—said Doughty "broke a road" for other Westerners, among them Lady Anne Blunt and her husband, Wilfred. The Blunts crossed central Arabia from Damascus to the Persian Gulf in 1878.

In the depth of the desert one day,

Penitents and fakirs under a banyan tree appeared in a popular 17th-century guidebook for adventurers in India. Numbers 2 through 5 identify shrines. Penitents display painful, lifelong postures, maintained day and night in hopes of rewards in a future life. The book's French author, Jean-Baptiste Tavernier, made five trips to India, where he amassed a fortune as a gem dealer. Curiosity led him to study Indian customs on his excursions.

Niccolao Manucci (below), a Venetian soldier of fortune, lived by his wits in India for 54 years. Masquerading as a doctor, he grew rich applying commonsense remedies to wealthy patients. To embellish his memoirs Manucci commissioned the miniature showing him in upper-class dress.

the Blunts rode out with their Bedouin companions, spurring swift mounts between towering red sand dunes toward Ha'il, a distant oasis city where Emir Ibn Rashid had a renowned stable of horses.

The emir could have beheaded these infidels at a whim. But perhaps because he had spent many hours with Doughty, he instead shared with them his love of horses. The Blunts brought to England a sheaf of Lady Anne's evocative paintings of desert life and several magnificent Arabian horses that made their stud world famous.

Only Tibet, girded by deserts and the world's highest mountains, surpassed Arabia in hostile remoteness. The Dalai Lama, Tibet's ruler, enforced its isolation to guard the power of the maroon-robed monks and the colorful pantheon who shaped its life. Expulsion or execution faced foreigners who trespassed, and death awaited Tibetans who were found to have helped them.

Spheres of influence became deadly rivalries as Britain and Russia pressed toward Tibet, then under the political control of China. To map Tibet as a step toward control, the British used ingenious ruses. In the 1860s Indians, trained as surveyors and spies, entered Tibet posing as merchants or Buddhist pilgrims. They counted their footsteps on prayer beads to calculate distances, took secret measurements with hidden instruments, and figured out latitudes and altitudes.

Caravans ply the Silk Road's southern branch through the Pamirs. Empires clashed here in the 19th century as Russia and Britain pressed toward eastern central Asia, a little-known region nominally ruled by China.

Col. Nikolay Przhevalsky, Russia's foremost explorer, made four expeditions into the deserts and mountains south of Siberia in the 1870s and 1880s, aided by a retinue of guides, interpreters, and sharpshooting Cossacks (below). Camel loads of scientific instruments yielded route surveys, maps, botanical collections, and new knowledge about the area. Though Przhevalsky failed to reach his goal —Lhasa, Tibet's capital—he is remembered for other discoveries, including the world's last wild horse, which bears his name (Equus caballus przewalskii).

The Russians openly backed their brilliant explorer, Colonel Nikolay Przhevalsky. Geographer, botanist, zoologist, and crack marksman, he longed to find Lhasa. In 1872 he climbed from the Gobi into northern Tibet. When he faced down both Tibetan bandits and bandit-hunting Chinese cavalry, villagers regarded his lack of fear as saintly magic. But winter and short supplies kept him from striking on toward the capital.

Expeditions in the Gobi led to a second try six years later. Camped on Tibet's soaring, treeless plateau, Przhevalsky and his Cossack escort were barely a week's march from Lhasa. Rumors raced through the capital that a Russian force was bent on kidnapping the Dalai Lama. Mobs of burly Tibetan guards in sheepskins blocked Przhevalsky's path. Przhevalsky's 13 men were so far outnumbered that he turned back, bitterly disappointed. They were only 160 miles from their goal.

An unlikely group from England almost succeeded. Mr. and Mrs. St. George Littledale, with their nephew and their fox terrier, took a caravan onto Tibet's plateau in 1895. Their caravan leader was Rassul Galwan, a Ladakhi with an appetite for adventuring with sahibs.

The Littledale pack animals died from altitude sickness and exposure, Mrs. Littledale became ill, but the caravan struggled on. Eight days' ride from the forbidden city, some 300 Tibetans tried to force the tattered party to halt. Rassul boasted, "These two are English sahib, and the other one are very big lady, relative of queen of English." That claim gained them only a brief advantage. Then Rassul had to threaten: "In these boxes we have enemy-killing thing. If put fire to a box, then burn all men of country." The gullible locals, scoffed Rassul, were "jungly men, believe to that matter."

They marched on, but Mrs. Littledale's illness worsened, and they had to give up and return to India. Rassul wrote a book about his travels, with an introduction by Col. Francis Younghusband, the self-confident star of British imperialism who would finally force Lhasa open.

As a young army officer Younghusband had crossed Asia from Peking to India, and explored the Karakoram Range and the Pamirs. He dreamed of entering Lhasa in disguise. When India's viceroy panicked over rumors of a Russian pact with Tibet, the British government authorized Younghusband to "show the flag" and compel exclusive agreements with Britain.

Younghusband led a small army across the Himalayas in December snow, 1903, accompanied by a caravan of thousands of mules and yaks, six camels and several correspon-

dents from newspapers in London.

Tibetans armed with swords, muskets, and magic charms gathered at Guru. Shooting began by mistake. Horrified, Younghusband watched a four-minute massacre that left 700 Tibetans dead or dying. An ancient superstition held that if the fortress at nearby Gyangze ever fell to invaders, Tibet would be lost. Younghusband took the fortress, then marched on to Lhasa. The Dalai Lama had fled, and the regent signed England's treaty. London set up a flourishing trade mission in Gyangze and, with Tibetan cooperation, banned foreigners—except for the English and the Chinese.

Infuriated, a French Orientalist named Alexandra David-Néel entered Tibet without permission. Her books about this strange land, where nomads lived on neighborly terms with demons and a cranky sorcerer might bombard his enemies with flying barley cakes, encouraged the new field of Tibetology.

With Tibet, Asia was yielding its last secrets to Europeans. For 700 years, gate-crashers seeking wealth, souls, power, and knowledge had brought tales of Asia's startling ways back to Europe. Now Europeans would try to coerce the one continent to serve the desires of the other. But as Jesuit explorers had learned, Asia would receive the touch of the West on Asia's own terms. Generations later, many an Asian businessman would wear a gray flannel suit—and worship at a Buddhist shrine.

Comment comence le liure de mar pul des meruecilles dine la grant et dõ
de la minour armenie.   Et des diuerses regions du monde.
                            ur sauoir la pure verite de diuerses regions du mon
                            de. Si prenes ce liure cy et le faictes liue. si y trouueres les
                            grandismes merueilles qui y sont esclaptes. De la grãt
                            armenie. et de perse. et des tartars. et dinde et de main
                            tes autres prouinces. si comme nře liure compterá p
                            ordres appartenent. de quoy messur mar pol. sages z
                            nobles ciuoiens de venisse raconpte pour ce que il le

By James A. Cox

"How about here?" said one of the voices around the bed. The old man heard pages turning. "Here, where you say the mountains are so high and cold that *fire does not burn so brightly, nor give out so much heat as usual, nor does it cook food so effectually.*

"How can you expect people to believe such lies, Uncle Marco? Repent, while there is still time before you die!"

Marco Polo, merchant of Venice, formerly in the service of Kublai Khan, ruler of the Mongol Empire, and now a tired old man of 70, lay in his bed, eyes closed, and did not answer.

Almost half a century had passed since 1275, when he arrived in Cathay with his father, Niccolò, and his uncle Maffeo; 29 years since their return to Venice; and 26 years since the appearance of his book, grandly titled *Description of the World.*

Ah, the book. He had written it in 1298, after the Venetian fleet in which he was serving as a gentleman commander suffered a humiliating defeat. Marco spent three years in a Genoese jail as a prisoner of war. To while away the hours, he related his experiences in the Orient to his cell mates. One of them, a scholar and romancer from Pisa named Rustichello, said the world would enjoy hearing of all these wonders; why had Marco never written them down? Marco laughed. His friends in Venice didn't believe the tales when he told them; what good would a book do? But Rustichello persevered, and at last Marco gave in, dictating the stories as his cell mate scratched them down on parchment with goose quills.

And so the book was born. Rustichello was right: Within a few years after Marco was released from jail, the book was translated and transcribed in a number of versions, and the name of Marco Polo became well known. And Marco was right, too, because most of the people who read or heard about the book didn't believe it.

The Polos leaving Venice on their second journey to China and the court of Kublai Khan.

"Lies!" they cried. "All lies! A book of a million lies!"

In Venice, his own city, he was jeered. For many reasons they called him Marco Milione—Marco of the Millions—and referred to the ancestral Polo home as the Court of the Millions. Even friends and relatives accused him of lies and exaggerations.

And now several of those friends and relatives were gathered about his bed as he lay dying, begging him to retract the incredible statements made in his book: "The end is near, Marco. For the sake of your immortal soul, tell the truth!"

The old man heard them, but his mind was in the past, in 1269, when he was a stripling of 15. The Polo kinsmen had gathered at a feast to welcome home Niccolò and Maffeo from a trading voyage that had lasted 15 years and taken them far to the East, to Cambaluc, capital city of the great Mongol emperor, Kublai Khan, in fabled Cathay. Marco listened excitedly as Niccolò and Maffeo told of the Khan. The Khan had asked the two Venetians to be his ambassadors to Rome, to carry costly gifts for the Pope—and an offer. The Pope was to send to Cambaluc a hundred wise and learned men to teach the arts of Western culture in the Khan's court. And if they could prove Christianity to be superior to all the other religions flourishing in Cathay—Confucianism, Buddhism, Zoroastrianism, Islam, Judaism, and others—then he, the Great Khan, and all his subjects would become Christians.

If his father and uncle were headed back to Cathay, Marco didn't intend to be left behind. He eagerly presented himself to them with his qualifications: He was inquisitive, could read and write, do sums, and having grown up along the quays of medieval Europe's greatest commercial port, could probably handle a ship in a squall. Niccolò and Maffeo signed him on.

In 1271 Pope Gregory X gave them gifts and letters for Kublai Khan. They also carried oil from the sacred lamp in Jerusalem. But the Pope could not muster a hundred wise men—only two timid and unworldly Dominican friars, who fled back to Rome before the journey was fairly started.

Undeterred, nor worse off than before, the three Polos pushed on. Their route led through Armenia into Persia, Afghanistan, and the great Pamir plateau, lands where only a handful of Europeans had traveled. In his dreamlike retracing of that momentous journey, the withered old man saw himself as a robust lad of 17, with a lively curiosity and a passion for taking notes, recording the passing scene: the snow-covered mountain where the ark of Noah was said to rest; in Persia, the tombs of the Magi and the castle of the fire worshipers; and at Baku, on the Caspian coast—

His nephew's voice interrupted his reverie, reciting familiar words: *"a fountain from which oil springs in great abundance, insomuch that a hundred shiploads might be taken from it at one time. This oil is not good to use with food, but*

152

> *Their arms are bows and arrows, sword and mace; but above all the bow, for they are capital archers, indeed the best that are known.*
>
> MARCO POLO

'tis good to burn, and is also used to anoint camels that have the mange.'' The voice went on, with an edge of mockery, "Really, Uncle Marco—oil, squeezed from the ground as from olives? For the sake of your immortal soul, we beseech you. . . ."

The old man closed his ears and continued his mental journey. Climbing the mountains of Afghanistan, he marveled at oxen white as snow, great hairy yaks, pheasants with six-foot-long tail feathers, sheep with thirty-pound tails. And up on the Pamir plateau. . . .

Another voice: *"wild sheep of great size, whose horns are good six palms in length. From these horns the shepherds make great bowls to eat from, and they use the horns also to enclose folds for their cattle at night. Who ever heard of such creatures? For the sake of your soul, Marco. . . ."*

Sighing, the old man closed his eyes and fled within himself. Down from the mountains, the travelers entered the Gobi, that great sea of pebbly sand, following the route of the jade caravans and emerging deep in Cathay. They spent almost a year at Kanchow, the heart of the Mongol homeland, learning the customs of the nomads, who carried their tent dwellings on huge wagons as they followed their cattle from plains to highlands with the changing seasons. In time of war, the Mongol men endured great hardship, sometimes riding for ten days without lighting a fire or taking a meal. . . .

"They also have milk dried into a kind of paste to carry with them. . . . on an expedition, every man takes some ten pounds of this dried milk with him. And of a morning he will take a half pound of it and put it in his leather bottle, with as much water as he pleases. So, as he rides along, the milk-paste and the water in the bottle get well churned together into a kind of pap, and that makes his dinner.

"Ah, Marco! Think of the family's reputation!"

Eyes and fists clenched, the old man paid no heed. Eastward, then northward they journeyed. At last, three and a half years and some 7,000 hard miles out of Venice, they reached the magnificent summer capital of Kublai Khan in Shangdu—Xanadu to the poets. The Khan received them warmly in the great audience hall, and after they had knelt and bowed their heads to the carpet four times he bade them rise and tell of their journey. He was a heavyset man of late middle age and middle height with black eyes, a fair complexion, and a well-proportioned nose. For his part, the Khan was pleased to see a young man of 21, with a bright face and eyes that sparkled with intelligence, who, during the long trek, had learned to speak and write the four main languages of this vast empire, and therefore promised to be useful.

The Venetians prospered in the court of Kublai Khan. Soon the Great Khan began to employ Marco on public missions that took him to distant parts of the country. Marco had noted that the Khan yawned in boredom over the usual dry recital of facts from a returning commissioner, but took delight in reports that included unusual facts and odd customs from the far reaches of his empire. Marco continued making notes of his travels, to please the Khan as well as himself.

In moving about the country he cited such things as excellent roads

aquesta carauana es partida de l'impi de sarra panar al catayo

tprsgdos

fugur

iachion

taiui

febur

From a 14th-century atlas painted on wooden panels: The Polos' caravan crosses Asian mountains. At the court of the Great Khan the merchants kneel to present papal letters.

with highly developed land communications by postriders; paper money accepted as legal currency; and . . .

"*black stones existing in beds in the mountains, which they dig out and burn like firewood. If you supply the fire with them at night, and see that they are well kindled, you will find them still alight in the morning. Oh, Marco, Marco, for the sake of your soul. . . .*"

The old man ignored the interruption. He was back in the southern regions of the Khan's empire, where he came upon primitive people tattooed from head to toe; crocodiles with mouths big enough to swallow a man at one gulp; tribes that were addicted to eating human flesh, deeming it more delicate than any other. He sailed to Ceylon in a fleet of four-masted junks under orders to purchase for the Khan the world's largest ruby and a begging bowl said to have belonged to the Buddha himself. On the way, stopping off at Sumatra, he had made a discovery that would, he knew, generate intense interest in the mercantile centers of Europe. Spices! "All the precious spices that can be found in the world," he mumbled, remembering the words in his book.

Now he thought of the Khan's winter palace at Cambaluc, an immense marble structure set in a maze of walls, parks, gardens, copses, grazing lands, and game preserves, all surrounded by outer ramparts. It was the time of the Mongol New Year, early in February. The Khan and his subjects, all dressed in white, the color of good luck, were attending a parade of 5,000 royal elephants, each piled high with samples of the royal treasure. Later, the Khan entertained 6,000 guests at a huge celebration and feast in the grand hall of the palace, and graciously accepted gifts to the crown. There were jewels, jade vases, pelts of sable and ermine from the north, silver and gold. . . .

"*On that day, I can assure you, among the customary presents there shall be offered to the Khan from various quarters more than 100,000 white horses, beautiful animals, and richly caparisoned. Ah, Marco, your time is so short—why won't you retract these exaggerations?*"

Lips pursed stubbornly, Marco continued his journey through the past. When the snows melted, the Khan and his court, a vast assemblage of men and women, left Cambaluc on the great spring hunt, a leisurely tour of the provinces. Kublai Khan rode on four elephants in a howdah covered with tiger skins and gold leaf, while his barons rode horses and the ladies reclined in palanquins. They were accompanied by huntsmen, beaters, falconers, hounds, and birds, with servants at everyone's beck and the whole guarded over by troops of soldiers.

Then it was on to the summer court at Shangdu, in the cool western hills. Shangdu was a walled park with winding waterways, meadows, wild animals, and a stable of pure white mares whose milk was drunk only by the Great Khan and his family and favorites. In the park were two palaces. One was marble, decorated with gilded paintings of trees and flowers, birds and beasts. The other was a marvel of construction made of polished bamboo canes embellished with gilt and brilliant lacquers, and carved dragons clad in gold. . . .

"*The construction of the Palace is so devised that it can be taken down and*

155

Dragons of Yunnan from a 14th-century French version of Marco Polo's book.

In Xanadu did Kubla Khan
A stately pleasure dome
    decree:
Where Alph, the sacred
    river, ran
Through caverns measureless
    to man
Down to a sunless sea.
SAMUEL TAYLOR COLERIDGE
"KUBLA KHAN"

put up again with great celerity; and it can all be taken to pieces and removed whithersoever the Emperor may command. When erected, it is braced by more than 200 cords of silk.

"Your soul, Marco. Think of your soul!"

The old man kept his eyes closed. After 17 years in the service of the Khan, the Polos had begun to think wistfully of home. Niccolò and Maffeo were showing their age and so was Kublai Khan, now well into his 70s. He would be joining his ancestors soon enough, and who knew what the new ruler would think of the white men from the West?

At first, the Khan would not hear of their leaving. But fate intervened. Ambassadors arrived with a request from Arghun, King of Persia, that the Great Khan send him a new wife from the same Mongolian family as his favored queen who had died. A 17-year-old beauty named Cocachin was selected, but fighting among princes in the western provinces had closed the overland route back to Persia. Reluctantly, the Khan agreed to let the Venetians, excellent mariners, deliver the bride by sea in return for the privilege of regaining their homeland.

A fleet of 14 four-masted junks was prepared for the voyage, while the Polos converted their considerable holdings into gems and jewelry, which they carefully sewed into the linings of their woolen garments. The old man in the bed was too weary now to linger on the two years of that arduous trip to Persia, through uncharted seas, with many stops

156

along the way—Sumatra, Java, Malaya, Ceylon, India. They delivered Cocachin to her queenship and sailed on to Venice.

They arrived in 1295, after an absence of 24 years, in queer Oriental clothes, travel stained and tattered, stray dogs yapping at their heels. At first they were denied entrance to their ancestral home, now occupied by relatives who believed them long dead. Marco remembered how remarkably they had returned to life when, having argued themselves inside and donned fresh silken robes of crimson hue, they tore open the linings of their rags and dumped forth diamonds, pearls, sapphires, emeralds, and rubies.

Jewels that could be held in the hand were proof enough that the three wandering Polos had indeed done something out of the ordinary. But the stories they told—especially Marco—stretched belief. Great wealth can make all sorts of eccentricities acceptable, so the relatives did nothing foolish. But Marco knew how they shook their heads among themselves and shuddered when some of his tales began to be repeated along the Rialto.

Matters went from bad to worse when hand-transcribed copies of his book appeared. As fast as words can travel, much of the Western world was laughing its incredulity. Once again, the old man marveled at it: People so willing to believe that alchemists could transmute base metals into gold, that an infinite number of angels could dance on the head of a pin, that fire-breathing monsters gobbled ships as they tumbled over the edge of a flat Earth, such people could not accept a Mongolian emperor rich and powerful enough to command a gift of 100,000 white horses. Or paper money. Or trees that grew nuts as big as a man's head.

The old man hoped that not everybody disbelieved. There were some—better educated, perhaps, or more worldly, or blessed with greater imagination—who lusted after islands where all the world's spices grew. Perhaps there would be men who would carry his book with them on voyages of exploration across unknown seas.

It would be vindication, of sorts. But too late now, in 1324, as he lay on his deathbed, listening to friends and relatives, with sneers or pious horror in their voices, importune him to admit that the things he had seen with his own eyes, heard with his own ears, were all lies.

"The end is near, Uncle Marco! For your soul, tell the truth at last!"

The old man opened eyes filled with memory, and whispered back:

"I have not told half of what I saw!"

Europe had received Marco Polo's book with enthusiasm, but to readers it seemed more like enjoyable fiction than fact. Scribes who hand copied the book sometimes added their own embellishments. Nevertheless, later explorers, including Columbus and Magellan, read Marco Polo's book with care. Marco's friends and relatives may not have quoted from it at his bedside as we have conjectured, but the story goes that they did gather there to implore him to recant and so provoked his famed deathbed response.

Alexandra David-Néel

By Elisabeth B. Booz

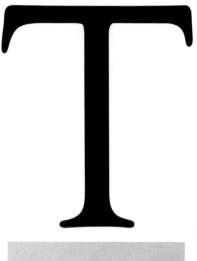

Visions of the high lamas: Grotesque masks worn by Tibetan Buddhist dancers depict mythological fairies and demons that inhabit spiritual trances.

The British Trade Agent in Gyangze was taking his afternoon nap. It was April 1924 in southern Tibet. An agitated servant tapped at his bedroom door: Sorry to disturb him but two common-looking Tibetans, a man and a woman, were outside. The woman was asking to see the sahib, in a peremptory tone. She behaved just like a European.

"Oh, God," groaned David Macdonald. "Send her in here."

His nine children took glee in practical jokes. He was not about to be taken in. When he heard footsteps, he rolled over and pretended to snore. Without turning, he said crossly, "I know perfectly well who you are! Now get out of here and stop acting the fool!"

He sensed a shocked silence. A voice with a French accent replied, "You are speaking to Madame Alexandra David-Néel!"

His Majesty's Trade Agent jumped out of bed. The owner of that name, a thorn in the side of the British Raj for the past decade, was a tiny, frail woman in Tibetan dress, barely five feet tall and 55 years old. In a flurry of apologies, Mr. Macdonald summoned the family and escorted her to the drawing room, where tea was served.

Eight years earlier the British had deported Alexandra David-Néel for illegally entering Tibet. She had vowed then and there to reach its heart, Lhasa. The capital was so inaccessible and so tightly sealed against foreigners, under pressure of world politics, that only a handful of men from the West had ever seen it—and never a woman. Outrage motivated her as much as her aim to discover the mysterious life of the Tibetan people by living as one of them. This was a startling idea in 1916. No outsider had ever attempted it.

David-Néel had the resources she needed. She had gained acceptance in France as a serious Orientalist. As a former actress, she could disappear into the scenery. She had a journalist's sharp eye. And she

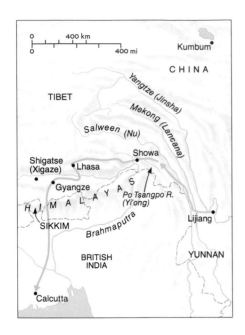

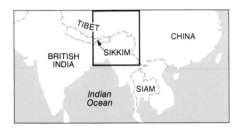

had enough money. At age 36 Alexandra David had married Philippe Néel, a distant cousin. They rarely lived together, but he supported her financially and they remained intimate friends through a lifelong exchange of letters—the material of her books.

In 1911 David-Néel left for India, hoping to write articles for the French press. Tibet's Dalai Lama, in exile there, granted her his first interview with a foreign woman. After a learned discussion of Buddhist doctrine he advised, "Learn the Tibetan language."

In Sikkim David-Néel hired her indispensable companion-servant, a 15-year-old Sikkimese monk named Aphur Yongden, who practiced Tibetan Buddhism. She deepened his understanding of the doctrines and eventually became his adoptive mother. Yongden never left her side until his death, in France, 40 years later.

Her clandestine excursions into Tibet began in 1914. With camera and notebook, David-Néel reached Chorten Nyima, a tiny, ruined monastery just over the border from Sikkim, inhabited by three nuns. Their spiritual insight led her to seek a tutor like theirs, a hermit who lived in Sikkim's mountains. Throughout one winter she stayed as his apprentice in a cave at 13,000 feet. The anchorite shared secret knowledge and taught her Tibetan.

At Shigatse, deep in Tibet, Alexandra David-Néel met the Panchen Lama, Tibet's second most revered figure. He heard her debate with erudite monks and conferred on her the robes of a graduate lama, a sort of Tibetan Ph.D. Wearing the yellow silk bonnet of an abbess, she wrote to her husband, "I feel completely at home in this central Asian character." The British Raj got wind of it and deported her.

Two years later David-Néel struggled across China from Peking to Kumbum, a Tibetan monastery in the undefined borderlands. She and Yongden remained among its 3,800 monks for three years. Throughout these highlands, the lady lama traveled with a small caravan of mules, in local style. She blessed villagers and nomads while she learned their customs. One winter, on China's tea-trade route, she met an English geographer, who lent her his maps and pointed out an unexplored route into Tibet up the Salween River from China's Yunnan Province. The way continued through wild territory along the Po Tsangpo River to Tibet's main east-west caravan route—and on to Lhasa.

David-Néel prudently "disappeared" to the Gobi, to let border officials forget her. The mules and servants, her camera, her comfortable tent and zinc bathtub would all have to go. She and Yongden, in disguise, would risk it alone.

In late October 1923, two beggars joined the thousands of pilgrims who continually circulated throughout Tibet, visiting its sacred places. The poor young lama and his aged mother appeared to be the lowest of the low. But their knapsacks contained two compasses, a tiny tent, rope, and other necessities. Rough copies of the Englishman's maps lined David-Néel's boots. Under their clothing both pilgrims wore

revolvers and money belts with silver and gold. Because surveying instruments were out of the question, David-Néel guessed at altitudes. Where possible she followed rivers. Many times, when snow blotted out landmarks and trails, she was completely lost.

Discovery as a foreigner could mean death at the hands of superstitious Tibetans. At the very least it meant capture and an end to exploring. She blackened her hair with ink and lengthened it with skinny yak-hair braids. She darkened her skin with cocoa and soot. A dirty old fur bonnet found on the path completed her peasant's outfit. Filth was essential to the disguise, as Tibetans rarely washed. When chance brought them to a hot spring and a yearned-for bath, Yongden implored her not to wash her face, which finally had the right color.

Once, rinsing her cooking pot in a stream, she heard a woman whisper, "Her hands are like a foreigner's!" Washed clean, they were startlingly white. While frantically blackening them with soot from the pot, she overheard the general reprieve: She must be Mongolian.

They preferred to sleep in the open and cook their own food—barley

A tea porter on the main trade route of China-Tibet borderlands.

gruel and brick tea with butter. But as winter deepened, they accepted hospitality, usually in hovels at a level of society unknown even to many Tibetans. As a lama, Yongden was always welcome, badgered to give blessings and prophecies. In an ironic exchange of roles, Yongden sat on cushions by the fire while the worthless old woman was relegated to an icy corner on the dirt floor. She was gathering anecdotes for books, but the raw material was sometimes hard to live through.

They sometimes used people's superstition to good effect. When Yongden told fortunes, he prescribed cleanliness or an act of kindness as an antidote to demons. After crossing lonely passes into the kingdom of Po on the Po Tsangpo, they met robbers. Yongden was forced to surrender a couple of coins and would have had his money belt discovered had David-Néel not taken over. She screamed and howled at the theft of her son's fortune and called down vengeance from the most dreaded Tibetan deities whose names no common person dared pronounce. She later wrote, "I am a tiny woman with nothing dramatic in my appearance; but at that moment I felt myself rising to the height of a powerful tragedienne." She petrified even herself with the supernatural aura she had created. The terrified robbers begged her to stop, returned the stolen money, and retreated with a blessing from Yongden.

On a 19-hour march across uninhabited mountains, with winter snow closing the passes behind them, Tibetan lore came to the rescue. Exhausted and half-frozen, David-Néel tried to make a fire by moonlight—only to find that the flint and steel were wet. Without fire, in their sodden clothes, they would freeze to death. Yongden urged David-Néel to try *thumo reskiang* to raise her body heat. Not unlike modern biofeedback, this art had been used by Tibetan hermits for centuries to survive at high altitudes with the scantiest of clothing.

She put the flint, steel, and a pinch of kindling under her dress and began to concentrate. Imagining fire blazing around her, flames curling over her head, she became semiconscious until the loud snap of ice cracking on a nearby stream jolted her awake. She found herself feverishly hot and deliciously comfortable. She lit a fire with ease, and awoke the next morning, refreshed.

David-Néel and Yongden approached the big caravan route with dread, knowing they must obtain travel permits at a toll bridge. But their disguises held up. Yongden dealt with officialdom while his old mother, muttering prayers by the doorstep, went unnoticed. Luck stayed with them all the way. When they reached Lhasa among throngs of pilgrims for the New Year celebrations, nature supplied a sandstorm to cloak their entrance into the holy city.

Alexandra David-Néel must have mentally thumbed her nose at the British as she followed other pilgrims to the roof of the Potala, the Dalai Lama's magnificent fortress. Panic struck when an officious palace monk made her take off the dirty fur bonnet, exposing brown hair from which the ink had long worn off—but she passed as a Ladakhi, from India's borderland. Under the full moon of the New Year, David-Néel and Yongden joined the festival crowds around Lhasa's ancient Bud-

162

A ruined shrine, three Buddhist nuns, and Alexandra David-Néel, who admired the independence of these women in their mountain isolation.

dhist shrines. Larger-than-life-size images of animals, men, and gods, sculptured of butter and vividly colored, lined the streets. Nomads burst through the excited throng, "sturdy giants, cowmen clad in sheepskin, holding on to one another, ran for joy. . . . Their big fists belaboured the ribs of those whom bad luck had placed in their way."

David-Néel and Yongden stayed in Lhasa for two months. Then they changed disguise, adopting the dress of the lower middle class. David-Néel bought books and manuscripts to delight Oriental scholars in Europe, and a horse to carry her and Yongden on to Gyangze.

As she told it afterwards in the drawing room of His Majesty's Trade Agent, the whole trip had been a splendid adventure of "wanderings truly wonderful." It seemed hardly possible to her astonished audience that this small Frenchwoman could have crossed unexplored parts of Tibet in the middle of winter and lived in Lhasa, undetected. David Macdonald, a rare Tibet hand, could not hide his admiration.

Only in letters to Philippe did she admit that she had arrived in Lhasa "reduced to a skeleton . . . my skin hung from my bones in long folds, like a deflated balloon. . . ." and that nothing could ever induce her to repeat such madness again. But she had accomplished her goal. From lofty philosopher to squalid villager, Alexandra David-Néel had experienced Tibet. And told the world.

Alexandra David-Néel recounted her adventures in My Journey to Lhasa, Magic and Mystery in Tibet, *and other books.*

163

A Sea So Vast

By Robert M. Poole

Captain James Cook lay facedown in the Pacific Ocean. He was dead. A Hawaiian, part of a mob assembled on the shore at Kealakekua Bay, had clubbed him from behind. He fell from the black lava beach into the turquoise water, and two or three assailants splashed in after him. They stabbed him and beat him until he ceased struggling.

Silence spread from the shore, like the rain clouds that boil up daily from Mauna Loa and fan across the huge green island of Hawaii. Nothing about Cook's death on this day—February 14, 1779—made sense. He was revered throughout much of the world, a Briton sailing under the protection of the French, Spanish, and American governments.

On three voyages in ten years, he touched the ice of both Poles, explored the western shores of Canada and Alaska, and filled the vast blue spaces of Europe's maps with islands and peoples that were unimagined before he made them known.

Earth's largest ocean, the Pacific, stretches some 10,000 miles from east to west and 10,000 miles from north to south. All seven continents could fit within its boundaries.

That expanse of water, with so little land sprinkled through it, would defeat more than one explorer. In this emptiness a ship could sail for months without finding land, as Ferdinand Magellan learned on his frightful crossing. Those who followed also would suffer from starvation and scurvy—once the bane of Pacific exploration. If sailors survived these hazards, they might face death in a fight on a lonely shore, as Cook and Magellan had done.

But nothing that the Europeans endured compared to the sufferings they inflicted, deliberately or not, on Pacific peoples. For each European who died, many thousands of Polynesians fell victim to the guns and diseases the visitors brought.

The Polynesians, called savages by Europeans, had themselves settled the Pacific long before Magellan nosed his *Trinidad* into the Great South Sea. By then, Polynesians were scattered over a larger area than any other people on Earth.

They had settled island after island in the Polynesian triangle, defined by the Hawaiian Islands, New Zealand, and Easter Island. Living in a region of seventy parts water to one part land, the Polynesians naturally developed a mastery at sea. They navigated without compass or sextant, setting their course by the stars, by wind direction, by the pattern of ocean swells. A Polynesian sailor could dip his hand in the water and by its temperature detect a change of current. To his eye cloud formations reflected the shimmering waters of a lagoon, and thus announced the position of an atoll long before its palm trees appeared on the horizon.

What prompted the Polynesians to scatter? Perhaps a family had to flee for breaking *tapu*, the sacred

Besieged by the immense Pacific, spindly islands of the Tuamotu group shimmer in a relentless surf. Polynesian voyagers settled the far-flung lands in Earth's largest ocean, bringing coconuts, bananas, taro, and other food plants with them from other islands.

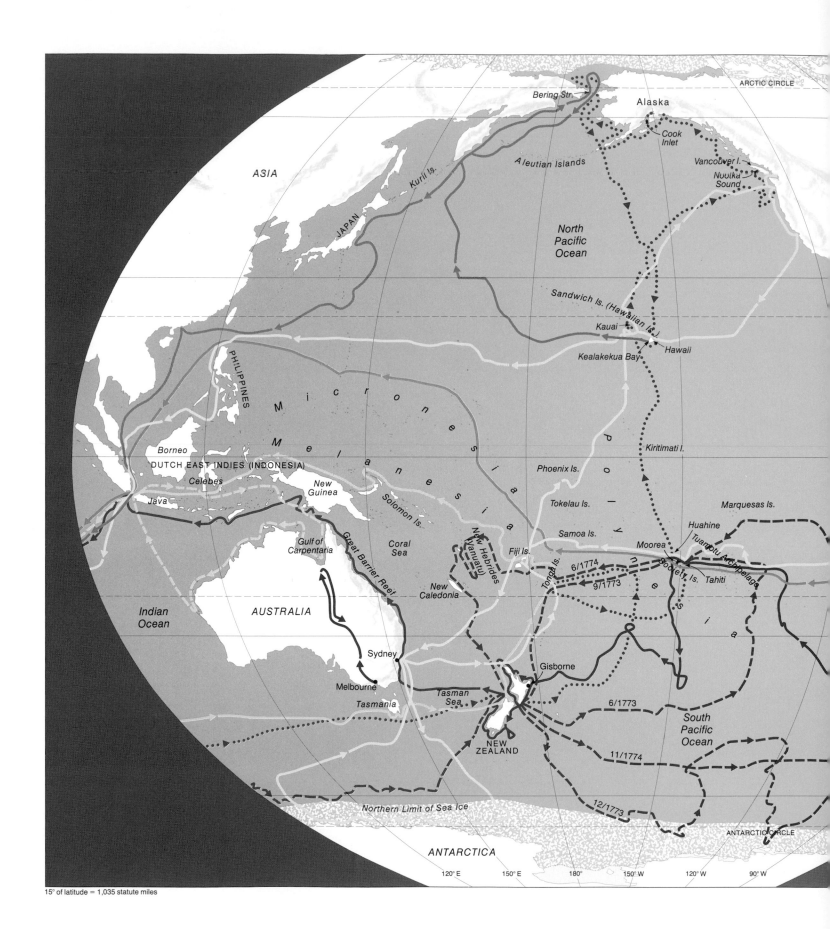

ASIA

JAPAN

Kuril Is.

Bering Str.

Aleutian Islands

Alaska

Cook Inlet

Vancouver I.

Nootka Sound

North Pacific Ocean

Sandwich Is. (Hawaiian Is.)

Kauai

Hawaii

Kealakekua Bay

Kiritimati I.

PHILIPPINES

M i c r o n e s i a

M e l a n e s i a

Borneo

DUTCH EAST INDIES (INDONESIA)

Celebes

Java

New Guinea

Solomon Is.

Coral Sea

Phoenix Is.

Tokelau Is.

Samoa Is.

Marquesas Is.

P o l y n e s i a

Huahine

Moorea

Tuamotu Archipelago

Society Is.

Tahiti

Gulf of Carpentaria

Great Barrier Reef

New Hebrides (Vanuatu)

Fiji Is.

Tonga Is.

6/1774

9/1773

New Caledonia

Indian Ocean

AUSTRALIA

Sydney

Melbourne

Tasmania

Tasman Sea

Gisborne

NEW ZEALAND

6/1773

11/1774

12/1773

South Pacific Ocean

Northern Limit of Sea Ice

ANTARCTICA

ARCTIC CIRCLE

ANTARCTIC CIRCLE

120° E   150° E   180°   150° W   120° W   90° W

15° of latitude = 1,035 statute miles

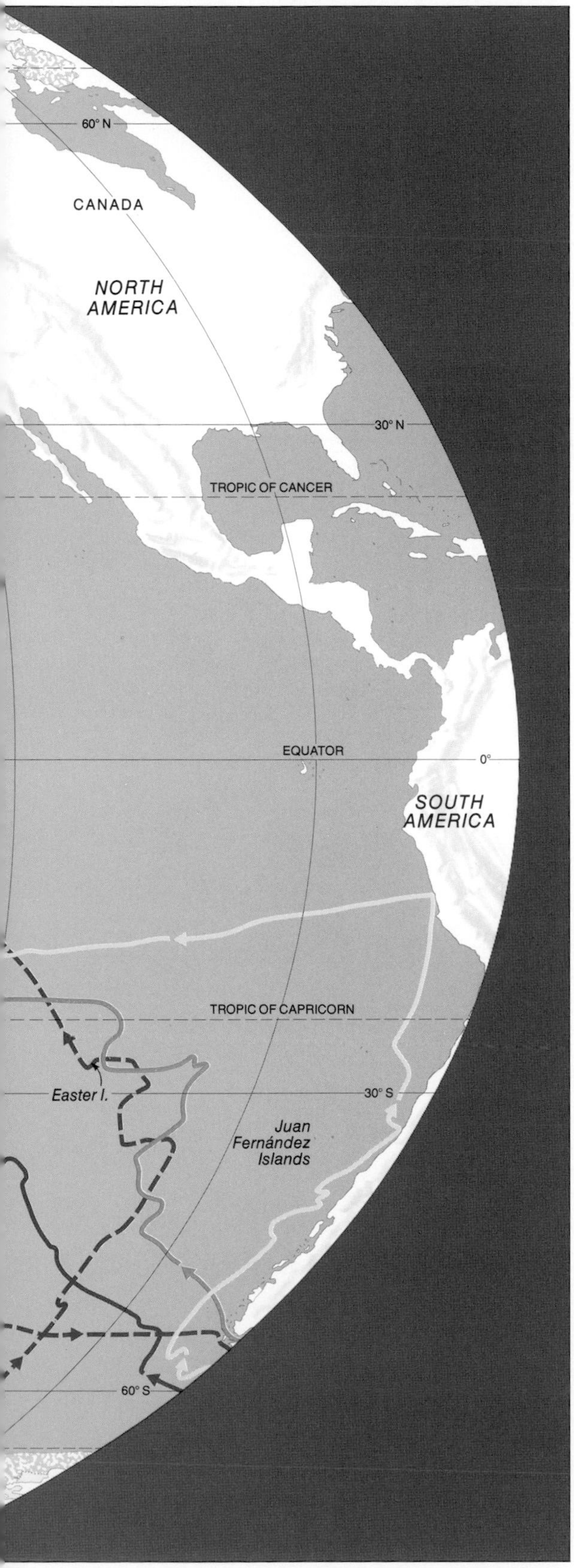

60° N
CANADA
NORTH AMERICA
30° N
TROPIC OF CANCER
EQUATOR
0°
SOUTH AMERICA
TROPIC OF CAPRICORN
Easter I.
30° S
Juan Fernández Islands
60° S

"He left nothing unattempted," said King George III of James Cook (below, right), who changed the map of the world, filling in blanks from the Antarctic to Alaska. On three historic Pacific voyages, Cook built upon earlier discoveries by Abel Janszoon Tasman, the Dutchman who first saw New Zealand, and Samuel Wallis, the English captain who found Tahiti. After Cook came Charles Wilkes, who confirmed Antarctica's existence while on the U. S. Exploring Expedition. On land, explorers Robert O'Hara Burke and William John Wills first crossed Australia from south to north.

But long before Europeans entered the Pacific, Polynesians set out on their early voyages of settlement. By A.D. *800 they occupied an area nearly twice the size of the continental U. S.*

OVERLEAF: *Polynesians glide an outrigger past Moorea's peaks. The stability of larger, seagoing outriggers enabled early voyagers to travel vast distances.*

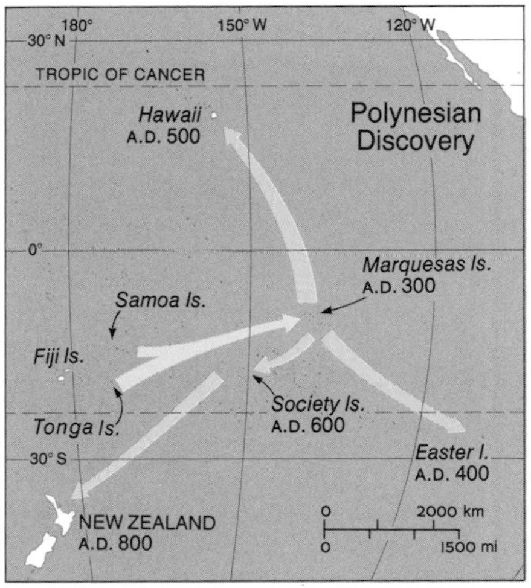

180°
150° W
120° W
30° N
TROPIC OF CANCER
Hawaii
A.D. 500
Polynesian Discovery
0°
Marquesas Is.
A.D. 300
Samoa Is.
Fiji Is.
Society Is.
A.D. 600
Tonga Is.
30° S
Easter I.
A.D. 400
NEW ZEALAND
A.D. 800
0 2000 km
0 1500 mi

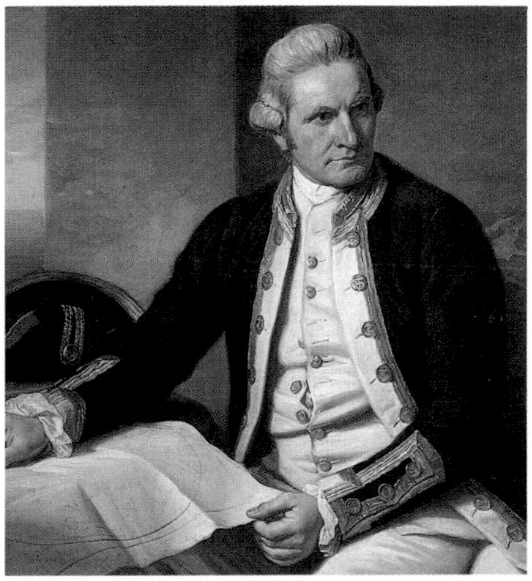

Tasman 1642
Tasman 1644
Wallis 1766-68
Cook 1768-1771
Cook 1772-75
Cook 1776-79
Voyage after Cook's death 1779-1780
Wilkes 1838-1842
Burke and Wills 1860-61
Early settlement
Dispersal

code. Perhaps others lost at war and sought peace elsewhere. Or perhaps a sailor wondered, as sailors will, what lay beyond the horizon.

Less mystery surrounds the motivations of the Europeans who first sailed into the Pacific. They wanted dominion and gold.

The Spaniards who came in the 16th century sought a quick route from the Americas to the Philippines, the center of what they hoped would be their eastern empire. The 17th century brought a wave of Dutch explorers searching for new trade routes to the East Indies. In the process, those first European sailors discovered an island here and there, but it was largely a matter of luck.

Both Spanish and Dutch explorers sought in vain for a rich continent known as Terra Australis Incognita, the unknown southern landmass that had loomed large in human imagination since ancient times, when Greeks reasoned that huge landforms existed in the Southern Hemisphere to counterbalance the lands that spread through the north. In the absence of fact, later travelers filled the unknown region with fantasy: It was rich in gold, with a mild climate and docile natives. Pedro Fernandez de Quiros, sailing under the Spanish flag in 1606, mistook an island of the New Hebrides for the continent and staged a High Mass and fireworks to commemorate his "discovery." Others glimpsed the continent's ghostly outlines in the

distance, only to see it vanish in clouds or turn into an island.

Still the legend of the Great South Land became an obsession of Europe, one that inspired the greatest era of Pacific discovery.

When James Cook turned toward that ocean in 1768, he had two sets of orders: He was to solve the continental question, once and for all. And he was to visit Tahiti to watch Venus pass before the sun. By observing the planet's transit, the Royal Navy could calculate Earth's distance from the sun, which would aid celestial navigation.

Cook was a natural choice as expedition leader: He was a masterful navigator, trained on the rough waters of the North Sea. There he had served on a merchant coal ship, or collier, before joining the Royal Navy for the Seven Years' War.

The North Sea experience prompted Cook to request a collier for his worldwide expedition. At 368 tons, the *Endeavour* was slow and homely, with the stout lines of a tugboat, but her flat bottom reduced the risk of running aground in unknown waters, and her vast hold could store provisions for a long voyage. Plain and practical, like James Cook.

The same could not be said of Joseph Banks, a wealthy young dilettante and amateur botanist who accompanied Cook as an unofficial observer. Other gentlemen would tour Europe to finish their educations, but not Joseph Banks. "Every blockhead does that," he scoffed. "My

Grand Tour shall be one round the whole globe."

For such a person, what better place to explore life, in all its raw beauty and variety, than Tahiti? Here was a place scarcely affected by civilization, an isolated society that had seen European ships on only two previous occasions.

When Samuel Wallis, an Englishman, discovered the island in 1767, Tahitians met him with a shower of stones—a common greeting for the first Europeans landing on many Pacific islands. Most natives assumed that strangers came to conquer, not to befriend. When the Tahitians resisted Wallis, he shot two natives, killing one. The Tahitians eventually yielded, and established friendly relations with the British.

Several months later, the Frenchman Louis-Antoine de Bougainville arrived at Tahiti, which he described as paradise on Earth: "Nature has placed it in the best climate of the universe, embellished it smilingly, enriched it with all its gifts, covered it with handsome inhabitants . . . ; she herself has dictated their laws," wrote Bougainville, thus beginning the romantic myth of Tahiti.

For a weary sailor who had been months aboard ship, Tahiti *was* a paradise, where coconut palms leaned to soft breezes and black sand beaches shimmered like polished onyx. Tahiti smelled of the sea, mingled with the fragrance of jasmine and gardenia. Fruits and other fresh foods abounded, and the Tahitian

people were willing to share them.

Cook and Banks arrived a year after Bougainville. While Cook made preparations to observe Venus, Banks plunged into island life. He got a tattoo, collected plants, noted how people worshiped, and how they cooked a dog (suffocate it, singe its hair, and roast it for two hours). When Banks heard about a mourning ceremony, he stripped off his clothes (including his white waistcoat with silver frog clasps) and participated, allowing the Tahitians to blacken him with charcoal. Reduced to a loincloth, the gentleman botanist marched around with the funeral party, stopping to pray here and there. He wrote about it, as he did everything, often without slowing for commas and the other impediments of punctuation.

Banks and his entourage of scientists examined all aspects of island life—animal, vegetable, and mineral—and thus began a new age of exploration that set high standards for later voyages by Charles Wilkes, Charles Darwin, and Jean-François de Galaup, Comte de La Pérouse.

Looking over Banks's botanical collections, the practical Cook wondered whether they served any purpose. Could his men eat them? Banks assured the captain that they could not. Like Banks, Cook recorded all he saw and tasted. This included Tahitian pudding, a concoction of breadfruit, plantain, nuts, and coconut, for which he carefully copied the recipe. "I seldom or never dined without one when I could get it," wrote the great navigator.

That attention to detail, reflected in the writings of Cook and Banks, exploded the myths of idyllic Tahitian life that Bougainville and others had promoted. In fact, Cook wrote, Tahiti's natives stole anything that glittered, often warred with their neighbors, and practiced human sacrifice—hardly the stuff of paradise.

Still, Cook much admired the people. He later worried about how Europeans would ruin Tahiti. "It would have been far better for these poor people never to have known our superiority," Cook wrote in sorrow. Less than a century later, the island's culture was a shambles. First came disease, then missionaries who sacked temples and banned native dancing and religion. Then the settlers came, leaving only the Tahitian language as a cultural vestige.

Leaving Tahiti, Cook turned the *Endeavour* westward toward the neighboring islands, which he named the Society Isles "as they lay contiguous to one a nother." Here as elsewhere, Cook took on fresh fruits and meat, part of his campaign against scurvy, the crippling disease now known to be caused by a deficiency of vitamin C.

Cook recognized the importance of diet and cleanliness on long voyages. He kept the men's sleeping quarters scrubbed and aired. The *Endeavour* sailed crammed with experimental antiscorbutics, including malt, sauerkraut, and soup. Cook

used them all, and though he once whipped those men who would not eat their allotment of fresh food, he preferred subtler methods of persuasion. "Such are the Tempers and disposissions of Seamen," Cook wrote, "that whatever you give them out of the Common way... will not go down with them and you will hear nothing but murmurings gainest the man that first invented it; but the Moment they see their Superiors set a Value upon it, it becomes the finest stuff in the World and the inventer an honest fellow."

So when the men balked at sauerkraut, Cook had heaps of it served at his table. He instructed his officers to eat it with enthusiasm. Suddenly the crew craved sauerkraut. In less than a week, Cook had to ration it.

He had solved the problem of scurvy. Through ten years of hard sailing, not one man under Cook's direct command died from scurvy—a remarkable achievement for an age in which the disease had been the major obstacle to long voyages.

From the Society Islands, Cook ordered the *Endeavour* southwest, in search of the southern continent, and came upon New Zealand. He landed on North Island, near the present-day city of Gisborne, and anchored in a horseshoe bay. Buff-colored cliffs protected the waters, and steep green mountains rose in the interior. Land breezes carried the scent of black pine and rippled the bay: A quiet place and a good refuge—so it seemed.

Within hours, the British faced angry Maori natives who stood their ground on the gray beach. They hit the British with stones and swatted at them with war clubs, and one native was killed by gunfire. Next day, Cook resolved to capture a few Maori, take them to his ship "and by good treatment and presents endeavour to gain their friendship."

But the Maori resisted, and four or five more natives fell to the guns. Cook wisely turned away, naming the place Poverty Bay, "because it afforded us no one thing we wanted."

In retrospect, however, the experience proved valuable. Cook was remorseful. "Had I thought that they would have made the least resistance I would not have come near them," he wrote. Henceforth, he would approach unknown peoples gingerly, and he would insist on honest dealing with the local folk, even whipping one of his own men who stole a native's hatchet. Cook prevented his crew from felling a single coconut tree in New Guinea, for fear of offending the owners. And he ordered his men to fire wide of their attackers, to frighten, not to kill.

It is one thing to bump up against a new land and proclaim that you have discovered it, another to disprove the existence of a land, such as the illusory southern continent. To do that, you had to go to all the places the myth was thought to be, and discover that it was not there.

Now James Cook had to see whether New Zealand was part of the

"Our faithfull guide through all the vicissitudes of climates," said Cook in praise of the chronometer (left) he tested on his second voyage. The timepiece opened new possibilities for mariners, who could now calculate almost exactly their position at sea. Using the new clock, Cook compared Greenwich time to his local time, and thus pinpointed his longitude, the distance east or west of the Greenwich meridian. Before the invention of the chronometer, sailors judged longitude by complicated guess-work that sent many a ship wide of its target, often by hundreds of miles.

Less than a century after Cook, Americans explored Antarctica's fringes. An engraving, based on a sketch by expedition leader Charles Wilkes, shows some members of the Vincennes's crew skidding down an "ice island." Wilkes's dog, Sydney, lies in the foreground. "The icebergs were covered with penguins," wrote Wilkes, whose scientists collected more than 500 species of birds.

great continent, as Abel Janszoon Tasman, a Dutch explorer, had postulated more than 120 years before.

So Cook set out on a punishing six-month voyage to circumnavigate New Zealand. Gales and heavy surf pushed him away. He fought back, only to have the *Endeavour* buffeted away again, like a toy. Cook kept at it, sails split and rigging slipping, determined to complete his work. Inch by inch, a chart of New Zealand gradually appeared under Cook's hand, all 2,400 miles of ragged coastline. Tasman was wrong: The lands were not part of a great continent.

Terra Australis retreated a bit more, and Cook turned westward, sailing toward the eastern coast of Australia. There he stopped to take on fresh water and wood near the present site of Sydney.

In the baking sunlight of the beach, Aboriginals shook their spears and attempted to wave the newcomers away. The British landed anyway, and the natives vanished into the muffled gloom of the woods, where burrawangs and scribbly gums choked out the sun and parrots jabbered in the treetops.

That scene would be often repeated in Australia over the next century. As British settlers came, the Aboriginals retreated before them; thousands were killed in Tasmania, where the entire native population was almost exterminated. The people of this continent were not the main obstacle to exploration; the land was. Colonists began settling

OVERLEAF: *Killer whales knife through the waters near Canada's Vancouver Island. Cook spotted whales near here; Wilkes saw them in the Antarctic as well. The Wilkes expedition produced an unexpected wealth of natural history observations. And it collected 4,000 zoological specimens and 50,000 plants, which helped to start the Smithsonian Institution.*

Australia from the outside in, tentatively probing the continent's harsh interior. Charles Sturt explored the Murray-Darling river system in 1828 and 1829. In 1840 Edward John Eyre struggled toward the Sahara-like center until the barrenness deterred him. Twenty years later, that wasteland would doom Robert O'Hara Burke and William John Wills.

The continent's coastal fringes almost did in James Cook. Leaving the mainland, Cook made northward to chart Australia's eastern coast, not realizing that he was sailing inside the Great Barrier Reef, a 1,250-mile-long coral maze. Threading through this trap, the *Endeavour* ran aground, and was barely saved.

She arrived home three years after her voyage had begun. Though Cook's first voyage achieved much, the question of the southern continent remained. So in 1772, he set out again with two rebuilt colliers, the *Resolution* and *Adventure*. In three years he covered 70,000 miles, making a bold circumnavigation of the globe that took him as far south as 71° 10′. He proved that a habitable Terra Australis did not exist.

Cook crossed the Antarctic Circle on January 17, 1773—the first person to do so—and slowly worked his way around the pack ice.

"Excessive Cold," wrote Lt. Richard Pickersgill on the *Resolution*, "the people Numb'd, yᵉ Ropes all froze over with Ice & yᵉ Riggᵍ and Sails all covered with Snow."

Cook came close to Antarctica,

177

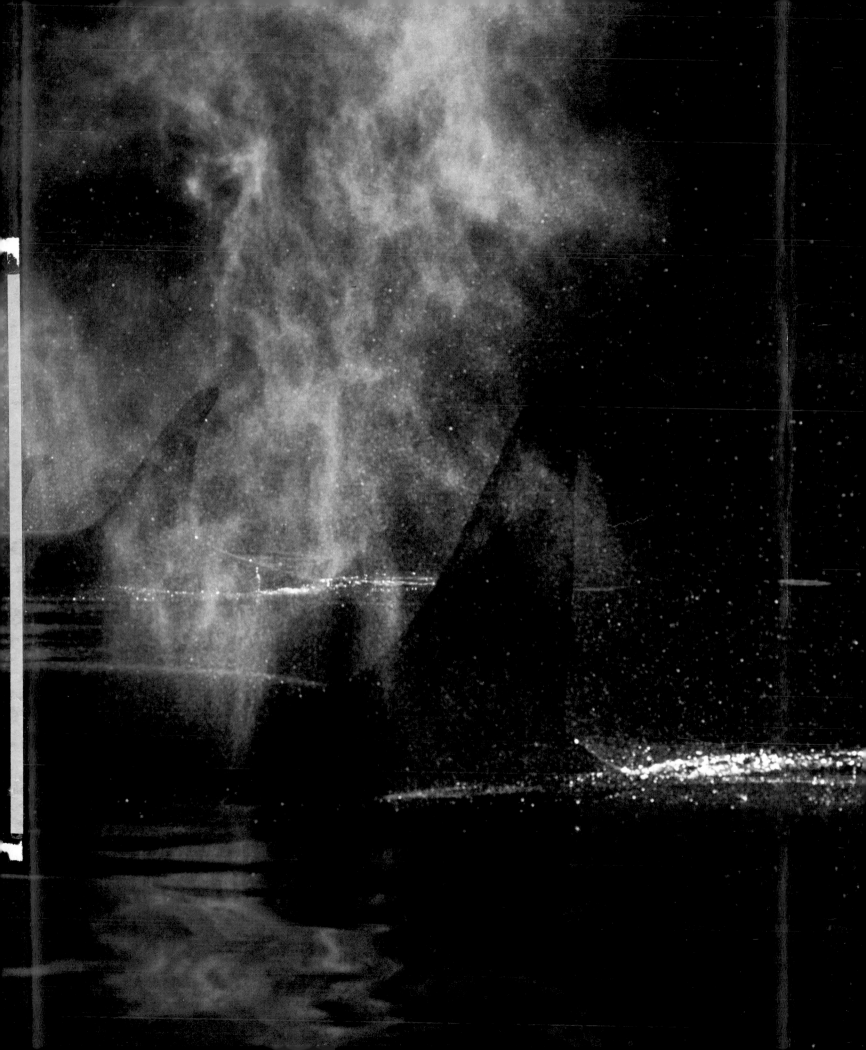

but saw no land. He guessed that the continent was the source of huge ice floes that threatened his ships. Near the end of his second voyage, Cook wrote: "The risk one runs in exploring a coast in these unknown and Icy Seas, is so very great, that I can be bold to say, that no man will ever venture farther than I have done."

For once, Cook was wrong.

Less than a century later, American sailors spied the mountains of the seventh continent and confirmed its existence. It was January 16, 1840. The squadron of six Navy vessels were sailing under Lt. Charles Wilkes. Self-righteous and aloof, Wilkes shared none of James Cook's generous spirit. But difficult as Wilkes was, his determination, scientific ability, and thorough professionalism made his voyage one of the most revealing in Pacific history.

Wilkes delved into a part of the Pacific that Cook had scarcely examined. This was Melanesia, a group of Pacific islands northeast of Australia. Melanesian lands were poor, with the meager food supply constantly threatened by hurricanes and the demands of other tribes. Little wonder that the Melanesians resisted when boatloads of hungry Europeans descended on them.

Fiji, part of Melanesia, was well known for its fierce inhabitants. And navigation was a nightmare among the three hundred islands of the Fiji group, where the ocean bottom could go from fifty fathoms to three without warning. As the U. S.

Serenity reigns in the Place of Refuge of Hōnaunau on Hawaii, as ukulele players greet the sunset. When Cook visited the island, strict taboos governed daily life: Commoners could not touch the chief's possessions; women could not eat with men; fishing seasons were limited. Executioners killed taboo violators, often by strangling, unless the offender escaped to one of these Hawaiian sanctuaries. There a priest would absolve the accused, who could return safely home.

expedition approached the Fijian maze in 1840, some of the officers began to write their wills.

The Americans found the inhabitants of Ovalau in an ugly mood, as if preparing for war. Fortresses and stockpiles choked the streets of its port, Levuka. The local people, their black skin daubed with soot and red paint, presented a "spectacle of mingled hideousness & ferocity," according to an awed visitor. One Fijian carried a cooked human head, from which he took an eye and ate it, "smacking his lips at the same time, with the greatest possible relish," wrote an American.

A few weeks later, the Americans displayed their own brand of savagery. On the island of Malolo to purchase food, a party of Wilkes's men came upon a group of natives. The Americans, thinking to ensure their safety, took a local man hostage. A crowd gathered, a struggle began, and two Americans were clubbed and stabbed to death.

In retaliation, Wilkes ordered his troops to storm Malolo's villages. Supported by rocket fire, the Americans went in with muskets blazing. In half an hour, about 80 Fijians were dead. A calm descended, disturbed only by the moans of the injured and the crackling of flames. Into the fire Wilkes's men piled spears, bows, arrows, and clubs. Then to mock the natives' cannibalism, they tossed in a warrior's corpse, along with some yams.

Some of the Americans seemed shocked by their own behavior. "I hope I am not a savage in disposition," wrote one, "but . . . I felt a degree of savage like satisfaction every time I did or thought I had Killed one of those Miscreants." The travails of a long expedition, piled one upon the other, could transform the most humane of people.

Even James Cook was not immune. He rested for just a year after his second expedition before the Admiralty called on him again, this time to search for a northern passage between the Pacific and Atlantic.

In the process, he discovered Hawaii, mapped the northwest coast of North America, charted unknown parts of Canada and Alaska, and crossed the Arctic Circle. He reached northward to 70° 44′. Here he found no passage between the oceans—just a 12-foot-high barrier of ice, stretching across the horizon "compact as a Wall," wrote Cook. He turned southward, for Hawaii.

Despite his achievements, Cook had been in no condition for another worldwide voyage. Although still shy of 50 when selected for the third expedition, he was worn down by the unending stress of exploring. Day after day, he faced unknown waters or unknown lands. One misjudgment could doom ship and crew. His men, as always, were a hard-drinking, hardheaded lot plucked from the dregs of society. They had to be watched, cajoled, and outmaneuvered. And on this last voyage, Cook's *Resolution* was a constant

Serrated mountains plunge to the sea on the coast of Kauai, one of the Hawaiian Islands discovered by James Cook in 1778. The "prodigious surf," he wrote, "broke so high against the shore that we could not land. . . ."

In more than a decade of Pacific voyaging, Cook's masterful seamanship saved his ships from disaster. But even this great navigator could not steer clear of the cultural misunderstandings that bedeviled many explorers in this region: Hostile Hawaiians stabbed and clubbed Cook in an argument over a stolen boat at Kealakekua Bay, where just weeks before the captain had received a god's welcome.

Cook's wide-ranging travels opened the Pacific to a tidal wave of change. After him came whalers, missionaries, and colonists who remade most aspects of native life including diet, religion, work, and language—forever altering this once secluded ocean realm.

problem. Though she had performed nobly on the second voyage, she was hastily and improperly refitted for this one. She leaked steadily, prompting an officer to write home: "If I return in the *Resolution*, the next trip I may Safely Venture in a Ship Built of Ginger Bread."

Finally, there were the thefts. Everywhere Cook landed, it seemed, the native people stole from him. A sextant vanished in Huahine, a goat at Moorea, a 20-pound anchor hook in Nootka Sound. One light-fingered Indian even managed to pinch Cook's gold watch—while his cabin was under guard. Pacific cultures did not cherish private property as Europeans did. Usually the thieves meant no harm; stealing

from Englishmen was largely a matter of sport.

For a weary Cook, the thieving was a final insult. He ordered floggings. He jailed offenders. He slashed their arms. He sacked a village and burned canoes to punish one thief, and cut off another man's ears to make an example of him.

Was this the same Cook who had worked so hard to prevent bloodshed on earlier voyages?

The answer came at Kealakekua Bay, where Cook called after his arduous northern passage of 1778 and 1779. Learning that Hawaiians had stolen one of his ship's cutters, Cook went ashore to take a local chief as hostage, thinking this would secure the boat's return.

Cook found the chief and began walking him toward the shore. The old chief's wife and others rushed out to protest, and a crowd gathered, menacing the British with stones, spears, and taunts. Cook the humanitarian spoke: "We can never think of compelling him to go on board," he told a marine, "without killing a number of these People."

Too late. Someone threatened Cook with a dagger and a stone, and Cook answered with a load of shot from his musket. The crowd advanced. Now Cook fired with ball, and a Hawaiian fell. For the last time, the captain turned toward his ship—perhaps to retreat, perhaps for reinforcements—but by then, the mob was already upon him.

Robert O'Hara Burke
William John Wills

By Edwards Park

Last day's trek to the false promise of safety: Weak from hunger, Burke, Wills, and King struggle toward Cooper's Creek and the end of their journey across Australia.

In Melbourne in the late 1940s, you could see their giant statue from the lawns outside the old Parliament House of the state of Victoria. You could eat lunch and look at them.

Burke stood, bearded and gaunt, beside the seated Wills, his hand on the other's shoulder. Both looked away as though searching. For what? The way across the wild, unknown continent? The way back?

Melbourne perches on the very fringe of a vast and still relatively empty landmass. Drive northwest past the suburbs, and you can see the green ridge of the horizon. Climb it, and you see another ridge beyond, and then another, and another. And hundreds of miles beyond them, the green turns to the brown-yellow plains and downs of the Outback. And much farther beyond that, cracked claypans and stone deserts shimmer in blazing heat: the Never-Never, where the crystalline air makes nameless hilltops and rock formations on the horizon seem close enough to touch. And still farther north, the tropics wait, breathless, dank, soul rotting.

Many Australians have never seen this—just the first part. Burke and Wills saw it all, struggled through it on an epic journey, a journey you could envy, except for the end.

Robert O'Hara Burke, originally a Galwayman, was a police superintendent in the mining district of Castlemaine in the 1850s. He was a strangely driven man—a little fey. Sturdy, black-bearded, he had pale, brooding eyes. He cared little for his own appearance. His trousers sagged around his heels, and often saliva dribbled down his beard.

Though Burke ran his police station well, he made his neighbors wince by sitting stark naked, except for his helmet, reading a book in the wading pool behind his house. Notoriously apt to get lost in the bush, he nonetheless would gallop hell-for-leather through the woods, 30 miles, just to swing on the front gate of a certain magistrate who danced with rage if anyone swung on his front gate.

At 39, Burke was unmarried. When he cleaned himself up, however, he could charm the ladies with small gallantries and Irish wit. He had, recalled a Melbourne hostess, "such a daring, reckless look about him."

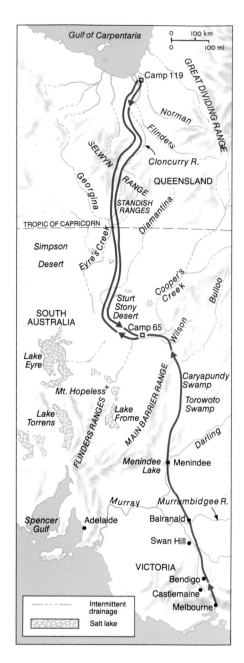

AUSTRALIA

Gold had made Melbourne prosperous at mid-century. A new Royal Society determined to explore the great unknown to the north. Plans were laid. It would be a big expedition, using camels, and would be the first to traverse the country northward to the Gulf of Carpentaria. To find a leader, the Exploration Committee scanned 14 applications and chose the ingratiating policeman from Castlemaine, Robert Burke.

On August 20, 1860, Burke led a small army out of Melbourne town while the crowd cheered and little boys ran beside the caravan. With him rode 3 scientists and 14 assistants, followed by 27 camels and several horse-drawn wagons bearing 21 tons of supplies.

The winter month of August brings rain to Victoria, and the expedition inched north through black mud. But in every town and mining camp, settlers turned out to cheer the explorers, who took almost three weeks to reach the little settlement of Swan Hill near the Murray River.

Burke's second-in-command, George James Landells, had earned his position by selecting the Indian camels and shipping them to Melbourne. But he had insisted on lacing their rations with rum, for the salubrious effect it would have, so the expedition lugged 60 gallons of it. News of the rum reached some sheepshearers on a remote station near the Darling River. They broached the supply and got howling drunk.

That was enough for Burke. Out went the rum—and Landells. The camels were taken over by his assistant, a former soldier in India named John King, a capable and biddable man. For his new second-in-command, Burke chose the youngest of the scientists, William John Wills.

He was a handsome athlete of 26, son of an English doctor who had come out to the goldfields. Young Wills worked on a sheep station, helped his father in medicine, and finally got a job at the Melbourne observatory. Fond of mathematics, he had taught himself surveying and delighted in astronomy. Burke thought the world of him, and Wills complemented his leader with his careful work and undeviating loyalty.

The party stopped at Menindee, then an outpost of civilization. Beyond it lay the Never-Never. Here Burke picked up William Wright, a local character who offered to guide the group on the next leg of the journey, a 400-mile hike to Cooper's Creek (now Cooper Creek), which previous explorers had found to be a reliable oasis.

Burke split the party. Eight men, 15 horses, and 16 good camels would go ahead to set up a supply depot at Cooper's Creek. The rest would hole up at Menindee, await the lagging supply train, and continue to the Cooper. On October 19, Wright led Burke, Wills, King, the foreman William Brahe, and three assistants northward.

October is a bad time to head toward the Australian center, for the sun sends the mercury out of sight. Through the fierce heat the party struggled, finally reaching the Torowoto Swamp with its reliable water. Burke sent Wright back to Menindee, where he was to gather the supplies and bring them up to the depot at the Cooper.

Wright headed south and the other seven plodded through rocky

188

An Aboriginal guide, known only as Dick, who led a search party in a futile hunt for Burke and Wills.

> He was a wild, eccentric daredevil. . . . Either he did not realise danger or his mind was so unhinged . . . that he revelled in it.
>
> A CONTEMPORARY, SPEAKING OF BURKE

plains, from water to water. Each distant cluster of trees marked a creek bed—often, in that wet year, a series of water holes, or billabongs, where they could camp.

Cooper's Creek was the largest of these, a string of splendid billabongs shaded by trees. The party arrived on November 11, were driven from their first camp by a plague of rats, then settled comfortably beside a large billabong near an old coolabah tree. Here they built their depot. They also rested, prepared supplies for the long push to the gulf, and waited for Wright to return with the reserves. Young Wills, feeling wonderfully fit, explored the area, looking for various routes north.

By mid-December, Burke was ready to go. Wright must show up any day now, and the leader felt his men were capable of a mighty effort—nearly 1,500 miles to the gulf and back. Burke split the group again. With Wills, King, and one assistant, an ex-sailor called Charley Gray, he would make the dash north. He would take his own horse, Billy, and the six best camels. Brahe and the others would man the depot at Cooper's Creek. "It is my intention," Burke optimistically wrote to the committee, "to return here within the next three months at latest."

"Sunday, Dec. 16, 1860," begins an entry in the journal that William Wills kept. "The two horses having been shod, and our reports finished, we started at forty minutes past six a.m. for Eyre's Creek." Brahe rode with them to their first camp, then headed back to Cooper's Creek. He turned and called out his own estimate to his friend, "Goodbye, King, I do not expect to see you for at least four months."

Burke's diary is a scrappy, messy collection of notes—some of them merely tantalizing: "Made a creek where we found a great many natives. They presented us with fish, and offered their women." Wills's more detailed journal fills in facts and figures, as well as descriptions of the countryside and its life: ". . . red-breasted cockatoos, pigeons, a crow, and several other birds . . . two wild plants of the gourd or melon tribe;

one much resembling a stunted cucumber, and other . . . very similar to a small model of a water melon. . . ." He reflects the then current attitude—haughty yet fearful—of white settlers toward the natives: "A large tribe of blacks came pestering us to go to their camp and have a dance, which we declined. They were very troublesome, and nothing but the threat to shoot them will keep them away. . . ."

At first the going was faster than they'd dared hope, the country better watered. Of western Queensland Wills noted, "fresh plants met our view on every rise; everything green and luxuriant. The horse licked his lips, and tried all he could to break his nose-string and get at the food."

Gradually the land changed. They came among giant anthills, then the Standish and Selwyn Ranges. Here, Wills noted, "Pieces of iron ore, very rich, were scattered in great numbers over some of the hills."

Unluckily, the party arrived in the tropics at the same time as "the wet." During this rainy season the flat land turned into huge marshes, and the camels slid and plunged in the mud. Camp 119 (the 119th since leaving Melbourne) was about 30 miles from the sea. Burke and Wills

left the other two there and slogged on toward the northern coast.

They waded through a bog, then found a streambed and followed it. "We passed three blacks, who, as is universally their custom, pointed out to us, unasked, the best part down. This assisted us greatly. . . ." When they camped for the night, that Sunday, February 10, they tasted the water. Brackish. They noted an eight-inch tide. They were at the Gulf of Carpentaria. Mangrove swamps barred them from the shore, but they had made it.

"It would be well to say that we reached the sea," wrote Burke, "but we could not obtain a view of the open ocean." Still they were the first white men to link the north and south coasts of Australia.

Weary but proud, the two rejoined King and Gray. However, there was no time for celebration. Terribly short of food, they knew they must head straight back south. So, with the rain pelting them and the ground giving way underfoot, they began their laborious back track.

Fatigue began turning Wills's entries to short scraps—sometimes the bare mention of a camp. Often, now, he gave the camps names instead of numbers: Recovery Camp, Saltbush Camp. At Eureka Camp they stumbled across a huge snake, killed it, and ate it. Burke promptly came down with dysentery. The others didn't feel too well, either.

Through the first three weeks of March it rained almost steadily, and their going was painful. The tough Gray began to complain of headaches. By the end of March they were back at last in the dry country, but all were weakened by lack of food. On April 8, they were held up by Gray, "who gammoned he could not walk." On the tenth, they had to kill Billy the horse and cut him up for meat. "We found it healthy and tender, but without the slightest trace of fat. . . ."

Only two camels remained, and since Gray now couldn't walk, they strapped him to a saddle. On April 17 Wills made a terse entry: "This morning, about sunrise, Gray died." They buried him as deep as they could dig—three feet. And only seventy miles from safety.

Safety? At the depot at Cooper's Creek, Brahe was at his wit's end. Wright had never arrived from the south with the supplies that he was supposed to have delivered almost six months ago. Burke and Wills and the others had never returned from the north. They'd now been gone more than the generous four months Brahe had estimated.

Brahe and his colleagues waited—week after week of steeling themselves to the persistent flies, keeping fires going to drive off mosquitoes, shooting rats. Aside from guarding the grazing animals and preparing meals, they had nothing to do but gaze out at the serene water hole and watch the birds. The lassitude of the Outback was sapping their will. They stopped fishing and shooting ducks. They simply ate meals of rice and tea and salt beef and pork and damper, a bread baked in the ashes of a campfire. And now William Patton, the blacksmith, was sick, his limbs swollen, his gums too sore to chew. Most of them felt these symptoms of scurvy, though not as badly. The sickness comes with the

191

territory, unless you're willful enough to break the spell of this eerie, peaceful land and look after yourself.

Brahe couldn't. Day after day of heat and stillness and nothing to do . . . night after night of silent stars . . . the growing sense of human puniness in the vastness of eternity . . . all these produced a lassitude that has an almost crippling effect on those who venture into Australia's remoteness. They stare endlessly at the coals of a dying fire in the silent wildness, and simply give up thinking and planning.

Where was Burke's party? Had they died in the emptiness, or had Burke headed east to Queensland's coastal settlements? Brahe couldn't answer, and the need for an answer, a decision, became more and more compelling as the days passed. What was he to do? Remain and rot?

It never occurred to Burke, less than 50 miles away, that Brahe would do anything but stay. On the 20th they continued, Burke riding one camel, Wills and King switching off on the second. They camped that night with only one day's journey to go, so they divided up most of the last rations and downed them. At dawn on the 21st, they set forth.

Brahe had fixed on the 21st as the day to give up waiting and break camp. He buried a large share of the rations under the coolabah tree, then raked over the spot so the natives wouldn't see it. On the tree trunk the men carved: DIG / 3 FT. N.W. / APR. 21 1861.

They loaded the camels, strapped poor Patton on one, and painfully trudged southward from the Cooper. It was about 10:30 in the morning.

Less than 30 miles to the north, the gulf party was forcing itself to a final, desperate effort. On they went, passing landmarks that they remembered, feeling the closeness of their goal. The early night of April fell on them, the camels lurching behind the men. By moonlight they continued, sure now that they could see the tents of the depot.

At about 7:30, only nine hours after Brahe had left, they arrived at Cooper's Creek, Camp 65. There was no answer to their shouts, no joyous congratulations, no tender care, no triumph at all in the end.

And that *is* the true end of the Burke and Wills expedition. Of course they found the buried cache, and the food restored some strength. But it was not enough to repair weakness gone bone deep. The men headed for the settlements near Mount Hopeless, some 150 miles away, but had to give up and return to the Cooper. They were too weak. Ironically, it was the natives they had so scorned who now nursed them and taught them to make flour out of the seed of the nardoo fern. The little cakes tasted good, but they couldn't fend off starvation.

Near the end of June or the beginning of July, Wills died, then Burke. Wills kept his journal going to the end, even with a touch of humor: "My pulse are at forty-eight, and very weak, and my legs and arms are nearly skin and bone. I can only look out, like Mr. Micawber, 'for something to turn up. . . .'" And Burke, too, wrote a few words. Like a good officer, he tried to look first to the welfare of his men: "King has stayed with me till the last. He has left me, at my own request, unburied, and with my pistol in hand."

King was found alive by one of the rescue teams that started out after

Nothing now but the greatest good luck can save any of us.
JOURNAL OF WILLS

192

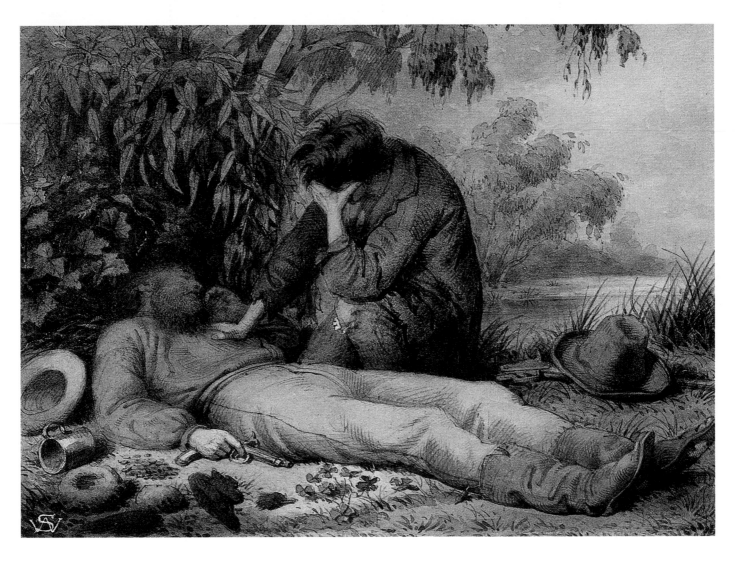

Death in the Outback—Burke with his pistol, mourned by King.

Brahe returned from Cooper's Creek (meeting Wright who, undone by lethargy and logistical problems, was just setting out). The blacks had nursed King and led the rescuers to him. He told of the triumphant attainment of the gulf, of the heartbreaking return to the deserted depot, and of the deaths of Burke and Wills. Brahe, who had been guiding the rescue team, heard King's story. His feelings can only be imagined. The Royal Commission that later looked into the affair chastised him.

In Melbourne, a monument was raised to Burke and Wills, along with a statue. The latter has been moved from its old place near the Parliament House and now stands by a gurgling fountain in a shopping center at City Square. But perhaps people still eye the statue as they munch a meat sandwich and sip a little good, brown beer. Perhaps they see that look in the sculptured eyes, that seeking. For what?

Perhaps for nine hours.

The journal of Wills was published in Melbourne in 1861. Alan Moorehead has written an absorbing narrative of the expedition, titled Cooper's Creek.

Fatal Africa

By Denis Hills

"He had long hair . . . interwoven with the bowels of oxen. . . . He had likewise a wreath of guts hung about his neck, and . . . about his middle." His body was wet with running butter. This Galla chief, mounted on a cow and decked out in all his finery to meet the ruler of Ethiopia, was one of the characters described by James Bruce, a wealthy Scottish laird, on his return to London from Ethiopia in 1774. Before Bruce's visit, Ethiopia and its ancient Coptic Christian Church had been a mystery to Europeans for 150 years—ever since the country had expelled its Portuguese Jesuit missionaries in a fit of nationalism.

But people scoffed at Bruce's descriptions of the handsome, cruel Ethiopians; at his tales of banquets at which raw beefsteaks were hacked from a living animal and chewed and swallowed on the spot, and guests of both sexes, gorged and drunk, gave themselves up to orgies of shameless debauchery. Then there were the massacres: Dismembered bodies, said Bruce, lay scattered about the streets of Gonder, and his own hunting dogs had brought home heads and arms.

His stories seemed too farfetched to be true and cast doubt on his claim to have discovered the source of the Nile—a goal sought since antiquity. Word went round that Bruce was an impostor. He withdrew in a huff to his estate in Scotland.

Bruce in fact had got his geogra-

phy wrong. It was not, as he boasted, the source of the Nile that he had found but of its tributary, the Blue Nile. And he wasn't the first European to see it. Some Portuguese priests, whose accounts Bruce tried to discredit, had been there a century or more before him. But Bruce's observations about Ethiopia's terrain and customs proved essentially sound, being confirmed by other travelers after his death in 1794. He had lifted the veil from one corner of the African Continent and brought the question of the Nile's source dramatically to public attention.

"Travellers like poets are mostly an angry race," wrote explorer Richard Burton. He could have been thinking of Bruce and his anger over lack of recognition, or of many other European explorers of Africa, including himself. Most had a single-minded tenacity that brooked no rivalry. Africa, with its unknown interior, offered adventurers a new path to glory in an era of geographical curiosity awakened by Captain Cook's explorations of the Pacific.

In that new spirit of geographical inquiry, Sir Joseph Banks, the English botanist who had sailed with Cook, helped found the African Association in 1788 to fill in the "wide extended blank" of the African interior. Within this vast unmapped area lay the source of the Nile in central Africa and most of the Niger in West Africa. No European had explored the Niger or even identified its outlet, and reports from African and

A boatman pilots his dugout canoe through early morning fog on southern Africa's Okavango River, which Swedish naturalist Karell Johan Andersson explored in 1859. Many explorers took to rivers to avoid slogging across fiery sands or hacking through jungle, but cataracts, malarial swamps, and floating vegetation often blocked their way. Most Europeans who ventured inland in the 18th and 19th centuries lost their health, if not their lives, in the land one explorer dubbed Fatal Africa.

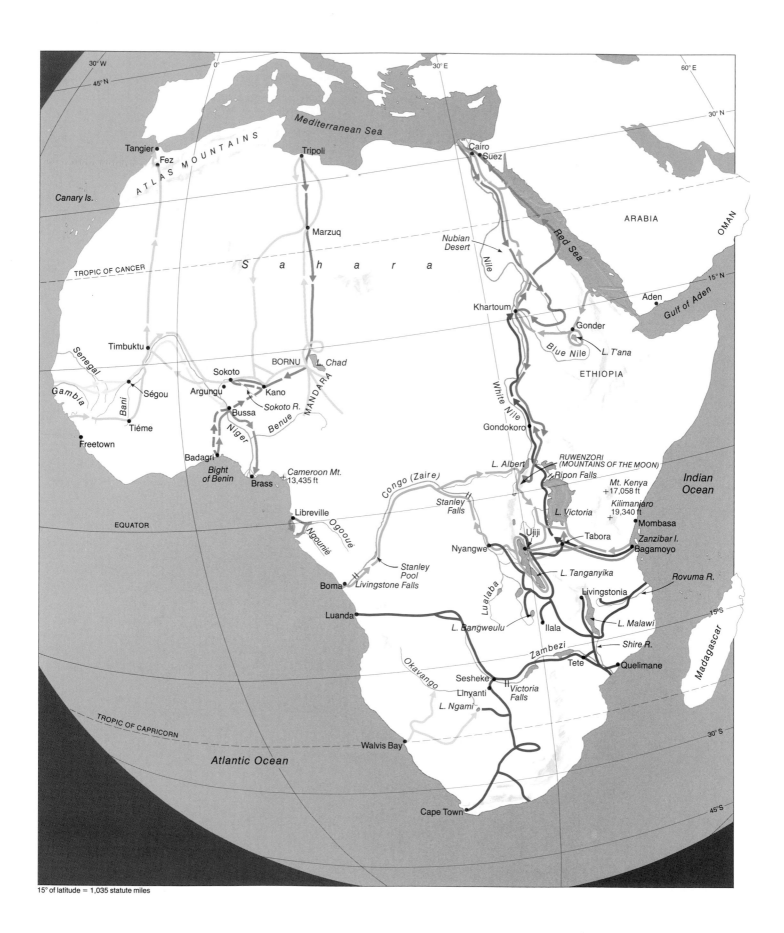

30°W · 0° · 30°E · 60°E

45°N

30°N

Mediterranean Sea

ATLAS MOUNTAINS

Tangier
Fez
Tripoli
Cairo
Suez

Canary Is.

Marzuq

ARABIA

OMAN

TROPIC OF CANCER

S a h a r a

Nubian Desert

Nile

Red Sea

15°N

Aden

Gulf of Aden

Khartoum

Gonder

Timbuktu

BORNU
L. Chad

Sokoto
Kano
Sokoto R.
Argungu
Bussa
Benue
MANDARA
Niger

Blue Nile
L. T'ana

ETHIOPIA

Ségou
Bani
Senegal
Gambia
Tiéme
Freetown

White Nile

Gondokoro

Badagri
Bight of Benin
Brass
Cameroon Mt.
+13,435 ft

Congo (Zaire)

L. Albert

RUWENZORI
(MOUNTAINS OF THE MOON)
Ripon Falls

Mt. Kenya
+17,058 ft

Indian Ocean

Libreville

Stanley Falls

Kilimanjaro
19,340 ft
+

L. Victoria

Mombasa

EQUATOR

Ogooué
Ngounié

Ujiji
Tabora

Zanzibar I.
Bagamoyo

Nyangwe

Stanley Pool
Livingstone Falls
Boma

Rovuma R.

Lualaba

L. Tanganyika

Livingstonia

Luanda

L. Bangweulu
Ilala

L. Malawi

15°S

Zambezi
Shire R.

Tete
Quelimane

Madagascar

Okavango

Sesheke
Linyanti
L. Ngami

Victoria Falls

TROPIC OF CAPRICORN

30°S

Walvis Bay

Atlantic Ocean

45°S

Cape Town

15° of latitude = 1,035 statute miles

Adverse winds and currents delayed exploration of the African shoreline by European ships, but Portuguese, British, French, and Dutch traders had coastal toeholds by 1600. Deserts, disease, and hostile inhabitants kept them from mapping the interior for nearly 300 more years. Arabs led exploration in the north. Beginning in the 600s, Arab traders crisscrossed the Sahara, establishing Muslim settlements. By the 1800s Omani Arabs controlled much of the East African coast and the slave trade on the island of Zanzibar.

A fanciful engraving (below) shows Scotsman James Bruce, one of the first European explorers to push inland, drinking a toast in 1770 from the source of the Blue Nile in Ethiopia. Bruce mistakenly claimed his find to be the chief source of the Nile. He brought back tales of brutal justice in Ethiopia, where the scavenging striped hyena (sketched by Bruce) roamed Gonder by night, feasting on the flesh of mutilated or executed criminals.

OVERLEAF: Kebbawa fishermen surge into Nigeria's Sokoto River at Argungu, a town that German explorer Heinrich Barth described in the 1850s as a center of Kebbawa rebellion against the local sultan. The tribesmen perform an ancient ritual: Using nets with calabash floats, hundreds of men compete to catch the largest fish. Its size foretells how the gods will favor the Kebbawa in the coming year.

- Bruce 1768-1773
- Park 1795-1806
- Clapperton, Denham, and Oudney 1821-25
- Clapperton and Lander 1825-27
- Caillié 1827-28
- R. and J. Lander 1830
- Livingstone 1841-1873
- Barth 1850-55
- Andersson 1853-59
- Burton and Speke 1857-59
- Speke and Grant 1860-63
- S. and F. Baker 1861-65
- Stanley 1871-1889
- Kingsley 1895

Arab travelers differed as to its direction of flow. In 1794 the African Association chose a young ship's surgeon, Mungo Park, as its geographical emissary to trace the Niger to its outlet and visit Timbuktu with its rumored hoards of gold.

The growing antislavery campaign in England had focused attention on West Africa. If slavery were abolished, perhaps the loss of profits could be made up by developing new markets for British commerce in the African interior. The coast had long been exploited for trade, mainly in slaves, but there had been no lasting white advance into the hinterland. Travel was hazardous, the inhabitants hostile, the climate lethal. The fever-ridden coast had earned the name "the white man's grave." (Africans today say that the mosquito was the black man's ally in keeping the white invaders out.) Slavers found it easier to wait off the coast for the black ivory to be brought to them by chiefs and slave dealers than to go hunting for it inland.

Mungo Park set off eastward from a town near the mouth of the Gambia in December 1795 with six Africans. As a white Christian bound for fanatically Muslim territories, poorly armed, and with few goods to barter for the favor of local chiefs, he was taking an enormous risk. But, avid for fame, Park was ready to gamble his life to achieve it. Throughout his journey he was insulted, threatened, and robbed. Moors hissed and spat in his face and his companions left him.

"A lonely captive, perishing of thirst," Scotsman Mungo Park drops to his knees and drinks with cows. Reduced to begging for sustenance during four months' captivity in a nomadic Muslim ruler's camps, Park often found himself too thirsty to sleep. On this night an old man yielded to his pleas but, fearing that Christian lips would taint the bucket, dumped the water in a trough.

Fired by youthful ambition, Park scouted the Niger River in West Africa in the 1790s and early 1800s, search-ing for its outlet. On his second Niger expedition, malaria and dysentery killed most of his European compan-ions, but Park struggled onward in a vessel patched together from the best parts of two rotting canoes.

At Bussa, by one account, tribes-men bombarded the explorers with rocks and poison arrows (opposite). The men returned fire until their ammunition failed. Then, all hope lost, they leapt to their deaths in the rushing waters of the Niger.

He was accused of being a spy and held captive for four months. Escap-ing, he struggled on to Ségou and at last caught his first glimpse of the "majestic Niger . . . as broad as the Thames at Westminster and flowing slowly to the eastward."

Park was by then starving and penniless. He was about to spend the night in a tree when a woman took pity on him, showed him to her hut, and cooked him a fish. Other women entertained him with an impromptu song—"Let us pity the white man; no mother has he," they sang.

A slave trader offered Park protec-tion during the 500-mile return jour-ney to the coast, which he reached in June 1797. In 1805 he was back again to search for the Niger's outlet, but this attempt failed too. Park and the few members of his party who survived the overland trip to the Ni-ger vanished. Their exact fate is un-known, but Africans said all the Eu-ropeans died in a fight on the river.

Mungo Park's account of his earlier Niger trip helped inspire a frail-looking young Frenchman named René Caillié. Caillié had dreamed of Africa since boyhood and was driven by a romantic ambition to visit the golden city of Timbuktu. Like Park, he resolved to reach his goal or perish in the attempt. In 1827, disguised as an Arab pilgrim, he joined a small caravan leaving the west coast. Experience had taught him to travel light, and one of his few, prized possessions was an umbrella.

At Tiéme he fell ill with scurvy: "The roof of my mouth became quite bare, part of the bones exfoliated and fell away, and my teeth seemed ready to drop out of their sockets. . . ." A village woman nursed him, forcing him to drink rice water. "At length, after six weeks of indescribable suffering . . . I began to feel better."

Caillié continued his journey by canoe down an upper tributary to the Niger—he traded his precious umbrella for a passage—and reached Timbuktu. But he was bitterly disappointed. "I had formed a totally different idea of the grandeur and wealth of Timbuctoo," he wrote. The fabled city was a dump of mean mud houses with a few stunted trees, roasting under a burning sun, and besieged by marauding bands of Tuareg horsemen. The grand myth died. Golden Timbuktu was nothing but a desert trading center whose main resource was salt.

To return home to France, Caillié traveled north to Tangier, crossing the Sahara with an Arab caravan, a journey no other European had completed. When he published the account of his travels, many readers disbelieved it. The British even accused him of finding and copying the journals of Maj. Alexander Gordon Laing, who was murdered on an earlier visit to Timbuktu. In 1838 Caillié died embittered at the age of 38.

No explorer had yet reached the lower part of the Niger, so the Colonial Office in London organized a fresh expedition, this time from the north. In 1822 two former navy men, Hugh Clapperton and Walter Oudney, and army major Dixon Denham left Tripoli for the kingdom of Bornu near Lake Chad. Clapperton and Oudney, who had planned the trip on their own, were furious when the Colonial Office sent Denham too, without even making clear who was the leader. Angry rivalry between Denham and Clapperton reached such a pitch that they parted ways. Denham turned east to explore the Lake Chad region. Oudney died while traveling west with Clapperton toward the Niger.

At Sokoto the sultan refused to let Clapperton continue to the Niger, only 150 miles away, and he retraced his steps to England in 1825. Later that year he tried again, taking along his servant Richard Lander, a young man of 20 who was to show heroic qualities of stamina and enterprise. They traveled north from the Bight of Benin. At Sokoto, Clapperton was reduced to a skeleton by dysen-

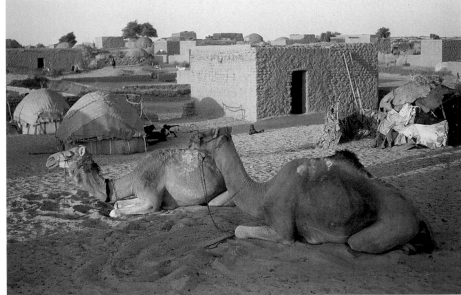

"Nothing but a mass of ill-looking houses, built of earth," wrote French explorer René Caillié in dismay. The first European to return from Timbuktu, in 1828, he exploded the myth of a glittering desert center of wealth and culture. Caillié's sketch of the city (left) with its mosques and crowded dwellings—an illustration in his 1830 book of travels—reveals an eye for detail. In modern Timbuktu (below), camels rest beside houses that might have come from Caillié's picture.

Timbuktu's inhabitants were devout Muslims. To travel in Muslim territory, Caillié posed as an Arab. Aware that Tuareg nomads had murdered Scotsman Alexander Gordon Laing near Timbuktu in 1826, he feared for his life if revealed as a Christian. The Frenchman hid notes and drawings when anyone approached and pretended to be studying loose pages of the Koran. He returned across the Sahara with an Arab caravan, limping into Tangier a sun-blackened skeleton.

tery. Lander, sick himself, nursed his master night and day, but in vain. Three days before he died, wrote Lander, Clapperton said "that he had heard with peculiar distinctness the tolling of an English funeral bell." He died in Lander's arms.

Determined to complete his dead master's task, Lander mounted a second expedition with his brother John in 1830. They reached the Niger, obtained canoes at Bussa, and traveled downstream through luxuriant scenery: "Magnificent festoons of creeping plants, always green, hung from the tops of the tallest trees, and dropping to the water's edge, formed immense natural grottoes," wrote John Lander. Surviving attacks by suspicious villagers, river

pirates, and "an incredible number of hippopotami," the brothers journeyed successfully to the river's outlet at Brass. The mouth of the Niger, sought by the British for over 30 years, had been discovered, an Admiralty spokesman said, "by a very humble but intelligent individual."

But still, the prime geographical mystery of the day remained the source of the Nile. German missionaries Johannes Rebmann and Johann Ludwig Krapf reported seeing snow on the peaks of two huge mountains near the Equator, Kilimanjaro and Kenya. Maybe melting snow drained into a great basin that gave birth to the Nile. Arab traders had spoken of a vast inland sea. Indian Army officers Richard Francis Burton and

John Hanning Speke set out from Zanzibar to investigate these reports.

Burton certainly fitted his own epithet of the angry traveler, as did Speke. Jealousy would destroy their relationship. They were an ill-matched pair. Burton, an irascible intellectual with a gift for languages, had an almost perverse curiosity about native customs—in India his overzealous investigation of Hindu lovemaking and of homosexuality in the male brothels of Karachi had brought charges of ungentlemanly conduct and wrecked his army career. Speke had a passion for hunting and collecting specimens. He smarted under an imagined accusation of cowardice by Burton on a previous trip. Setting off in June 1857 with a well-equipped party of soldiers, porters, and baggage animals, Burton and Speke were soon plagued by sickness, desertions, and theft.

In February 1858 they came to Lake Tanganyika at Ujiji. Here, as today, egrets stepped delicately among the gentle wavelets and the fish eagle, poised on a bone white tree, uttered its witchlike scream. But Speke, temporarily blinded by ophthalmia, could not see the lake and Burton, weakened by malaria, had to be carried to its shore. After a brief canoe trip to the north end of the lake, they turned back for the coast, pausing to rest at Tabora. Here Burton remained, to question local sheikhs about the area, while Speke traveled north to check Arab reports of a great lake larger than

Lake Tanganyika. Within a few weeks he was back with astonishing news. He had seen an immense stretch of water, which he named Lake Victoria. He had no doubt that it was the true source of the Nile.

Burton ridiculed Speke's impulsive claim—"The fortunate discoverer's conviction was strong; his reasons were weak"—but the subject was dropped for the time being. Speke sailed ahead for England, promising to say nothing about the expedition until Burton got back. He broke his word, announcing his discovery while belittling Burton's part in the expedition, and soon returned to Africa with an old Indian Army friend, James Augustus Grant.

Grant was the ideal partner, loyal and compliant. Turning north from Tabora the two men traveled toward the court of Mutesa, king of Buganda, at the northwest corner of Lake Victoria. Grant was held up with an ulcerated leg, so Speke went on alone. He was impressed by the spacious reed huts of Mutesa's capital, by the neatly made cloaks of bark cloth and antelope skin the men wore, and by the people's courtesy. But the cruelty horrified him. Ears were cut off in punishment for negligible crimes, and for minor breaches of court etiquette young women were instantly executed.

The king regarded Speke, the first white man he had seen, as a rich prize and was unwilling to let him go. He fleeced him little by little of cloth, beads, guns, and ammunition until Grant arrived. Finally the king gave them permission to proceed. Grant marched north with the main party to Bunyoro. Speke turned east along the lake.

So Speke was alone with his bearers when on July 28, 1862, he stood at last at the waterfall where Lake Victoria poured into the Nile. He was entranced by "the roar of the waters, the thousands of passenger-fish, leaping at the falls . . . hippopotami and crocodiles lying sleepily on the water." He had managed to keep this ultimate triumph to himself.

Speke joined Grant near Bunyoro, where the ruler, Kamrasi, detained them for many weeks. Then they proceeded to Gondokoro. Here Speke's old sporting friend, Samuel Baker, met them with supplies. "The Nile is settled," Speke cabled London on his arrival in Cairo.

Back in England many people remained unconvinced by his claim, and a debate was arranged in September 1864 between Speke and Burton. As Burton awaited Speke on the platform, news came that he had shot himself accidentally the day before while out hunting. Burton broke down in his hotel and wept.

A fellow explorer at the debate would continue the search for the Nile's source: David Livingstone.

It was a humanitarian anger that first spurred Livingstone's forays into southern Africa after his arrival in 1841. He combined missionary and antislavery zeal with a practical interest in opening up routes for trade

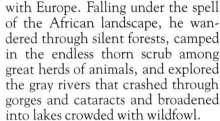

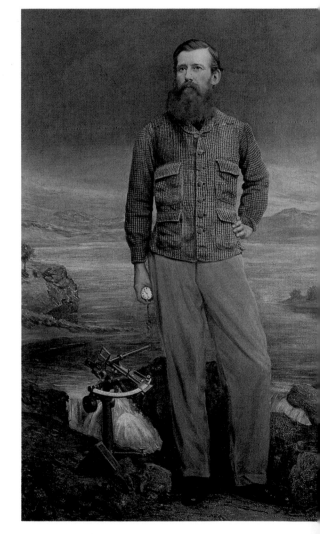

with Europe. Falling under the spell of the African landscape, he wandered through silent forests, camped in the endless thorn scrub among great herds of animals, and explored the gray rivers that crashed through gorges and cataracts and broadened into lakes crowded with wildfowl.

One major journey took Livingstone northwest from Linyanti across well over a thousand miles of almost unknown country to Luanda on the coast, which he reached in May 1854. After recuperating, he turned back the way he had come and proceeded east along the Zambezi River. Upon reaching Quelimane on the east coast, he became the first European to cross Africa. But his repeated attempts to establish a trade route on the Zambezi were thwarted by miles of rapids, and the Shire and Rovuma Rivers proved little better.

By now famous in England for his geographical exploits, Livingstone agreed to a proposal by the Royal Geographical Society to pursue the question of the Nile after Speke's death in 1864. Combining exploration with God's work, he could also check on the Arab slave trade. In 1866 he embarked on a lengthy search for the Nile's source, losing contact with the outside world. Everywhere he went, he found alarming evidence of the slave trade that supplied East Africa, Arabia, Persia, and India. Reduced to destitution by desertion and theft, he had to travel with Arab slave caravans himself, often marching with the victims.

Scottish missionary-explorer David Livingstone (right) reads the Bible to African villagers. He used it as a spiritual Baedeker to guide him, by example, through the tribulations that beset him as he explored southern Africa and challenged slavery, which he called the "great open sore of the world."

In 1853 he set out to "open up a path into the interior, or perish." While following the Zambezi east across the continent, Livingstone, mounted on an ox (below, right), glances back over his

shoulder to see a wounded buffalo toss one of his bearers in the air. The man had stabbed the buffalo when it charged the line, and it turned on him. The bearer landed on his face but suffered no cuts or broken bones. "We shampooed him well," wrote Livingstone, "and then went on."

Artist Thomas Baines joined Livingstone's next venture in 1858 and painted "Poling up the Zambesi" (below, left). The boatmen found punting faster than rowing in shallow water.

In 1871 he witnessed a shocking incident. It started with a quarrel over the purchase of a fowl in the market of Nyangwe on the Lualaba and turned into a massacre. Livingstone was appalled as he watched Arabs shooting down helpless villagers, who tried to escape by canoe or by jumping into the river. He felt he was in hell. "I hear the loud wails . . . over those who are . . . slain," he wrote in his journal. "Oh, let Thy kingdom come!" He decided to halt his explorations and repair to Ujiji.

At this low point in his fortunes the miracle occurred. A column emerged out of the bush firing off salutes, with a white man striding forward and a servant carrying the American flag. It was Stanley. The

American newspaperman had found the missing wanderer. Livingstone and Henry Morton Stanley greeted each other with a grotesque pretense of reserve. "Dr. Livingstone, I presume?" "Yes."

Newly equipped by Stanley, Livingstone set off on his last march. By now his search for the Nile had become an obsession. Sick, almost toothless, scarcely able to walk, he turned into a wandering guru seeking, if God willed, a lonely grave in the forest. In 1873 he finally collapsed in Ilala near Lake Bangweulu, where a servant found him dead one night, kneeling beside his bed.

Despite Livingstone's efforts, the slave trade was worse at his death than he had found it when he came

OVERLEAF: "The smoke that thunders" was the Makololo name for the Zambezi's Victoria Falls, whose billowing vapor Livingstone spied from five miles away in 1855. Perched at the brink, he watched the river "roll and wriggle" away from the 350-foot-deep chasm that slashes across its course.

Brash adventurer and revered missionary meet beneath the American flag: Tipping his pith helmet, Henry Morton Stanley inquires, "Dr. Livingstone, I presume?" The New York Herald had sent Stanley to find the famous explorer and interview him. Livingstone, sick and destitute, thought the journalist's arrival in 1871 at the Arab trading post of Ujiji was God's handiwork and persuaded Stanley to help him explore Lake Tanganyika. They became close friends. Trekking back to the coast,

quick-tempered Stanley threatened to shoot a bearer (left) who stumbled midriver and nearly lost the letters and journal Livingstone was sending home.

In 1873 Livingstone's ruined body gave out. His African companions buried his heart and entrails under a tree, embalmed his corpse, and carried it to the coast—an eight-month journey. One of the Africans, former mission pupil Jacob Wainwright (below), sailed with Livingstone's coffin on the explorer's final voyage home to England.

to Africa. His report of the massacre at Nyangwe, however, so shocked the British government that they forced the sultan of Zanzibar to close his slave market.

During his brief friendship with Stanley, Livingstone had fired the imagination of the ambitious journalist. Angered by being considered an upstart in England and a fraud in America, Stanley was determined to prove his detractors wrong. He got two newspapers to sponsor an expe-

dition to resolve the pattern of lakes and rivers in central Africa—to finish the work of his avowed hero.

He left Zanzibar late in 1874 with a huge caravan. Reaching Lake Victoria, he assembled his portable 40-foot boat, the *Lady Alice*, and sailed around the lake—establishing that it was a single lake and that Speke had been right about the Nile—and surveyed Lake Tanganyika.

He confirmed that the Lualaba flowed into the Congo (now the

Zaire), which he followed westward to the coast. It was an epic journey. Only 115 of his original party of 356 reached the sea. His men starved, drowned, and fell sick. The riverbanks resounded with war drums, and tribesmen attacked the party. Stanley retaliated by burning villages. He proved a harsh taskmaster, sometimes flogging offenders or putting them in leg chains. Under his relentless drive, men mutinied and deserted. His methods brought criticism, but they got results—a portent of the ruthless approach employed by the great powers in their scramble for Africa from the 1870s to the 1890s.

In contrast, Mary Kingsley's role in Africa was refreshingly humane. Any anger she felt was aimed at people who derided African religion. As an amateur English ethnologist striving to understand the Africans, she was ahead of her time.

After two earlier trips to West Africa, she sailed again for Freetown in 1895, dressed as always in severe Victorian clothes and a bonnet. She went on to spend about a year in the French Congo, Gabon, and Cameroon, journeying rough, often by canoe. Here she befriended the cannibal Fang tribe, whom she called "Fan," to avoid unfortunate associations. She learned to understand the reasons for witchcraft, or fetish, as it was called: Africans believed that misfortune and death were the work of malignant spirits whom it was necessary to propitiate by magic.

Once she fell into a 15-foot game trap, but her "good thick skirt" saved her from being "spiked to the bone and done for." Another time, in a village hut, she noticed a strong smell of "unmistakably organic origin" and found some bags full of human remains—a hand, "three big toes, four eyes, two ears, and other portions of the human frame." She learned that the Fan "like to keep a little something . . . as a memento."

On her return to England, she campaigned for colonial government that stressed justice, medical care, and anthropological study. She did not share the view commonly held by Europeans that the Africans were cruel or depraved children.

During Mary Kingsley's time, the exploration of Africa entered a second phase. Earlier explorers had only filled in the major geographical blanks—the river systems, the lakes, and the mountain ranges. Their accounts of the African people were often prejudiced by their own viewpoints and religious convictions. And they overestimated Africa's potential wealth and fertility.

From the 1890s to the 1920s, hundreds of colonial officials, army officers, and adventurous traders, whose names have mostly been forgotten, mapped Africa and did the donkeywork that made possible roads, railways, and cities. The traces of such men's devoted works remain in cairns or signposts on African hilltops. They paved the way for modern Africa and the independent black states that succeeded the colonies.

By James A. Cox

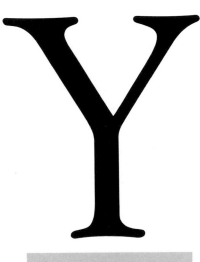

Tribal inspection: The Bunyoro people greet Sam and Florence Baker.

You could make a movie about them—a real Saturday-afternoon-at-the-Bijou flick. The true-life experiences of Sam and Florence Baker as they search for the source of the White Nile! It's set in central Africa in the 1860s. The kind of tale that kept you riveted to your seat when you were a kid. And a great love story, too.

Sam Baker is positively larger than life. A British clubman. Widower in his late 30s with four daughters. Heir to a modest fortune. Solid, conservative, convinced of his own and Britain's superiority. Also strong and fearless, a sportsman who hunts stags on foot with only a knife because shooting them is too easy. *Also* a writer and artist, a skilled linguist, and a practical man who is at home in the wilderness, yet capricious enough to buy his second wife, a beautiful Hungarian refugee named Florence Finnian von Sass, in a Turkish slave market.

That's the scene to open with, the slave auction in 1859. Decadent Ottoman town on the lower Danube in what is now Bulgaria. Minarets reaching skyward, half-starved dogs scavenging in the streets below. Rough-voiced men—soldiers, Turkish traders, elegantly attired pashas—gather in a noisy crowd. Off to one side we spy a cluster of government officials and two visiting big-game hunters—a slim Indian maharaja and Sam Baker. The slaves—young white women and children—huddle together in terror. Now the auctioneer hauls forward a slender, teenage girl, her long golden hair swept back into a loose braid. Leering pashas begin the bid. Suddenly Sam charges through the crowd waving a fistful of Turkish liras and throws down the winning bid. The film title superimposes as he leads his purchase away.

The music stops abruptly, the scene begins to fade. We'll have a woman's voice—old but firm, with a lingering Balkan throatiness—say something like: "And that was how I met my Sam!"

We move to the formal English garden of a neo-Gothic stone manor

Sam fleeing the charge of a screaming
bull elephant that he has wounded.

house where an old woman is tending roses. She is Lady Florence Baker, grande dame of the manor and alone since 1893, when Sam went to his reward. For our movie, she reveals the secret past that she only hinted at in real life. She explains briefly how she came to be sold as a slave: bloody uprisings in Hungary and the Balkans, her entire family slain, rescued by a faithful nurse, but finally left alone and defenseless. Florence ends by saying simply, "I owe everything to Sam."

She tells how Sam took her to the Black Sea, where he was involved in building a railroad. "But his heart was never in that," we'll have her say. "Africa—that's where he yearned to be, with the great explorers. Again and again he wrote to the Royal Geographical Society, hoping to join an expedition, but always he was turned down. So one day he decided to go up the Nile on his own. And I went with him." She laughs softly as the scene fades. Other people might worry about whether they were married then, but she would have followed Sam anywhere.

Now we see Sam and Florence in a kaleidoscope of scenes, all from Sam's journals: gliding up the Nile on a dahabeah, a small lateen-rigged houseboat; struggling across the Nubian Desert with 2 servants, 16 camels, and assorted baggage under a blazing sun; settling down beside a river in the Sudan, where Florence converts a round thatched hut into "the perfection of neatness," with a chintz- and muslin-covered dressing table and hunting knives on the wall; Sam hunting on horseback with the fearless Hamran Arabs who, armed only with swords, go after mighty elephants; Sam and Florence exploring and mapping the tributaries of the Nile that tumble out of Ethiopia, learning Arabic and as much of the central African languages as they can pick up.

After a year they decide they're ready for the big push. On to Khartoum, capital of the Egyptian Sudan, a frontier town built on the ivory and slave trades, and the jumping-off place for the interior.

Sam and Florence hate Khartoum. It is filthy, untamed, rotten to the core. Everyone, from Governor-General Moosa Pasha down, has a finger—or a fist—in the illegal slave trade. Sam presents his firman from the viceroy of Egypt, a permit that instructs local officials to give him every assistance. He is greeted with resentment, apathy, and antagonism. No one wants a meddling English gentleman poking about the slave-producing regions of the upper Nile. But Sam plows right ahead. He puts together an expedition of 3 boats, 40 boatmen, assorted horses, donkeys, and camels, an escort of 45 armed Arabs, and supplies for 4 months. Destination: Gondokoro, 1,000 miles south of Khartoum and the last stop before the vast unknown of darkest Africa.

The mail from England has brought a request from the Royal Geographical Society. Consul John Petherick was supposed to leave supplies at Gondokoro for the Speke-Grant expedition that is trying to pin down the source of the Nile. But no one has heard from Speke and Grant for a year, and Petherick is missing in the jungle and rumored dead. Will Sam take supplies to Gondokoro? Sam eagerly agrees. If he

A sudden storm on Lake Albert. The Bakers' canoe races for shore.

I at once named it the Albert N'yanza—N'yanza being the native name for "lake" or any sheet of water.
SAMUEL BAKER

finds the explorers before they reach the Nile's source, perhaps he will share in the glory. If they're dead, he may finish the search himself.

We follow Sam and Florence to Gondokoro. It turns out to be a string of riverside camps where traders keep slaves and ivory while awaiting the annual boats from Khartoum. The traders spend their time drinking, quarreling, killing each other, brutalizing the slaves, and terrorizing the local tribes. The place stinks of ordure and rotting food. Flies everywhere. Hordes of sleek rats. Clouds of mosquitoes, "the nightingales of the White Nile." Sam calls the place "a perfect hell."

Quickly Sam and Florence learn they are even less welcome here than they were in Khartoum, and for the same reason. The message rings loud and clear when a bullet shatters the skull of a boy in their boat. But they cannot leave without news of Speke and Grant. The threats escalate. When mutineers attack Sam, Florence rushes into the fray and fast-talks the ringleader into begging Sam's pardon. Their entourage begins to break up with desertions.

Finally one morning the rattle of gunfire from the south heralds the approach of a caravan. Sam's men race to his boat with news of two emaciated white men. *Speke and Grant!* Bursting with excitement, Sam ushers his bedraggled countrymen back to his dahabeah for refreshments. They are exhausted, their clothes in tatters, but they have much to tell, especially of Lake Victoria. The question of the Nile's source, Speke says confidently, is settled.

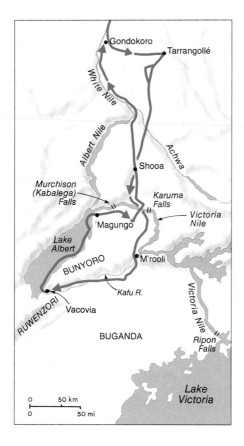

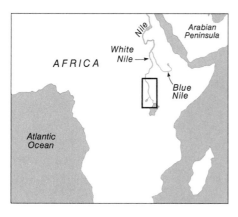

Sam cannot hide his disappointment. "Does not one leaf of the laurel remain for me?" he blurts. Speke tells him of rumors of another large lake to the west of Victoria that might also feed the river, and Grant draws up a rough map. To get there, they warn, glancing at Florence, will require hiking hundreds of miles, through the lands of implacably hostile tribes to the kingdom of Bunyoro, ruled by Kamrasi, "a sour, greedy African" who is likely to strip them of every possession. The grim warnings do nothing to dim Sam's enthusiasm. He can barely wait to get started. But their force has dwindled to only 17 men of doubtful loyalty, too small a party to travel on its own. They are forced to attach themselves to the caravan of a slave trader.

Now, by Sam's account, begins an almost unbelievable odyssey. The trading party takes its time. The rains come. Rivers are unfordable. Fever prostrates Sam and Florence for weeks on end. They run out of quinine. Their baggage animals die. Their food supplies dwindle, and they're reduced to eating grass. White ants and rats invade their hut. The war drums of the harassed tribes thump incessantly, spelling out a message of hatred for the slavers and all who associate with them. Even a friendly chief, Commoro of the Latooka, asks Sam: "Suppose you get to the great lake; what will you do with it? If you find that the large river does flow from it, what then? What's the good of it?"

In almost a year they move barely 150 miles closer to their goal. Shorthanded and ill, they cannot break away from the traders. At last, in January 1864 they reach the Victoria Nile and look across into Bunyoro. Kamrasi's tribesmen line the far bank. Sam puts on a tweed suit similar to that worn by Speke, and his interpreter calls out that Speke's brother has come to visit. The natives dance and sing in great excitement. But it is Florence who creates a sensation the next day when she undoes her hair and lets the golden tresses drop to her waist. The Bunyoro have never seen anything like it.

For all this brave show, Sam and Florence are so weak with fever by the time they reach Kamrasi's capital at M'rooli that Sam has to be carried into the king's presence. (Or at least Sam *thinks* he's the king. He's really the king's brother, M'Gambi, acting as stand-in, for security.) Sitting on a copper stool set on leopard skins, he counters every request for porters and a guide to the mysterious lake in the west with a demand for presents. The game goes on for days. Beads, shoes, a gun, necklaces, a sword, a cashmere shawl, a Persian carpet. Finally convinced he has picked his guests clean, M'Gambi says that Sam can go to the lake, but Florence must remain. He fancies her for a wife. It is not a mean-spirited demand: In exchange he will give Sam a pretty Bunyoro wife.

This is the last straw. Enraged, Sam hauls out his pistol and threatens to shoot him dead on the spot. Florence rises from her seat in wrath and screams at M'Gambi in Arabic. He doesn't understand the language, but he gets the meaning. He shrugs and tells them to go.

With porters and escort grudgingly supplied by M'Gambi, they set off. Food is scarce—their escort of Bunyoro warriors ranges ahead and

223

Women of Shooa dancing to celebrate the Bakers' return from Lake Albert.

strips villages along the way of everything edible. Fever and exhaustion dog every step. They have to cross the Kafu River, which is covered two feet deep with a matting of water grass and other plants. The porters run across, sinking only to their ankles. Sam starts after them. Florence can't make it. Sam looks back to see her doubling over, her face contorted and purple, sinking through the weeds. He races back and drags her to dry land, but she lies as if dead, her hands and teeth tightly clenched, her eyes wide and staring. Acute sunstroke!

They must keep moving. Sam trudges beside Florence's litter each day, keeps vigil at night. On the third morning she awakens, thrashing, raving deliriously with "brain fever." They reach a village—no food there. Sam dismisses the armed escort. He and his porters shoot some guinea fowl and find wild honey in the forest. Sam has been seven days with no sleep and little food. He reaches the end of his endurance. He covers Florence with a plaid and collapses, unconscious. His men fit a new handle on a pickax and look for a place to dig a grave. Fade out.

Fade in, many hours later. Sam wakes up. No longer is Florence thrashing about. She lies serenely, her face like marble. Sam is in agony, thinking she died while he slept. But then—a miracle! She opens her eyes for a moment and gives him a calm, clear look.

After two days the little caravan moves on. They are heading directly toward a high mountain range. Their hearts sink. There is no way they will be able to cross those towering peaks. But wait! Their guide tells them the mountains are on the *far* side of the lake; if they start early in the morning, they will reach the big water before midday!

Barely able to sleep, Sam rouses the expedition before dawn. They set out at a swinging pace, Florence and Sam riding oxen. The sun comes up on a beautiful day. They toil up a hill—and there, a quarter of a mile below them, stretches the lake, glittering like a sea of quicksilver, blue mountains rising from the far shore some 50 miles away. Sam had planned to lead his band in three lusty cheers. Instead he offers up a fervent prayer of thanks. Then he names the expanse Albert N'yanza—Lake Albert—for the late husband of Queen Victoria. At the shore he drinks deeply from this important secondary source of the Nile.

The scene shifts back to the manor garden in England, where the elderly Florence picks up the story. Explorers have two main problems, she explains. One is getting there. The other is getting back home. She and Sam did not have it easy (now another kaleidoscope of scenes): a stormy trip across the lake; their canoe almost capsized by a hippopotamus in crocodile-infested waters; an outbreak of plague; skirmishes with hostile villagers and Arabs; a trip in a dirty troop transport up the Red Sea. But at last, more than four years after they first set foot in Africa, they reach Suez. And for the first time Sam abandons Florence—for the hotel bar and a couple of tankards of ice-cold Allsopp's Pale Ale.

They land in England in October 1865, and almost right away they get married—a quiet ceremony—in St. James's Church in Piccadilly. While they were still in Africa Sam was awarded the Royal Geographical Society's gold medal. Knighthood soon follows, but there is a hitch: Sir Samuel Baker, discoverer of Lake Albert, is accepted at royal functions, but Lady Baker will never be received by Queen Victoria. *Nice* women do not share intimacies with men until they marry them.

We'll give Florence the last word, confident in her role as Sam's partner and adviser—his "prime minister," as he came to call her. A fine Hollywood speech: "I never thought I could forgive that woman. But then I realized something. What did a queen know of anything, locked away in a sterile court? How could she possibly know what it means to live in desperation, to face death day after day, and to love and be loved in spite of it all? There was nothing we could say to each other."

The scene dissolves to a green hilltop where Sam and Florence, holding hands, gaze proudly down at the lake they have discovered, their figures silhouetted against a blazing African sun. . . .

You'll find most of the details of our movie outline in Samuel Baker's book, The Albert N'yanza, *including quotations, except where we've indicated dialogue in the spirit of Hollywood. Richard Hall's* Lovers on the Nile *provides a gripping modern account. Sam's family loved and admired Florence. Descriptions of her come from a biography written by a great-grandson's wife and called by the name the Bunyoro gave Florence:* Morning Star.

Possessing a share of sangfroid *admirably adapted for African travel, Mrs. Baker was not a* screamer, *and never even whispered; in the moment of suspected danger, a touch of my sleeve was . . . a sufficient warning.*
SAMUEL BAKER

The Last Wildernesses

By Douglas H. Chadwick

"What a fabulous and extravagant country we're in!" marveled German naturalist Alexander von Humboldt when he arrived in South America in 1799. "Fantastic plants, electric eels, armadillos, monkeys, parrots. . . ." Such tropical wonders—here represented by macaws clustered near an Amazon River tributary—drew a new breed of explorer: the scientist in search of knowledge. Naturalists, geographers, and anthropologists now probed the world's intractable wilds in their quest to unravel nature's mysteries.

The sun has melted, red as macaw plumes, into the simmering mist. Now heat lightning blossoms from the Amazon twilight, flashing images of an earth-colored river flowing through walls of vegetation. And the swoosh of big bats chasing the lightning bugs blends with the jungle song: of a distant jaguar, whose eyes burn through the dark; of birds and frogs, Indians in the village, cicadas shrilling a wall of sound—of countless voices, most of them as yet uninterpreted.

In the 2.3-million-square-mile basin known as Amazonia, and in other tracts of wilderness surviving here and there on the globe, lie the major challenges for modern exploration: To find not just what is out there, but how it works. To understand the potentials of the last great wildernesses even as we transform them.

Scientific exploration came into its own in the 18th century, the Age of Reason as it was called. Earlier explorers sought glittering riches, slaves, souls, or imperial dominion. Now a new breed, the scientist-explorer, set out to learn about Earth's living resources—its flora, fauna, and indigenous cultures.

Charles-Marie de La Condamine, a friend of Voltaire's, descended the Amazon in 1743, after a visit to Ecuador. He was the first to map this largest of rivers using scientific instruments. The baggage he delivered to Europe was as promising as it was exotic: quinine-producing cinchona trees; the insecticide rotenone; platinum; and rubber, which he used to coat his quadrant. He also carried tales of a natural canal, the Casiquiare, linking Venezuela's Orinoco river system to that of the Amazon.

Determined to map this legendary stream—as well as to observe and study "the harmony in nature"—Alexander von Humboldt explored the Orinoco in 1800 with French botanist Aimé Bonpland. Humboldt touched barometer and thermometer to practically everything in his path. Meeting electric eels, he promptly started shocking himself with the long wriggling generators and dissecting them to learn about their anatomy. Humboldt's experiments would cause a sensation back home, where Alessandro Volta had just displayed the first electric battery.

Humboldt and Bonpland found the Casiquiare. It was real. The mystery there was how so many biting bugs could fit into the air at once. Day after ripe, green, windless day, the pair twitched, slapped, and mapped along the river, their big canoe awash with pressed plants and rock samples, its live cargo of seven parrots, a toucan, a motmot, and eight monkeys shrieking amidst the insect drone. At night, they built fires to smoke out the pests, while Humboldt recalled an Indian's words: "How comfortable must people be in the moon! . . . She looks so beautiful and so clear, that she must be free from mosquitoes."

Croaking like frogs, curl-crested tou-
cans swoop at British naturalist Henry
Bates (opposite) during his 1848-1859
study of the Amazon and its tributaries. In Bates's day, few uncharted
areas remained on maps of the world.
Into these came explorer-scientists to
study what—and who—lived there.
South America's sprawling forests
and volcanic peaks enticed Humboldt,
then Charles Darwin and Brazilian
explorer Cândido Rondon. The Villas
Boas brothers—Claudio, Orlando, and

Through Colombia, Ecuador, and
Peru, Humboldt's curiosity played
across the landscape like sun shafts
through clouds, illuminating tropical storm patterns, geomagnetic
fields, the way elevation affects plant
distribution, the strange behavior of
animals just before earthquakes, the
geology of volcanoes, and the cold
coastal current that now bears his
name. He marched up the Ecuador-
ian volcano Chimborazo, to an elevation of 19,286 feet by his calcula-
tions. He suffered altitude sickness.
He also figured out why, relating it
to a decrease in oxygen.

Another amateur naturalist with
boundless curiosity, Charles Darwin
took Humboldt's *Personal Narrative
of Travels* along on his 1831-36 journey on the *Beagle* around the world.
He also carried a just-published work
entitled *Principles of Geology*. Its author, Charles Lyell, argued that the
Earth was older than the 6,000 years
some biblical scholars had set, and
that its crust was continuously being
reshaped. Those were radical notions then, but the fossil seashells
Darwin collected at 12,000 feet in
the Andes would eventually make
him wonder: If the environment is so
changeable—evolving over time—
what of the organisms that dwell
within it? Tradition taught that species were immutable—fixed for all
time. After his return home, the
young man who had once entertained the notion of entering the
clergy found himself in a state of
creative flux that, years later, would

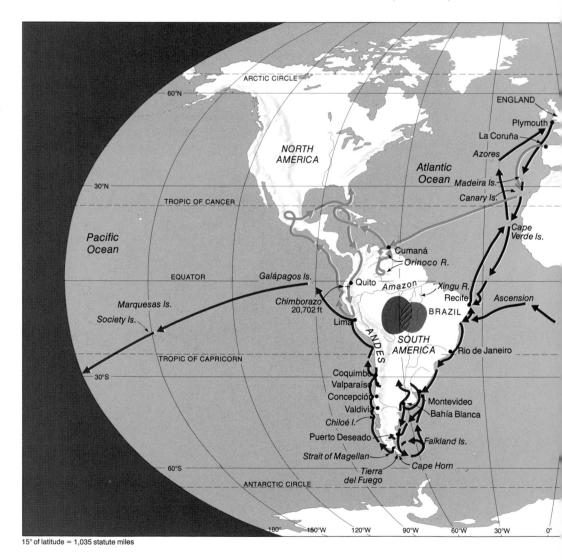

15° of latitude = 1,035 statute miles

228

Leonardo—followed, seeking isolated Indian tribes. Even today scientists from many nations probe this still largely unknown realm.

The deserts and mountains of central Asia also proved daunting; not until the late 1800s did scientists mount major expeditions to fathom their secrets. Swedish geographer Sven Hedin charted windswept deserts and Himalayan heights; American botanist Joseph Rock trekked central China in search of plants and anthropological knowledge; Roy Chapman Andrews, an American zoologist, searched the Gobi for fossils.

Italian naturalist Luigi D'Albertis and government officials of New Guinea challenged that island's tangled terrain, emerging with tales of cannibals, headhunters, birds of paradise—and with some of the last missing pieces of the mapmakers' global puzzle.

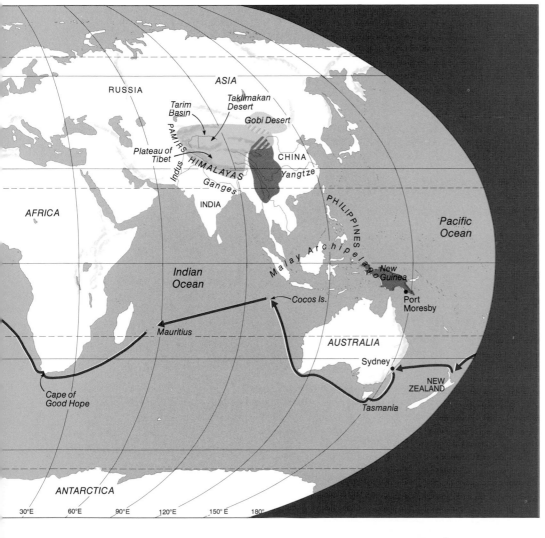

Hedin 1890-1935
Andrews 1922-1930
Rock 1922-1949
D'Albertis 1872-77
MacGregor 1888-1898
Champion 1926-1940
Hides 1935

Humboldt 1799-1804
Darwin and the *Beagle* 1831-36

Rondon 1907-1914
Villas Boas brothers 1943-1973

All bluff and no bite, an emerald tree snake no thicker than a finger shows its toothless gape in a forest in Amazonia. Most snakes in the Amazon basin pose little threat to humans—including a "wonderfully slender" six-foot serpent that dropped on Henry Bates and tangled him in its coils.

Serpentine tributaries writhe through a rain forest on their way to the Amazon. Using rivers as roads, scientists have explored the forests of Amazonia for more than two and a half centuries. The region may support 30 percent of Earth's species of plants and animals. Darwin's visit to Brazil in 1836 led him to describe the land as "one great wild, untidy, luxuriant hot-house which nature made for her menagerie."

culminate in the theory of evolution.

In the dreary factory town of Leicester, in the English Midlands, a hosier, Henry Bates, and a schoolteacher, Alfred Wallace, would read Darwin's *Voyage of the Beagle* and dream of orchid jungle light. In 1848, the two friends broke out for the Amazon, having arranged to sell specimens to wealthy collectors at threepence each.

Over the next 11 years, Bates amassed specimens of 14,712 species, 8,000 of them—mostly insects —previously unknown to science. From just one area in the state of Pará, Brazil, he netted 700 butterfly species, 310 more than inhabited Europe. Bates chased more than new creatures to classify. He also stalked relationships, focusing on how a single species of butterflies varies subtly from one habitat to the next, and how certain palatable varieties resemble noxious-tasting ones—an adaptation for fooling predators that we now term Batesian mimicry. "Nature writes, as on a tablet, the story of the modifications of species," he concluded and went on to publish eloquent proof.

Wallace, returning home earlier, had lost his hard-won collections during a fire at sea. He was quickly off again, though, this time to the steaming Malay Archipelago. Resting between malarial attacks and forays through lush tangles of life forms, he independently conceived the principle of natural selection at about the same time Darwin brought

forth his *Origin of Species* in 1859. Already systematic exploration of nature was offering glimpses of the unifying laws that shape existence— including, it would become apparent, our own.

More details of our past awaited discovery in central Asia, an expanse just as wide and uncharted as the Amazon. In 1893 the Swedish explorer Sven Hedin journeyed through southern Russia and on to the Taklimakan Desert, west of the

Names of more than a hundred plants crowd a slice in the flank of Chimborazo, a 20,702-foot volcano in Ecuador. Alexander von Humboldt devised this composite view of South American volcanoes to show how plant types change from tropical to temperate to arctic as altitude increases. He climbed mountains with a barometer to measure his altitude and ascended rivers with chronometer and sextant to fix his position. With thermometers he recorded air, ground, and water temperatures and with hygrometers, humidity; with compasses he took magnetic readings; with telescopes he studied meteor showers—and with a microscope he delighted the ladies of Cumaná, Venezuela, with visions of strange beasts that were their own head lice.

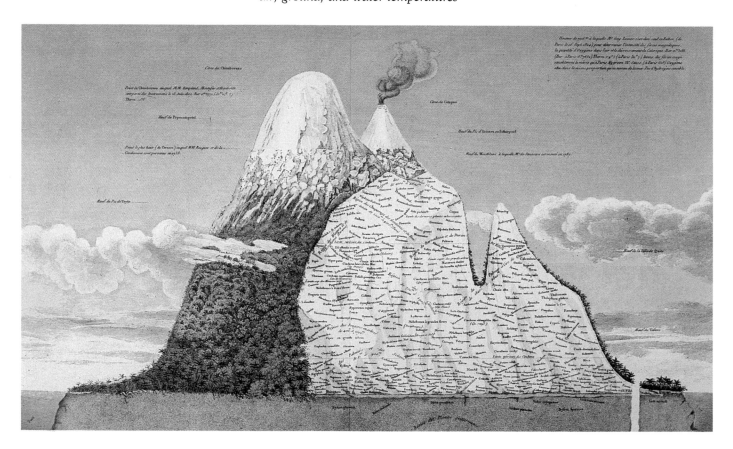

Gobi, to fill in what he called the "white spots" on maps. Some of the arid wilderness proved nearly as blank in reality; he soon ran out of bearings, then out of water. Two of his Muslim assistants drank camel urine. They died bloated with salt. Hedin crawled on for five nights, burrowing into the sand by day, until he found moonlight reflected in a muddy pool.

Once reoriented and reorganized, he pressed onward. From the dunes he sifted traces of forgotten, 2,000-year-old cities: Taklimakan and Karadong, flourishing when Buddhism spread northward from India. Later, along a spur of the old Silk Road, he located ruins of the Chinese city of Loulan. Within, preserved by the endless drought, bundles of some of the first paper invented proved to hold some of the first bureaucratic paperwork. Yet these writings whispered details of the daily commerce and administration, hopes and wor-

A Cacajao monkey sits for a sketch by Humboldt. Indians on the Casiquiare River sold him the small primate for a pet. It soon died of a stomach ailment —but not before Humboldt had studied its behavior.

Seated among instruments and specimens, Humboldt and his colleague, botanist Aimé Bonpland, are themselves captured on canvas by a 19th-century artist. Darwin praised Humboldt as "the greatest scientific traveler who ever lived."

ries, of a society old a millennium before Marco Polo passed that way.

White spots drew Hedin toward the Tibetan plateau. Ever since Alexander the Great first swept into India, geographers had assumed that the south-flowing Indus, Brahmaputra, and Sutlej Rivers originated in the Himalayas, the tallest mountains on Earth. Hedin proved that they flowed through that barrier and that their true sources lay in a more northern range, which he mapped and named the Transhimalayas.

Hedin kept crisscrossing white spots for more than 40 years. After a Mercury astronaut photographed Tibet from space in 1963, NASA used Hedin's surveys to help decide which wrinkles were which. Maybe the spacemen could imagine him somewhere among those map contours, watching stars blaze above his yak-dung fire, or fashioning ice skates from knife blades to carve sparkling free tracks across a frozen lake in the Tarim Basin.

Roy Chapman Andrews planned more elaborately for each of his five expeditions to the Gobi between 1922 and 1930. The zoologist from the American Museum of Natural History sought proof there for theories of mammalian evolution. Priding himself on overlooking no detail, he took care to select a team whose specialties would complement one another: surveyor, geologist, paleontologist, archaeologist, and others. He was among the earliest explorers to rely on 20th-century technology,

feeling that automobiles could cover ground ten times as efficiently as camel caravans.

Some overlooked details came calling anyway one cold night at an old Buddhist monument. For some reason, every poisonous snake in the area seemed bent on warming itself at camp. Vipers got into cots, shoes, a chauffeur's hat, gun cases; they lay in braids across the tent floor.

"Perils," Humboldt once said, "elevate the poetry of life." Here, then,

in the slithering dark is Andrews, stepping on a coil of rope and elevating straight for the ceiling while Walter Granger, patient analyzer of rock strata, stabs furiously at what turns out to be a pipe cleaner.

There were more reptiles along Flaming Cliffs, old ones: the first dinosaur eggs ever recognized, and to go with them, skeletons of embryonic dinosaurs. Until then, no one was certain whether the colossal reptiles laid eggs at all. Equally important

"A knot of enormous, clustered masses of snow-covered mountains, from which radiate the highest and mightiest ranges of the earth," wrote Sven Hedin of central Asia's Pamir mountains. Beneath this awesome backdrop amble a Kirghiz elder and his son. Hedin rode on camelback into these mountains in the 1890s to explore western China's Taklimakan Desert. Continuing on his way to Peking, he paused for a portrait with a Mongolian herdsman by a yurt of heavy felt.

was the discovery of small mammal remains in rock dating from the Age of Dinosaurs. The find continued the tradition of Darwin, tracing back our line toward its beginnings.

The Men of the Dragon Bones, as the local Mongol bandits called Andrews and his team, also unearthed bones of the largest known terrestrial mammal, *Baluchitherium*. And they found the largest known carnivorous mammal, hyenalike *Andrewsarchus*, as well as flint and fossil remnants of a people they named the Dune Dwellers. In one place, the crew found fragments of dinosaur eggshells worked into squares; the original discoverers of dinosaur eggs had been the Stone Age Dune Dwellers.

Elsewhere in the world Stone Age cultures still lived, many of them in New Guinea, an island long enough to reach from London to Istanbul. In 1876 a bearded, aria-singing Italian naturalist named Luigi Maria D'Albertis charged up the Fly River in a steam launch so loaded with crew, arms, and ammunition that its decks barely rose above water. For 45 days his men sweated and suffered from flies and monotony while D'Albertis collected natural specimens and cultural artifacts. To get the latter, he lobbed skyrockets into riverside villages, looting huts abandoned by the terrorized inhabitants. He even stole skeletons from their burial platforms. "Exclaim if you will, against my barbarity," he later wrote. "I am too delighted with my prize to heed reproof!" No one accused D'Albertis

of being a dull scientist. Or a very good one. But he did make one of the first significant penetrations of New Guinea's interior.

Fourteen years later, William MacGregor, the rugged administrator of British New Guinea, pushed 535 miles up the Fly River by steam launch. He was as keen to study natural history in the island's interior, with its spine of snowbound equatorial peaks, as he was to extend colonial authority. Blocked by rapids, his

235

expedition beat its way overland.
Blocked by walls of bush, thunderstorms, and spear-tipped tribesmen,
MacGregor had to call it quits just
six miles short of the mountains.

On a later patrol, he topped the
divide. Breaking out of the cloud forest on his way up one 13,210-foot
summit, he found alpine meadows of
daisies and buttercups. He found
three new bird species there as well.
Unfortunately, his assistant Joe Fiji
ate two of them.

It wasn't until 1927-28 that the
wider part of the island was traversed, from the Fly to the Sepik
Rivers. On their second try, government officers Ivan Champion and
Charles Karius bested an eerie central ridge of labyrinthine limestone
so sharp that later visitors dubbed it
"broken bottle country."

In 1935 a police patrol headed by
Jack Hides explored the upper
Strickland River in the southern
highlands. After weeks of incessant

toil on short rations, Hides and his
men crested a mountain wall.

"My mother!" blurted a sergeant,
"What people are they?"

A huge, heavily populated valley
dotted with cultivated fields of
"mathematical exactness" lay before
them. New Guinea had spawned
legends aplenty but none as exotic
as the truth. Hidden among those
forbidding mountains were broad
valleys of grass; terraced gardens sil-
vered with the smoke from untold
huts; battlegrounds and watchtow-
ers. Explorers would find headhunters, pygmies, blond-haired people,
eaters of their enemies, eaters of
their own dead, people with jawbone
belts, snake earrings, gourds on their
penises, and feathers through their
noses. You might say we had been
speaking of mankind for centuries
without fully knowing what we were
talking about, for New Guinea supports perhaps the densest array of
tribal cultures on the globe—some
three million inhabitants, speaking
more than 700 languages. About 40
percent dwell in the highlands.

Unlike Hides, who was attacked 9
times and who shot at least 32 natives while crossing the highlands,
Champion usually avoided inci-
dents. But then his idea of courage
was different; he refused to raise his
rifle even when bows were drawn
taut against him.

The precedent had been set by a
Brazilian explorer, Cândido Ron-
don, in his surveys of the Amazon's
Mato Grosso hinterlands for the

An aerial view of New Guinea's upper Ramu River hints at the rumpled terrain—furrowed peaks, dark gorges, surging rivers, tangled forests, malarial swamps—that for centuries stymied explorers. But the sky opened pathways to inaccessible areas; in the 1920s floatplanes began bringing expeditions into the hinterlands, scouting routes from the air, and hauling supplies to remote camps.

A 1929 expedition (opposite, upper) mounted by the U. S. Department of Agriculture found itself mobbed by curious Papuans during a search for a disease-resistant strain of sugarcane. Using aerial photography, expedition members charted large parts of New Guinea that had never been explored by white men.

Arms in the air, explorer Jack Hides and a Tarifuroro tribesman discuss a safe route during the government official's 1935 trek, the last major expedition to probe the island's interior without radio or air support.

government, beginning in 1907. "Die if need be, but kill, never," was his motto. Part Indian himself, Rondon helped establish his country's first Indian protection agency.

His work continued under the Villas Boas brothers, Orlando, Claudio, and Leonardo. From the 1940s into the 1970s they probed the heart of the Amazon, seeking out remote, often unfriendly Indian tribes, some of whom had never seen a *civilizado*. It was delicate, dangerous work: leaving gifts, patient waiting, sudden flight when arrows whistled through the trees, more gifts—and at last the first wary encounter, the first touch, the first attempts at communication.

Humanitarianism is not the only reason for preserving tribal cultures. For much of the past decade, Darrell Posey, an American-born ethnobiologist, has lived among Kayapó Indians along a tributary of the Xingu River. He and a team of 20 specialists are conducting a study of Amazonia through native eyes.

Posey often works with Beptopup, a shaman. Beptopup claims to "speak" with certain animals, the spirits of dead people, and the world of energies beyond normal senses. You can make what you want of that; the practical point is that Beptopup carries volumes of unwritten information in his head. His specialty is the treatment of snakebites and scorpion stings. He knows how to graft wild medicinal plants onto fruit trees so as to have the remedies handy around garden plots. He knows how

239

Brazil's Waurá Indians hone their skills for games with rival tribes. Few outsiders knew much about the Waurá and neighboring tribes until Orlando (below, left), Claudio, and Leonardo Villas Boas explored their homelands. In 1961 the brothers helped establish Xingu National Park for Amazonian Indians, mindful of what can happen when "waves of civilization crash against the shores of primitive cultures."

to mulch with ant and termite nests to encourage plant growth; how to "transplant" colonies of *Azteca* ants, with their chemical secretions, to drive leaf-cutting ants from the gardens; and how to identify some 35 types of ants that can themselves be used for medicine.

Hike with him, and you might recognize *Colias* butterflies, bright flakes of color racing each other down jungle paths—just as Bates described them. You won't recognize the bugs sipping sweat off your forearms as minuscule bees. The shaman will. That pink one's hive has wax he can use to treat dizziness. The wax of the black one with gilt edges cures burns. And these leaves, crushed and rubbed on the body, will repel bees when you raid their hive.

"With ethnobiology, I think we're on a very exciting frontier," Posey says. "It's one thing to try to research and save plants and animals. But knowledge of how to use them is one of the Amazon's greatest resources." The project team has learned of uses the Kayapó have for over 600 plants that grow in this area. "The Kayapó have brought in many of these plants through trade and travel with other Indians from a region roughly the size of Western Europe, and they have domesticated dozens of wild varieties for their own needs."

In other words, what the civilizado sees as wilderness—for some a pristine paradise and for others a sprawling green hell to be conquered—the expert, the native, knows as a manageable neighborhood. His skills in working with living resources while increasing their diversity provides a rich source of conservation ideas.

As the scientist-explorers have shown us, the ultimate treasures were right there all along: in the soils and waters, the roots and leaves, the chorus of animals, and the manifold cultures of humanity. The hard scientific data need not diminish our sense of awe before creation. It doesn't for Beptopup. It didn't for Darwin. Watch his pen fly across the notebook as he makes one of his first excursions to the Brazilian interior: "Twiners entwining twiners—tresses like hair—beautiful lepidopters—silence—hosannah."

241

Charles Darwin

Edited by Margaret Sedeen

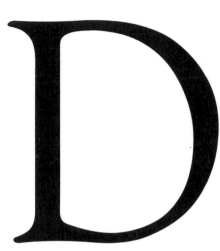

H.M.S. Beagle *at Sydney, Australia.*

At sea, February 1832

Dear sister Caroline,

We have crossed the Equator and are eight weeks out of Plymouth. Captain FitzRoy continues very kind to me in spite of my being underfoot in the crowded cabin we share. He is convinced that he can judge a man's character by his features, and tells me that when we first met he doubted whether anyone with my nose could possess sufficient energy and determination to voyage as naturalist aboard the *Beagle*. The Captain will be busy with coastline surveys for the Admiralty, and I will botanize and geologize to my heart's content at all our stops.

Our crew and passengers number above 70, including York, Fuegia, and Jemmy, the three natives of Tierra del Fuego whom Captain FitzRoy has educated in England. We are to bring them home. The *Beagle* is a splendid vessel, all fitted up with mahogany, brass armaments, 6 guns, and 24 chronometers! I find a ship a very comfortable house. Were it not for seasickness the whole world would be sailors.

I remember well the encouragement I received from Uncle Jos, that day when my mind was like a pendulum. Should I stay home, where all is familiar and my future as country parson a pretty sure thing? Or should I set out to explore a new world, to find I know not what? Well, I am here. My 23rd birthday has slipped by. My second life commences. Your affectionate brother, Charles Darwin

My dear Henslow,   *Rio de Janeiro, May 1832*

How are you all going on at Cambridge? But for your recommendation as my master in Natural History, I should not be aboard the *Beagle*. My first steps ashore, now some months ago, were in the Cape Verdes, where I feasted upon oranges and tasted a banana but did not like it. There I first saw the glory of tropical vegetation about which I have read

A Bible reading on board the Beagle. The devout captain, Robert FitzRoy, also led weekly Sunday services.

I think he was afterwards well-satisfied that my nose had spoken falsely.

DARWIN'S *AUTOBIOGRAPHY*

in Humboldt, and spent an unparalleled day hearing the notes of unknown birds and seeing new insects fluttering about still newer flowers. I examined there a white band which runs for some miles along the face of a sea cliff, about 45 feet above the water. Numerous seashells are embedded in this limestone band. It rests above ancient volcanic rocks and below a gently sloping stream of basalt which covered the shelly bed when it lay at the bottom of the sea. Geology is a pleasure like gambling. When speculating on what rocks may be, I often mentally cry out, "Three to one it is Tertiary!"

At Bahia I wandered in a Brazilian forest, delighted and bewildered by the novelty of the parasitical plants, the glossy green of the foliage, the flight of a gaudy butterfly. Already I am collecting and will send you specimens to study. I am red-hot with spiders, they are so interesting. I am overwhelmed by what I see, like a blind man suddenly given eyes. Yours affectionately, Charles Darwin

My dear Henslow,   *Tierra del Fuego, February 1833*
I have had my first sight of a real barbarian—of man in his lowest and most savage state. This is a mountainous land, partly submerged in the sea. A dusky mass of forest covers all the deep valleys. In the Strait of Magellan the distant channels between mountains seem from their gloom to lead beyond the confines of this world.

In December the *Beagle* got under weigh so that Captain FitzRoy

Charles Darwin in 1840, four years after the return of the Beagle.

could resettle York, Fuegia, and Jemmy. We had a smooth beginning, but Cape Horn demanded his tribute and sent us a wind directly in our teeth. Great black clouds rolled across the heavens, and violent squalls drove us into a cove. We pulled alongside a canoe with six Fuegians, the most abject creatures I anywhere beheld, with the rain trickling down their naked bodies. A woman suckling a child stared at our boat whilst the sleet fell and thawed on her bosom and on her baby.

We moored the *Beagle* and rowed in small boats with our Fuegians down a long channel where fires were lighted on every point. Men ran for miles along the shore and suddenly four or five came to the edge of a cliff. Their long hair streamed about their faces. They carried rugged staffs and waved their arms and sent forth hideous yells.

A few nights later we took up our quarters with Jemmy's people, the Tekeenica. They behaved quietly and joined the seamen to sing around a blazing fire. Although naked, they streamed with perspiration. We built large wooden wigwams and planted gardens for our Fuegians, but it was melancholy to leave them amongst their barbarous countrymen. Your obliged friend, Chas Darwin

My dear sister Cathcrine,   *Puerto Deseado, December 1833*

I am become quite a gaucho, drink my maté, smoke my cigar, then lie down and sleep as comfortably with the heavens for a canopy as in a feather bed. The danger from Indians is small as they are now collecting in the Cordillera for a battle against the Argentine army, which pursues a bloody war of extermination. After returning north to the pampas I traveled 600 miles, with guides, through a region until lately traveled only by Indians and never before by an Englishman. So fine an opportunity for geologizing was not to be lost.

In the pampas I found more fossil remains of the *Megatherium,* an extinct sloth the size of an elephant. It is the same that I found at Bahía Blanca in September along with several other remains, including a horse, a huge rodent-like animal, and a relative of the armadillo. These bones were embedded along with ancient shells similar to species even now living in the same bay. Here is evidence of Mr. Lyell's law that the longevity of mammal species is inferior to that of shelled invertebrates.

The gauchos are a singular race of countrymen. One's diet, traveling with them, is meat alone—puma, rhea, deer, armadillo (very good cooked in the shell), jaguar, especially beef. When we were at Montevideo, one gaucho showed great dexterity in forcing a restive horse to swim a flooded river. He stripped off his clothes and rode the horse into the water. Then he slipped off and hung onto the tail, splashing water in the horse's face each time it turned around. When the horse touched bottom on the other side, the gaucho pulled himself back on and grasped the bridle. A naked man on a naked horse is a fine spectacle; I had no idea how well the two animals suited each other.

We have had our Christmas here. The land deserves the name of desert but it supports many guanacos. I shot a good big one, so that we had fresh meat for all hands on Christmas Day. After dining we all went

Eruption of the Andean volcano Antuco—the center, Darwin speculated, of a shock wave that rocked Chile in 1835.

Tekeenica tribesman of Tierra del Fuego—as draped by the artist to accommodate Victorian sensibilities.

ashore for Olympic games of running, leaping, and wrestling. Old men with long beards and young men without any were playing like so many children. With affectionate love to my Father and to all of you.
Yours very sincerely, Charles Darwin

My dear Henslow,   *At sea, March 1835*
    We are becalmed off Valparaíso, for which I am grateful as I am always sick when there is a sea. I have received a large bundle of letters from England. I hope you have gotten mine, as well as the collections I have sent. We have had a most interesting time progressing up the coast of Chile. Off Chiloé in January, at midnight on the 19th, the watch hailed me on deck when he saw on the horizon something like a large star. It increased in size and by three o'clock made a magnificent spectacle. The volcano of Osorno, 73 miles away was in action and cast a glare of red light on the water. We later heard that on this same night, 480 miles to the north, Aconcagua erupted, and Cosegüina, 2,700 miles farther north, where there was also an earthquake. Whether this coincidence is accidental or shows some subterranean connection is hard to say, but the three vents do fall on the same great mountain chain.
    In February at Valdivia I was at work ashore. Suddenly came on the great earthquake about which you have read in the newspapers. For two minutes the earth rocked. Standing upright made me giddy, as though I were skating on very thin ice. The earth, the very emblem of solidity, moved beneath our feet like a thin crust over a fluid.
    In the town of Concepción people told us that during the fatal convulsion they threw themselves on the ground and gripped it to prevent being tossed over and over. Poultry flew about screaming. Horses stood with their legs spread, trembling. The earth cracked open and houses and the cathedral fell in blinding dust. This is one of the three most interesting spectacles I have beheld since leaving England—a Fuegian savage; tropical vegetation; and the ruins of Concepción. The land around the bay was raised two or three feet. It is a bitter thing to see such devastation, yet my compassion for the inhabitants was banished by my seeing a state of things produced in a moment which one is accustomed to attribute to a succession of ages.
    Now I go to cross the Andes. Horsecloths, stirrups, pistols, and spurs are lying on all sides of me. So my dear Henslow, good night.
Your most obliged and affectionate friend, Charles Darwin

My dear Caroline,   *Coquimbo, Chile, May 1835*
    It is worth coming from England once to enjoy these views. At 12,000 feet a transparency in the air and a confusion of distances and a stillness give the sensation of being in another world.
    Our traveling from Valparaíso was delightfully independent. In the inhabited parts, we bought firewood, hired pasture for the animals, and bivouacked in a corner of the field with them. We cooked our suppers under a cloudless sky. My companions were my guide and an *arriero* with his ten mules and a *madrina,* an old, steady mare with a bell around

Movable feast: A gaff-wielding sailor prepares to overturn a giant land tortoise in the Galápagos Islands.

her neck. Wherever she goes the mules, like good children, follow her.

The short breathing from the rarefied atmosphere is called *puna*. I experienced only a slight tightness across the head and chest. The inhabitants all recommend onions as a cure for the puna—for my part I found no remedy so good as my discovery of fossil shells on the highest ridges!

At about 7,000 feet in the Uspallata Range I found some snow white columns on a bare slope. They were petrified trees. I stood where a cluster of fine green trees once raised their lofty heads on the shores of the Atlantic, when that ocean—now driven back 700 miles—came to the foot of the Andes. I saw that they had sprung from a volcanic soil which had been raised above the level of the sea and then let down into the depths of the ocean, covered by sedimentary beds, then by submarine lava. I now beheld that ocean bed forming a chain of mountains.

Yet I miss you all so much that Snowdon to my mind looks higher and more beautiful than any peak in the Cordillera. I never cease marveling at all the marriages you have told me about. What a gang of little ones have come into the world since I left England. Give my love to all. Yours affectionately, Charles Darwin

My dear Henslow,   *Galápagos Islands, October 1835*

We anchored in several bays here for our surveying. The black sand is so hot that even in thick boots it is disagreeable to walk upon it; fields of lava in rugged waves are crossed by great fissures and stunted, sunburnt brushwood. One night I slept on shore. The next day was glowing hot, and the pits and craters—ancient chimneys for subterranean vapors—reminded me of the iron foundries of Staffordshire. Because many of the lava streams are still distinct, I believe that within a geologically recent period the unbroken ocean was here spread out. Both in space and time, therefore, I felt near that mystery of mysteries—the first appearance of new beings on this Earth.

Three species of Galápagos finches: Their varied beaks suggest adaptation to different environmental niches.

These islands appear paradises for the whole family of reptiles. There are large, clumsy lizards as black as the rocks. So many reddish ones lived on one island that we could not for some time find a spot free from their burrows on which to pitch our single tent. Of the giant tortoises, the inhabitants say that on one island their shells are thick in front and turned up like a Spanish saddle, whilst on another they are rounder, blacker, and taste better when cooked. The tortoises drink from springs high in the center of their island. It was comical to behold these huge creatures on their broad, well-beaten paths, one group eagerly traveling upwards with outstretched necks, another group returning, having drunk their fill. At the spring, the tortoise ignores onlookers, buries its head in the muddy water above its eyes, and greedily sucks in great mouthfuls. They travel by night and day. One, which I watched, walked at the rate of four miles a day—allowing it a little time to eat cactus on the road. I frequently got on their backs; then giving a few raps on the hinder part of their shells, they would rise up and walk away. Believe me, my dear Henslow, your most faithful, Charles Darwin

My dear Susan,   *At sea, September 1836*

I have lately received several letters from you and the other sisters. When I read in one that Professor Sedgewick says I shall be a leading man of science, I clambered over the mountains of Ascension with a bounding step and made the rocks resound under my hammer. Captain FitzRoy is readying his account of the voyage for publication. It warrants that all we have seen is evidence of the biblical tale of the Deluge.

For myself, I have been thinking about these five years wandering, and my imaginings haunt me. I must recount to you a strange dream I had last night. I sat in the clouds. Below me, in a primeval, tropical forest, were many animals: great fossil creatures covered with polygonal plates of armor; horses and cows and dogs; tortoises and lizards; mockingbirds, finches, hawks; apes, seamen, and Fuegian men and women. Then, my dear sister—surely you will think me mad—I saw in the forest an old gentleman with a long, white beard and a lantern in his hand. It was I! The old man turned the lantern's beam upon the wildest sight. The armored fossils began to change into armadillos, and a Fuegian man into Captain FitzRoy. All the people and animals began to melt together in a great lump, as though we all have one common ancestor.

Is this not ridiculous and fantastic, my dear Susan? Thanks to God, we are steering a direct course to England. God bless you all. Your most affectionate brother, C. D.

While aboard the Beagle *Darwin kept a diary and wrote a stream of letters to family and friends, four of whom are addressed here. The diary and letters are the source material for these composite letters, where Darwin's own words are abridged, merged, and provided with transitions to make a coherent and completely faithful story. Only the dream event is made up, but it is not false: In words and images Darwin himself used later he "foresees" hints of the theory of evolution that came to him as a result of the* Beagle *voyage.*

The Call of the Ice

By Lynn Addison Yorke

Their shallow breathing made a rising, falling sea of fur. Huddled together, they lay untroubled, as if they knew—those 21 huskies—that their work was done. Thirty-five days of temperatures that dipped to minus 70°F, of hauling thousand-pound sledges over ice ridges 30 feet high. Now the plane's twin engines rumbled beneath them and they slept, going home.

Twenty-one others remained with six men and one woman on the ice of the Arctic Ocean. They were on their way to the North Pole in a 1986 reenactment of Robert E. Peary's 1908-09 trek. The removal of the dogs was one of the few concessions to modern sensibilities the explorers made; in another, two injured men were flown out, leaving the group finally at six. In an *exact* re-creation of Peary's expedition, the surplus dogs would have been killed and eaten as supply loads lightened; the injured men might have struggled on or turned back alone.

The expedition, led by Minnesotans Will Steger and Paul Schurke, had waited two days for the plane to come pick up the dogs. Flight was impossible while a four-day blizzard spent its fury nearly 800 miles south at their base camp in Resolute, Canada. The team had camped on ice that drifted west, drifted east, but somehow never toward the Pole. They had stayed behind waiting after the French doctor, Jean-Louis Etienne, passed them on his way to the Pole—skiing alone with a 110-pound sledge harnessed to his chest and shoulders.

Now, on April 11, they could move on. Each day since their March 8 departure from the northern tip of Ellesmere Island meant the possibility of warming temperatures and breaking ice. Any day they might find themselves confronted with an impassable lead of open water that would force them to radio for planes to come and take them home.

Even if they reached the Pole, they would not be the first. But they would be the first *undisputed* dogsled expedition to reach the Pole without being resupplied. Team member Ann Bancroft would be the first woman to trek to either Pole. If Jean-Louis Etienne succeeded, he would be the first to walk alone to the North Pole.

"First" is a part of polar tradition. At the turn of the century, expedition followed expedition in a mad scramble to get "farthest north." An American explorer, Adolphus Greely, nearly died from starvation after being the first to reach 83° 24′ N in 1882, some 450 miles from the Pole but 4 miles closer than Englishman Sir Clements Markham had stood in 1875. Norwegian explorer Fridtjof Nansen sledged to 86° 14′ N in 1895. Six years later Umberto Cagni planted the Italian flag 28 miles closer at 86° 34′ N. But none of these men was as obsessed with being first as Robert E. Peary.

The near-freezing water of an open lead makes little impression on hardy huskies bred to battle the killing temperatures and fickle ice of the Arctic. No other mode of transport has served polar explorers so well: Inuit komatiks—wood sledges—drawn by Alaskan and Canadian dogs carried Robert Peary toward the North Pole and back in 1909. Roald Amundsen shipped the same tried-and-true technology south and conquered the South Pole in 1911.

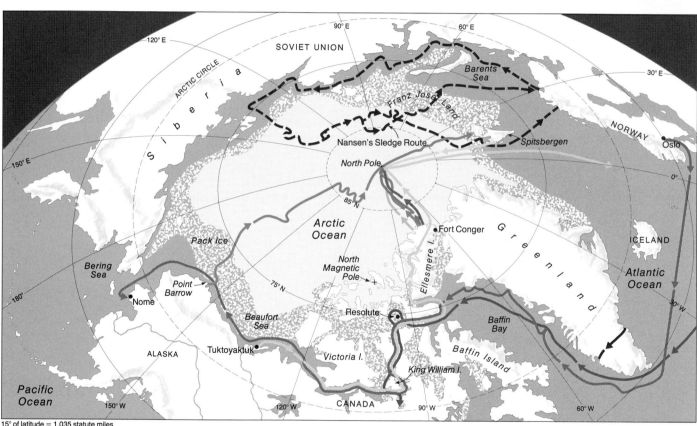

15° of latitude = 1,035 statute miles

▬▬▬	Franklin 1845-47
▬▬▬	Nansen 1888
▬ ▬ ▬	Nansen 1893-96
▬▬▬	Amundsen 1903-06
▬▬▬	Peary 1909
▬▬▬	Byrd 1926
▬▬▬	Plaisted 1963
▬▬▬	Herbert 1969
▬▬▬	Uemura 1978
▬▬▬	Fiennes 1979-1981
▬▬▬	Steger 1986

Whales first lured men to polar regions, but the dangers of the whale fishery (top) could not compare with the hazards that faced explorers who struck out over ice to reach the very ends of the Earth. The earliest Arctic expeditions attempted, like John Franklin, to navigate the icebound straits of the Northwest Passage. Later explorers headed for the Pole, sailing as far north as the seasonally fluctuating sea-ice limit allowed, then hauling sledges over the continually drifting, fracturing pack ice of the Arctic Ocean. The shortest route, chosen by Robert Peary, is from the tip of Ellesmere Island due north; many after Peary followed the same path by dogsled, by snowmobile, and on foot. Once the Pole was conquered, and outside support by airplane became available, explorers began to mastermind more challenging adventures like the long-range treks of Wally Herbert and Ranulph Fiennes.

252

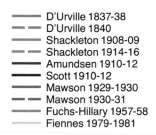

As with the North Pole, the shortest route to the South Pole was favored by the first explorers. Ernest Shackleton, Robert Scott, and Roald Amundsen all approached the Pole by way of the Ross Sea. More recent explorers have traversed the entire continent. Edmund Hillary and Vivian Fuchs started out from opposite coasts and met at a chosen spot—a supply depot near 83° S. Still others, in the pursuit of science, have devoted their explorations to the seas surrounding Antarctica.

———	D'Urville 1837-38
- - -	D'Urville 1840
———	Shackleton 1908-09
- - -	Shackleton 1914-16
———	Amundsen 1910-12
———	Scott 1910-12
———	Mawson 1929-1930
- - -	Mawson 1930-31
———	Fuchs-Hillary 1957-58
———	Fiennes 1979-1981

No ordinary ambition his; at 29, the young American naval officer planned a discovery as great as the one made by Columbus, "the man whose fame can be equalled only by him who shall one day stand with 360 degrees of longitude beneath his motionless foot, and for whom East and West shall have vanished; the discoverer of the North Pole."

Peary needed to be first because he needed to be famous. He wrote to his mother: "I *must* have fame and I cannot reconcile myself to years of commonplace drudgery and a name late in life when I see an opportunity to gain it now and sip the delicious draught. . . ."

Peary made four assaults on the Pole. During his second expedition, in 1899, he believed he was racing with Norwegian explorer Otto Sverdrup. In his effort to take the lead, Peary trudged through the darkness of midwinter in temperatures as low as minus 63°F.

When he arrived at Fort Conger on Ellesmere Island, his companion, Matthew Henson, had to peel the boots from Peary's frozen legs. As Henson ripped the rabbit-skin undershoes from Peary's bloodless feet, toes clung to the hide and snapped off at the first joint. "A few toes aren't much to give to achieve the Pole," said Peary. He lost them all.

In the end, he would lose more than toes in his pursuit of personal glory. Fifteen gold medals and three honorary doctorates could not wipe away the pain of bitter controversy

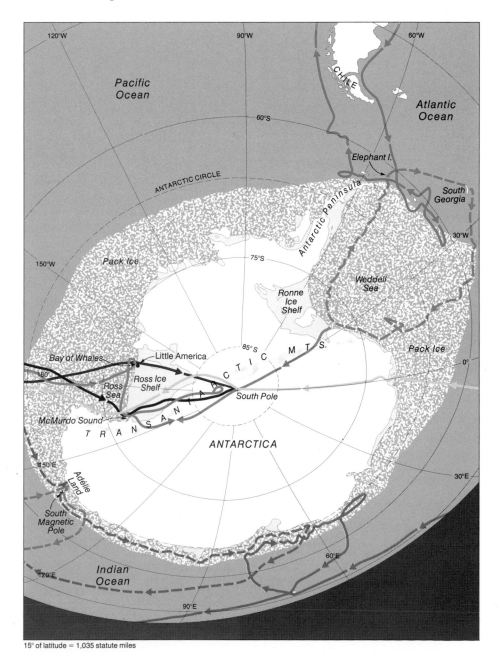

15° of latitude = 1,035 statute miles

253

Sea ice fractures under summer sun in Antarctica (right). Breakup here aids ships headed toward the continent. But once on land, explorers must negotiate glaciers laced with deep crevasses (below) before they reach more even terrain on the South Polar Plateau. In the Arctic, drifting floes mean treacherous going for explorers traversing the ice pack on their way to the North Pole; they dash across between March and May—after the minus 70°F days of winter but before summer breakup.

that followed the 1909 assertion of another American, Dr. Frederick Cook, that he had reached the North Pole a year before Peary. Neither claim could be verified and both men's records left room for doubt. Some said neither had reached the Pole. Peary's wife, Josephine, would write later that the congressional interrogation her husband underwent while his scientific observations were examined "did more toward the breaking down of his iron constitution than anything experienced in his explorations." Cook was eventually discredited and Peary vindicated by Congress, but Peary's bright star—his fame—was tarnished.

After 1909 it might have seemed that Peary had robbed the world of

256

one of its last great firsts. Not so. A string of successors contrived new ones. In 1926 Richard E. Byrd made the first flight over the North Pole, and in 1929 was first to fly over the South Pole. Ralph Plaisted reached the North Pole with a team of 12 men in 1968—the first to travel by snowmobile and the first arrival to be confirmed by airplane instruments. In 1978 Japanese Naomi Uemura was the first to journey solo to the North Pole by dogsled.

As polar firsts grew harder to conceive, they turned into "last great journeys." Even as Plaisted jounced to the Pole by Skidoo, British explorer Wally Herbert was traversing the Arctic Ocean by its longest axis—from Point Barrow, Alaska, to Spitsbergen, Norway, via the North Pole—in what he called "an epic trek . . . a journey that would complete the trilogy of the last three great pioneering geographical achievements" (the other two being the ascent of Mt. Everest by Edmund Hillary and Tenzing Norgay in 1953, and the Vivian Fuchs-Edmund Hillary Antarctic crossing in 1958).

Herbert, his three companions, and 34 huskies spent 16 months sledging over pack ice pressured by wind and current into a grinding, churning commotion of 30-foot ice walls and snow-filled valleys; knee-deep slush with all the characteristics of quicksand; young sea ice so thin and flexible that it bent like rubber nearly a foot from its normal plane as the sledges crossed it. They

257

"It is like a struggle between dwarfs and an ogre," wrote the Norwegian explorer Fridtjof Nansen (opposite) of efforts to break the stalwart Fram free from the Arctic Ocean's winter grip (left). But break free she did, north of Spitsbergen on June 13, 1896, after 35 months of drifting with the ice. The crew (below) guided the ship back to Norway, where they were reunited with Nansen and Hjalmar Johansen, who had left them to strike out for the Pole in March 1895. Nansen and Johansen made it to 86° 14′ N—a new "farthest north," but still some 260 miles short of the Pole. They struggled by sledge and kayak back to Franz Josef Land, where a British expedition rescued them just as the Fram began to break loose from the pack.

drifted on floes that cracked apart beneath their tents, leaving men leaping desperately to save their lives. After reaching Spitsbergen Herbert declared, "We'd done it. That was the end . . . the end of a period of history."

Not quite. Ten years after Herbert's voyage, British explorer Ranulph Fiennes masterminded—and completed—an epic trek to end all epic treks. He would travel around the world via the Poles. He called his expedition "the last major polar challenge. The joining-up of the feats of the Antarctic, Arctic Ocean and Northwest Passage pioneers into a logical conclusion."

Such grandiose schemes might have been plots concocted to attract movie producers. In a way they were. Great expeditions are expensive. Herbert wrote that he expected his expedition to cost around £53,000, and literary contracts to yield £48,000. No wonder he took along only three rifles for four men. "Just supposing a polar bear comes along," he said. "If you have four rifles, no one's going to pick up a camera."

All the razzle-dazzle has its roots in more pragmatic human endeavor. During the late 1500s, when the Spaniards and Portuguese held a firm grip on trade routes to the rich Orient, other European navies headed north seeking an alternate passage from the Atlantic to the Pacific. Before long they realized that the plan was not only impractical, it was dan-

Polar bears stroll on Arctic ice (opposite) as they might have in 1897 beneath the hot-air balloon of Swedish explorer Salomon Andrée and his two companions, Knut Fraenkel and Nils Strindberg. Their plan was to fly the Eagle across the Arctic Ocean from Spitsbergen to Siberia or Alaska. But not three days after lifting off, the balloon, leaking and ice coated, bounced through a debilitating fog to its final resting place on the sea ice. The explorers headed south by sledge and boat, but perished on an island east of Spitsbergen, where a ship passing 33 years later discovered their remains, diaries, and 17 rolls of film. The photographs (below), painstakingly developed by a Swedish technician, showed the downed balloon and a polar bear the explorers killed. One theory says the men died from trichinosis after eating undercooked bear meat.

gerous. Men fled ships locked and crushed in the ice only to die of scurvy and starvation. Their efforts were not entirely in vain, though: A succession of explorers mapped hitherto unknown areas, and reports like John Davis's of "great store of Whales" began a whaling boom that lasted until the early 1900s, when bowhead whales neared extinction.

The whales provided Victorian ladies with flexible baleen for their corsets. But from thousands of women over hundreds of years, the Arctic exacted a heavy toll. No fewer than 129 sons and husbands waved a final good-bye when they left British soil to seek the Northwest Passage with John Franklin in 1845. Forty rescue missions took ten years to turn up the frozen remains of some 30 bodies on King William Island.

"The British love for their heroes to die," Wally Herbert once said. Indeed, it was Franklin whom the Royal Geographical Society recognized as the discoverer of the Northwest Passage, even though the men who searched for him mapped most of the territory in which the passage lies, and even though Roald Amundsen finally navigated the labyrinth of icy straits north of Canada's mainland. By then it was 1906, 60 years after Franklin disappeared. And Amundsen was Norwegian. The British needed a new hero—a man who would conquer the South Pole.

It was December 7, 1908—summer in Antarctica. On their stomachs, Ernest Shackleton and his

Triumphant at the North Pole: Matthew Henson, Robert Peary's black companion, poses flanked by four of some fifty able Inuit who helped push Peary in stages toward the Pole in 1908-09. Able indeed—it was the Inuit who taught Peary to travel by dogsled and to make the fur clothing he wore (left, lower). But triumphant? Perhaps not. Some question the ambitious explorer's sketchy records, and wonder why his famous diary entry (opposite) was written on a loose sheet of paper inserted among four blank pages. Graver doubts surrounded the claims of Frederick Cook (left, upper): Five days before Peary's 1909 announcement, Cook said he had reached the Pole in 1908. Cook was discredited by the Royal Geographical Society, and Peary was declared by Congress to be the discoverer of the Pole. But with irrefutable proof absent in both cases, some say neither man stood there—and that no one did until the first confirmed arrival, by Ralph Plaisted, in 1968.

The Pole at last!!! The [...] of 3 centuries, my dream & ambition for 20 years. Mine at last. I cannot bring myself to realize it. It is all... all seems so simple & commonplace, as Bartlett said "just like every day". I wish [...] could be here with me to [...]

three companions peered over the razor edge of a deep crevasse on Beardmore Glacier, seeing nothing but blackness, hearing nothing but silence; Socks had vanished down there. Socks was the last of the four Manchurian ponies that had left Cape Royds on McMurdo Sound on October 29, 1908, pulling sledges and heading for the South Pole.

One by one the ponies had fallen—sinking up to their bellies in deep snow, skittering helplessly over the ice, always in danger of tumbling into the deep cracks that form in the surfaces of glaciers inching over the earth. It was a miracle that Frank Wild had not plunged with Socks to certain death—the pony had crashed through the fragile snow bridge that hid the crevasse moments after the others had crossed it. Wild, leading the unsteady pony, had fallen too, barely grasping the opposite edge of the chasm with his outstretched hands.

Now Shackleton and Wild and the two others, Jameson Adams and Eric Marshall, would share the burden of the pony's thousand-pound sledge. The men were bruised from countless falls as they tripped and stumbled through fields of sastrugi—wavelike snow ridges sculptured by the wind. Their feet and shins were slashed by sharp ice. Shackleton's heels were cracked open from frostbite and his head ached continuously as they climbed from the Ross Ice Shelf up the Beardmore Glacier to an altitude of nearly 10,000 feet in the Transantarctic Mountains.

In the even, dead white of sunlight diffused by clouds or mist, they could see no contours on the snow-covered ice. Snow blindness set in. It started with a runny nose, then they saw double, the blood vessels in their eyes swelled, and they felt a grittiness like sand under their lids. Their eyes streamed; their breath froze, then thawed in their beards, and condensed droplets trickled down inside their shirts to freeze again in sheets of ice on their chests.

On January 4, 1909, Shackleton wrote: "The end is in sight. We can only go for 3 more days at the most, for we are weakening rapidly." Five days later they turned around on the Polar Plateau, only 111 miles short of the Pole. The men barely made it back to the *Nimrod* in McMurdo Sound before she was forced in March to flee the encroaching ice of an Antarctic winter.

Shackleton would blame their failure partly on the loss of the pony. They had shot the other ponies, taking some of the meat and stashing the rest in depots for the return trip. If they could have eaten Socks, they might have made it farther south, maybe to the Pole.

Shackleton used ponies to haul sledges because he believed it was cruel to use dogs as pack animals. Even this was a concession to a British belief that nothing was so glorious as the triumph of human brute force over the power of nature. True achievement required true suffering.

An engraving of the north magnetic pole (below) by a member of James Clark Ross's party conveys a playfulness that matches the explorer's fanciful words about what might lie there: "an object as conspicuous and mysterious as the fabled mountain of Sindbad . . . or a magnet as large as Mont Blanc." In May 1831 he arrived at his goal—a featureless landscape near 72°N, 96°W.

Within the decade Ross turned south to circumnavigate Antarctica. In 1841 he entered the sea that would bear his name and encountered there the great tabular icebergs (opposite)—some more than 50 miles long—that calve from the Ross Ice Shelf.

OVERLEAF: Penguins like these might have greeted officers from the ship of French explorer Dumont d'Urville as they disembarked on Antarctica in 1840. D'Urville named the spot Adélie Land after his wife, Adèle. The penguins also inherited the name.

Real men walked, and pulled their sledges behind them.

No matter that experience proved otherwise—that huskies bred by the Inuit in the Arctic were surefooted and capable of pulling tremendous loads. Nansen and Vilhjalmur Stefansson, grandfathers of Arctic travel, knew that. Peary, and later explorers like Herbert and Steger, learned that. But back then, the British had to do it their way. That could be why Robert F. Scott, in 1911, lost the South Pole to Roald Amundsen, the Norwegian. And why Scott lost his life in the bargain.

To some extent, national chauvinism motivated most of them. Peary said in 1906: "To me the final and complete solution of the polar mystery, which has engaged the best thought and interest of some of the best men in the world, is the thing which should be done for the honor and credit of this country, the thing that I must do."

"What matters now," said Scott after Shackleton's failure in 1909, "is that the Pole should be attained by an Englishman."

Beneath the patriotic words, though, lay a drive so intensely personal that for some it approached compulsion beyond all reason.

Ambition. Says psychotherapist Evelyn Stefansson Nef, who traveled the Arctic with her explorer husband, Vilhjalmur Stefansson, before his death in 1962: "It's one of the characteristics that ties them together. The need to be famous."

She says Stefansson was different. "I am a scientist, not a tourist," he once replied when asked why he never cared to reach the North Pole. Stefansson, and others like him, eschewed the "firsts" and the "last great journeys." Dumont d'Urville, despite the orders of King Louis-Philippe in the late 1830s to penetrate as far south as possible in the Weddell Sea for the greater glory of France, cared far more about "the position of the magnetic pole, the knowledge of which is so important for the great problem respecting the laws of terrestrial magnetism."

Apsley Cherry-Garrard's only goal as a member of Scott's last expedition was to snatch a few emperor penguin eggs, incubated in the harsh winter darkness. "You will have your reward," he wrote in *The Worst Journey in the World*, "so long as all you want is a penguin's egg."

The scientists tend not to seek notoriety. But even they can display

On the deck of their corvette—a small ship ill suited to the crushing blows of Antarctic ice—Dumont d'Urville and his crew celebrated crossing the Antarctic Circle in 1840 (left). Their orders were to beat British explorer James Weddell's "farthest south"—74° 15'. But d'Urville was more interested in science than in flag-waving. His observations contributed to a 32-volume work containing watercolors of animals such as the leopard seal and the crab he named Lithodes antarctica *(above).*

curiously compulsive behavior at the ends of the Earth. They honor a tradition begun in 1912 by Australian explorer Douglas Mawson, who mapped over 1,800 miles of Antarctica's coast. They hack holes in Antarctic ice and skinny-dip in water that never gets much above freezing.

It helps to be compulsive. Filling a test tube with water from a frozen Antarctic lake involves hours with a gas-powered motor and a ten-inch-thick drill bit with enough extensions to reach 16 feet down. The setup has a torque so strong it drags the men who drive the drill in a slow circle on the ice. Wrote William J. Green of his scientific sojourn in Antarctica: "To be Ahab, to be monomaniacal in this polar quest, whatever its nature, is acceptable behavior. It is the norm."

It must be more than fame or national glory, more than adventure or science. It must be the wonder of a place as harsh as death. A place where in 1986 Steger and his five companions could arrive by dogsled at the North Pole; greet three planes carrying cameramen, reporters, and representatives from the National Geographic Society; and be forced to limit the festivities to a couple of hours so the planes, their engines left running because of the cold, would make it back to civilization on the fuel they could carry. A place where Etienne, arriving ten days later, had to pitch his tent and wait on the drifting ice pack for nearly four more, alone in his triumph, because

272

the weather would not permit flight.

And it must be the wind that blows the snow in gauze waves over the ice. It must be the blood red sunrise after six months of winter, the million shades of blue in a white landscape, the thunder of fracturing ice, the vapor trails that stretch out like veils behind the dogs.

It must be the place. Green wrote: "In the midst of a sentence that read, 'Water samples were collected with a 6.2 liter Kemmerer bottle attached to nylon line,' I wanted to say something about the afternoon shadows on the mountains or the murmuring of a distant stream or the way the wind was sapping my strength. I wanted to say something about the way water tastes on an antarctic lake after a ten-hour day. These things hovered like ghosts around the edges of scientific prose." They hover in the souls of explorers, adventurers, and scientists all, who answer the call of the ice.

When Richard E. Byrd piloted the Josephine Ford (opposite) over the North Pole in 1926, polar exploration entered a new age. Scientists could now fly to areas where even the most intrepid adventurers had never walked. In 1929 Byrd built an air base called Little America on the Ross Ice Shelf in Antarctica. He spent a winter there (opposite, below) and that summer became the first to fly over the South Pole. Today, scientists make regular visits to both Poles. Scientific bases surround the Arctic Ocean and drift stations float with the pack ice. In Antarctica, some 35 stations representing 18 nations coexist peacefully. During each Antarctic summer, expeditions such as the New Zealand geological survey (below) are dropped by plane into areas untouched by humans to continue exploring the mysteries of this frozen continent.

Roald Amundsen
Robert Falcon Scott

By Michael Parfit

Scott's expedition ship, Terra Nova, *seen from a cavern in an iceberg in McMurdo Sound.*

The canvas tent slapped and rattled under the lash of the Antarctic wind, and the three men inside listened without speaking. The wind was their mortal enemy—the wind that pressed through the cloth with its weight of cold, the wind that closed off their retreat, that pinned them to the ice of the Barrier and promised them that now, in the last days of March 1912, this tent would be their grave.

"The causes of the disaster," Robert Falcon Scott wrote slowly, "are not due to faulty organization but to misfortune in all risks which had to be undertaken." One of his feet was already frozen. He was failing of scurvy and cold. The last of the four men who had followed him to the end of the Earth—Birdie Bowers and Scott's old friend, Dr. Bill Wilson—were dying beside him. In the noisy little tent, the events of past years and months must have roared in Scott's ears like the drumming of the canvas: the daydreams of glory that drove him, the years of planning and preparation, and finally the endless toil of the great walk in the cold. Behind the noise, too, he must have heard whispers of the mistakes and defeats he acknowledged by writing those words of denial: the deaths of tractors, of ponies, of dogs, of Edgar Evans and Titus Oates; the triumph of Amundsen.

Amundsen! Amundsen, who left a flag to greet Scott at the Pole, the place that should have been virgin, who left a flag and a letter to be posted to the Norwegian king, as if Scott were a postman. Amundsen! Roald Engebreth Gravning Amundsen!

What did Scott know of this steady Norwegian who had beaten him so simply? He probably did not know his full name. He certainly knew his age: Amundsen was 39, four years younger than Scott. Amundsen was a civilian; Scott was a captain in the British Royal Navy. Amundsen had been to Antarctica in 1898 on the ship *Belgica,* and thus was among the first group of humans to spend a winter in the Antarctic

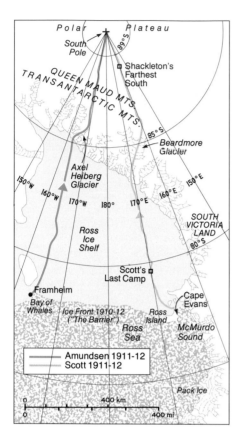

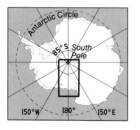

darkness; Scott had led an expedition south in 1901, and returned in 1904. Once, almost exactly two years ago—in March 1910—Scott had tried to meet Amundsen in Norway, but Amundsen, already planning his secret attack on the South Pole, had avoided him. The two men had never met. But in the tent, Amundsen was present—and triumphant.

If Scott let his mind wander back, he might have returned to Norway—his adversary's home. Scott had been there two years ago preparing for this journey. The motor-powered sledge he was depending on for travel on the Barrier ice had run beautifully. Scott had discovered how useful skis could be. He had thought himself a fortunate man.

He had also thought that Amundsen was going north. Amundsen had told the world that he was going to drift across the North Pole in the famous exploration ship *Fram.* The world believed him. Scott believed him. But when Amundsen's hopes of being first to the North Pole had been shattered by the claims of Peary and Cook, his mind had turned secretly but resolutely south.

Amundsen: that big black-and-white man, whom Scott had seen only in photographs, with his long steady face and his cursed equanimity. A man so unlike Scott—did he never have an emotion? Could he even imagine the swarms of doubt, the alternate despair and ecstasy, the agonies of self-evaluation that Scott endured? Amundsen: laconic, imperturbable. Always studying, considering methods: Inuit parkas, aerodynamic tents, the best use of dogs. Even when he was ill with scurvy on the *Belgica,* he made dispassionate notes to himself about how the illness softened and bewildered his own mind.

Were all those Norwegians so confoundingly cool? On his way south, at Melbourne, Scott had received a cable from Amundsen's brother: "Beg leave to inform you *Fram* proceeding Antarctic Amundsen." Suddenly Scott's ponderous expedition of motor sledges, ponies, and foot-slogging had become a race.

In the tent at the end of March, writing was bitter labor, but it was all Scott had left—of his strength, of his longing for glory. "I want to tell you that I was *not* too old for this job," Scott wrote as the snow hissed on the canvas. "It was the younger men that went under first. . . . After all we are setting a good example to our countrymen, if not by getting into a tight place, by facing it like men when we were there."

He wrote on, using his last energy on prose, gifted as few are with the chance to arrange and justify his life for others' eyes as his own filled with death. "I may not have proved a great explorer, but we have done the greatest march ever made and come very near to great success."

Confined by the flapping canvas, with his days full of the fury and cold of the storm, and his memory oppressed by nearly five months of steady plodding through snow and ice, he could have had only a glimpse of the full drama of the past two years. He could recall in detail the arrival of his ship, *Terra Nova,* at Ross Island in January 1911, and he knew Amundsen had disembarked at about the same time from *Fram* at the Bay of Whales, an indent in the enormous shelf of ice at the edge of the Ross Sea that both expeditions called the Barrier. Since the explo-

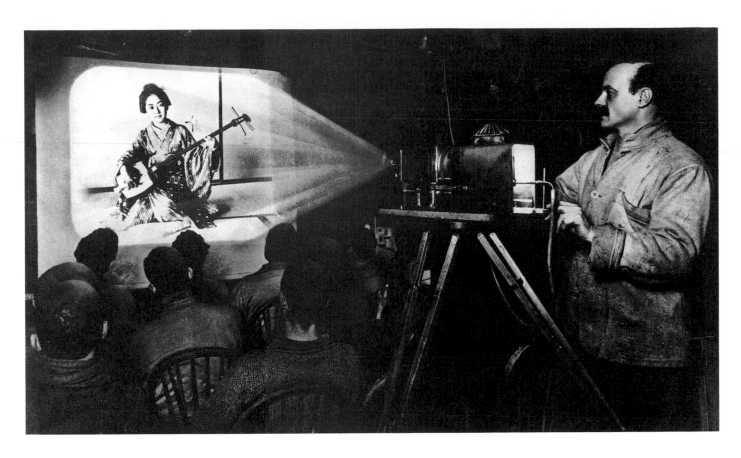

Work and play before the race: sewing at the Norwegian base, Framheim; movies for the British at Cape Evans.

ration season in Antarctica was so short, he knew that Amundsen too had spent the remaining months of daylight in 1911 planting depots of food up toward the Pole and testing his men and equipment.

For both teams the appearance of the sun in August signaled the start of the race to the Pole. Amundsen had begun fretting as soon as it was light. He was not, after all, immune to anxiety: "I always have the idea that I am the only one who is left behind," Amundsen wrote later. His haste drove him to an almost disastrous early start—September 8. Temperatures were in the minus 60s, so cold the heels of the men began to freeze. He had to retreat. He and the four others he had chosen to go south did not start off behind their dog teams again until October 19— but that was still 13 days before Scott harnessed his ponies and began.

"I don't know what to think of Amundsen's chances," Scott wrote in his diary just before he set off. "If he gets to the Pole, it must be before we do, as he is bound to travel fast with dogs and pretty certain to start early. On this account I decided at a very early date to act exactly as I should have done had he not existed. Any attempt to race must have wrecked my plan, besides which it doesn't appear the sort of thing one is out for." As if to persuade himself he wrote, "After all, it is the work that counts, not the applause that follows."

In the tent on the Barrier at the bitter end of March, the work was over, but Scott still must leave a record, as if he knew that the following spring expedition members searching from the base camp on Ross

279

> The English have loudly and openly told the world that skis and dogs are unusable in these regions and that fur clothes are rubbish. We will see—we will see.
>
> ROALD AMUNDSEN

A swig of whiskey for a chilled pony. Eventually, British ponies failed; Norwegian huskies fared better.

Island would find the tent and the bodies, the 35 pounds of geological samples they had hauled with them, scientific to the last; and the diaries under his shoulders. The wind and the noise of the slapping canvas went on and on, like torture. The three men spoke little in their pain and weariness, but Scott wrote. "Every detail of our food supplies, clothing and depots made on the interior ice sheet and over that long stretch of 700 miles to the Pole and back," he wrote in a statement he called message to public, "worked out to perfection."

In his delirium had he forgotten the disasters recorded in the diary he had written all those days? Could he forget the sight of those precious motor sledges broken down on the Barrier, the snow gathering around them like a shroud? Then the ponies had floundered and suffered so cruelly that they had to be shot far short of their goal, at the place called Shambles Camp. And there was the matter of dogs.

In the tent he yearned for the sound of dogs pulling sledges to his rescue—the dogs he had sent back to the base when he was more than 400 miles from the Pole. It was not just squeamishness at the "sordid necessity" of feeding dogmeat to dogs that had made him reject them; he was, after all, quite willing to shoot and eat his ponies. Nor was it just his expressed concern that dogs weren't reliable. He simply didn't want their help. In leaving the dogs behind he had chosen his daydreamed path to glory, the road, he had once written, on which men must struggle alone, and "the conquest is more nobly and splendidly won."

For Amundsen the only path that mattered was the one to the Pole. At about the same latitude at which Scott had sent the last dogs back to base, Amundsen had written: "It was a sheer marvel . . . that the dogs accomplished today. . . . 17 miles, with 5,000 foot climb. Come and say that dogs cannot be used here." In his last extremity, Scott must have had some idea how the dogs had pulled Amundsen away from him, so quickly and so far that on December 9, when Scott's team was killing ponies at Shambles Camp, 409 miles from the Pole, Amundsen had fewer than 115 miles to go. Even then, Amundsen was anxious. There, farther south than anyone had ever been, Amundsen and one of his men noticed a dog sniffing the southerly breeze and worried that Scott was ahead.

They needn't have been concerned. It had been warm on the high plateau for Amundsen—"Quite summer like:–0.4°F." But that same warm weather dumped wet snow on Scott, more than 200 miles behind, and raised the temperature at his lower altitude to above freezing; they joked about turning the tent into a boat. Melting snow soaked everything. "A hopeless feeling descends," Scott wrote in his diary, "What immense patience is needed for such occasions!"

But in the somber light of his canvas tomb, Scott found glory in the adversity he cursed. To him the greatness of the march was that the men did it all themselves, against odds that had been partly of their own making. When the machines were gone, and the ponies were gone, and the dogs were gone, Scott slipped into his harness and seemed, for once, content. The terrible hardship of the climb to the plateau's 10,000-foot elevation was simple and difficult; it cleansed him of his doubt. He just put on the skis, leaned to the harness, and pulled. "I was very jubilant; all difficulties seemed to be vanishing. . . ." On Christmas Day, Birdie Bowers wrote, "Scott got fairly wound up and went on and on. . . ."

On the journey went, day blazing into day, with no ease of darkness, no cease of wind. But by Christmas Scott had already been beaten.

On January 16—two and a half months from the start—Bowers saw a hump of snow that looked man-made. He chose to think it was built by the wind. Then, Scott wrote: "half an hour later he detected a black speck ahead. Soon we knew that this could not be a natural snow feature. We marched on, found that it was a black flag tied to a sledge bearer; near by the remains of a camp; sledge tracks and ski tracks going and coming and the clear trace of dogs' paws—many dogs."

Amundsen had been there just a month before. The Pole was conquered. All Scott could do was look at the things Amundsen had left there in a tent, pick up the triumphant letter Amundsen had written to the king of Norway to make his own simple record in case he didn't get home. The presence of the letter, with a note asking Scott to forward it, at least showed Amundsen's respect for Scott's ability to get to the Pole and back, but that was no solace. On the night of the black flag, Scott wrote, "All the day dreams must go."

This moment, more than any others, must have haunted Scott in his final days, two months later, after the long and bitter trek homeward, after the rations proved inadequate, the fuel dwindled, and the cold and the scurvy wore the five men down; after Edgar Evans, ill and injured, fell in the snow and died; after Titus Oates, ruined by his frozen feet, volunteered for death, leaving behind the legend that Scott's diary gave him: "He said, 'I am just going outside and may be some time.' He went out into the blizzard and we have not seen him since." But Scott, when he stood at the Pole and wrote in his diary, "Great God! this is an awful place. . . ." would have been astonished to know how ambivalent Amundsen himself was as the victor.

"I had better be honest," Amundsen wrote later, "and admit straight out that I have never known any man to be placed in such a diametrically opposite position to the goal of his desires . . . the North Pole itself . . . had attracted me from childhood, and here I was at the South Pole. Can anything more topsy-turvy be imagined?"

Late in March, trapped on the Barrier in the impossible wind, 12 miles from the food cache known as One Ton Depot, Scott could not have known what was to come: That Amundsen would return to muted acclaim and that he himself would be honored beyond any of those daydreams. In a sense the journey gave each his goal. For Amundsen, who disappeared on a rescue flight in the far north in 1928, the journey itself was, as the historian Roland Huntford has written, his work of art. To the world he became the man who had made it look easy. But he had never sought fame; exploration itself was enough. Scott had written what was true of Amundsen: The applause was less important.

I wish to repeat now, what I said when I first heard of the presence of Amundsen, that this Expedition is going to lay its plans and carry on with its work just as if Amundsen did not exist.
ROBERT F. SCOTT

A victorious Amundsen (middle row, center), with ship and expedition crews, heading home.

But Britain, sliding into a war, needed once more to hear of honor and death, of valiant defeat, of the tragedy of one man, trapped by his flaws, still giving all. England would forgive Scott his failings—even honor them—if he died well. So at last, in the tent, perhaps he knew: He had come to play the Light Brigade for the Empire. All he had to do was write the noble words. Kathleen, his wife, would edit them for strength. That was the gift he left beside his body: "We are weak writing is difficult but for my own sake I do not regret this journey which has shown that Englishmen can endure hardships, help one another and meet death with as great a fortitude as ever in the past."

Bill Wilson and Birdie Bowers died in their sleep, folded in their sleeping bags. Robert Falcon Scott pulled his coat open to the cold and did it the hard way.

Our story on the feelings and imaginings of Scott and Amundsen is based largely on their diaries, Scott's Last Expedition *and* The South Pole.

Into the Deeps

By Philip Kopper

T
wo scuba divers tumble off a boat anchored in Cozumel's lee, shatter the shimmering surface of the Caribbean Sea, and sink to the reef 40 feet below. They fall weightlessly through crystal blue and glide like birds, then drift down through gardens bright with fish. As a barracuda pauses on patrol, one diver snaps its solemn portrait. A squadron of iridescent squid jets by. The divers follow a bank of ghostly rocks and thread a maze of coral.

It could be called the oldest frontier. Since first we looked beneath the waves, humans have been drawn to the undersea realm. In Mesopotamia, archaeologists have uncovered mother-of-pearl inlays that date to 4500 B.C. And early Greek writers lavished praise on sponge divers, considered braver than warriors.

Yet it is also the newest frontier. Not until Jacques-Yves Cousteau introduced the Aqua-Lung could scientists freely explore the ocean's upper layers as these Cozumel divers do now. To go deeper was even harder; the first men to reach the lowest seafloor did so just 14 months ahead of the first to reach orbit. Within the past two decades, discoveries from the deeps have revolutionized long-held notions about our planet.

Our progress into the ocean's depths is a history of inventions. Although skilled swimmers like Japan's *ama* divers and Polynesian spear fishermen commonly plunged a hundred feet for food, coral, or pearls, no free diver could stay down longer than one breath of air lasts.

People used tools to increase that air supply. Ancient Greek sponge divers would lower an inverted pot into the water and breathe the air trapped inside. In Renaissance Italy, humans hung in the water on suspended platforms fitted with glass bells. In 1620 a Dutch inventor took King James I of England for a ride under the Thames in one of the first self-propelled underwater craft. Oars fitted with greased leather gaskets powered it, and air came through a tube from bellows on the surface.

In 1837 the invention of the helmeted diving suit brought shallow seafloors closer. Salvage and construction workers used these clumsy suits, tethered to the surface by air hoses. But if they stayed below for too long, or went too deep, they faced another problem: pressure.

With every 33 feet of underwater depth, pressure increases by 14.7 pounds per square inch—the weight of the atmosphere at sea level. Even at swimming pool depths, water pressure starts to squeeze nitrogen into the blood and tissues as bubbles, which are reabsorbed if the pressure eases slowly. But a diver who ascends too fast suffers the bends: crippling agony in the joints and muscles and sometimes fatal embolisms.

Late in the 19th century physiologists learned to prevent the condition by carefully timed ascent. Dives were still limited by the time needed

A sea fan and a group of redlings welcome a diver to the intricate ecosystem of a Red Sea reef. Plant and animal life abounds in the ocean's topmost layers, opened to explorers by the introduction of the Aqua-Lung in 1943. Farther down, by 5,000 feet, sunlight fades to darkness, and marine life dwindles to one-fiftieth of its surface numbers. This abyssal realm, where humans can venture only with submersibles, waits nearly untouched around a globe that is 70 percent underwater.

to decompress. Scientists discovered other dysfunctions caused by the gases divers breathed: Pure oxygen, pressurized at depths below 25 feet, caused convulsions. Nitrogen caused narcosis, the mind-addling "rapture of the deep," which could transform even experienced divers into giggling clowns willing to share their air with fish. The solution: Match gas mixtures to different situations.

While helmets, diving suits, and new breathing mixtures helped open the upper ocean to exploration, the first serious study of the deep ocean began on the surface, under the guidance of Matthew Fontaine Maury. A U. S. Navy lieutenant with a flair for prose, Maury was in command at the Navy's Depot of Charts and Instruments when he launched history's first major deep-sea survey in 1849.

Maury dispatched two ingeniously equipped research ships, *Taney* and *Dolphin,* to sound the Atlantic systematically. Using weighted lines, his ships made new readings of the ocean depths. They also collected seafloor samples that Maury called "the feathers from old ocean's bed," from depths never reached before.

His chart of the Atlantic was the first bathymetric picture of an entire ocean, but it erroneously showed depths of more than seven miles, a distortion caused, perhaps, by the ship's drift, currents, and other factors. *Dolphin* also recorded a rising bottom in mid-Atlantic, a plateau that he dubbed Middle Ground. Little did he know its true extent.

In 1855 Maury wrote the earliest oceanography text, with a characteristically exuberant pen: "The wonders of the sea are as marvelous as the glories of the heavens; and they proclaim, in songs divine, that they too are the work of holy fingers." His images were devout, but his goal concrete: to bring "the physical geography of the sea regularly within the domains of science."

A British square-rigger named H.M.S. *Challenger* advanced that aim in 1872. Outfitted with two well-equipped laboratories, she embarked on a three-and-a-half-year exploration around the world. Her five scientists, the first interdisciplinary oceanographic team, sampled ocean water at many depths and found that it varied in salinity and temperature. *Challenger* sounded the Pacific floor near Earth's deepest point, the Mariana Trench. The expedition collected sessile and free-swimming organisms, identified 4,417 new plants and animals, and compiled enough data to fill 50 volumes. When *Challenger*'s leaders announced the discovery of a ridge running south from Maury's Middle Ground, speculation revived about a "lost Atlantis."

Answers would only come with new technology, which military interests supplied. As navies deployed better submarines, they also developed echoing devices that could find an unseen hull or chart the seafloor with new accuracy. In 1925 the German research ship *Meteor,* armed with early sonar, set out to make

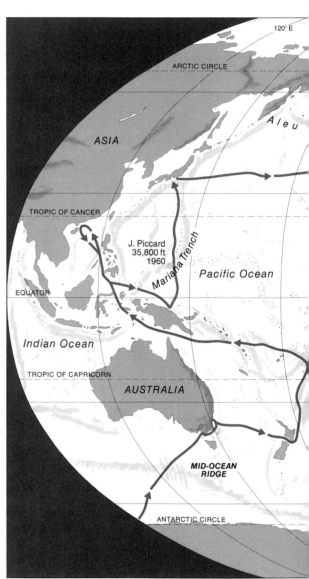

15° of latitude = 1,035 statute miles

Scientists peer through microscopes—one a long-barreled stereoscopic model—aboard H.M.S. Challenger. On her pioneering voyage of 79,292 miles, the British research vessel laid the foundation of modern oceanography, taking soundings around the globe with miles of hemp line. Dredges brought up samples for shipboard laboratories. Challenger returned with 13,000 kinds of plants and animals, proving the unexpected: Life could exist at great depths.

On a route crisscrossing the Atlantic (below), the German Meteor was first to record an entire ocean's currents. The succeeding decades brought more advances: William Beebe's bathysphere trips, Jacques-Yves Cousteau's Aqua-Lung, Auguste and Jacques Piccard's bathyscaph dives. Yet scientists have seen only a tiny fraction of Earth's 140 million square miles of ocean floor.

Not until the 1950s did geologists realize that a single feature, the Mid-Ocean Ridge, snaked through every ocean basin. While examining it with deep-towed cameras and an abyssal submarine off the Galápagos, startled investigators discovered unique colonies of sea life feeding around hot, mineral-rich springs far beyond the reach of sunlight. More vent systems were found at 21° North, and one rich in manganese on the Juan de Fuca Ridge. Project TAG (Trans-Atlantic Geotraverse) located the first vigorous vent system in the Atlantic.

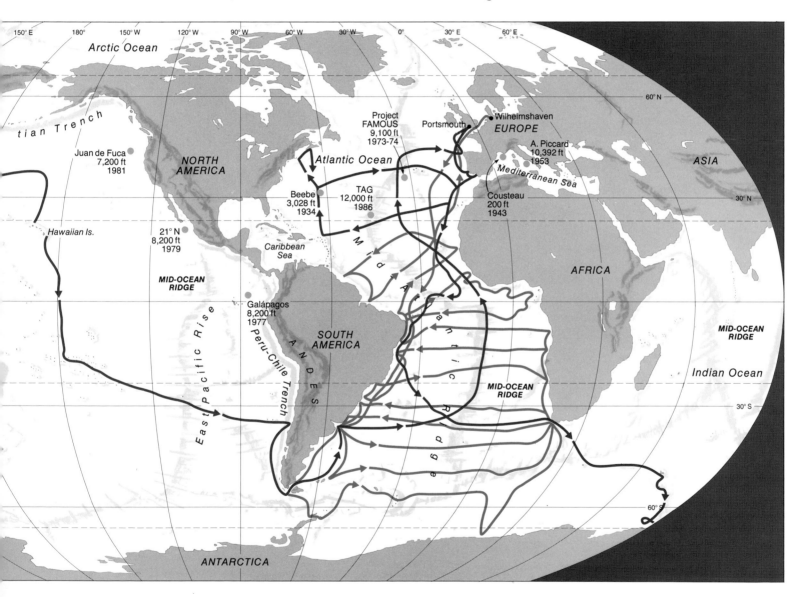

Challenger Expedition 1872-76
Meteor Expedition 1925-27
● Dive Site

In the three centuries since a crude diving bell took man 50 feet below, explorers have reached farther and farther into the deeps. Darkness and cold increase with depth, along with crushing pressure that tests the stoutest hulls. When Trieste hovered in the deepest known part of the sea, she had to withstand pressures of more than 960 atmospheres, or 960 times the weight of air at sea level. Scientists today often stay on the surface, operating their undersea vehicles by remote controls.

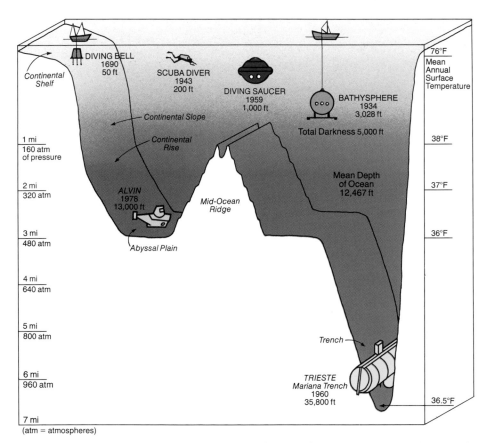

DIVING BELL
1690
50 ft

Continental
Shelf

SCUBA DIVER
1943
200 ft

Continental Slope

DIVING SAUCER
1959
1,000 ft

Continental
Rise

BATHYSPHERE
1934
3,028 ft

Total Darkness 5,000 ft

76°F
Mean
Annual
Surface
Temperature

1 mi
160 atm
of pressure

38°F

ALVIN
1978
13,000 ft

Mid-Ocean
Ridge

Mean Depth
of Ocean
12,467 ft

2 mi
320 atm

37°F

Abyssal Plain

3 mi
480 atm

36°F

4 mi
640 atm

5 mi
800 atm

Trench

6 mi
960 atm

TRIESTE
Mariana Trench
1960
35,800 ft

36.5°F

7 mi

(atm = atmospheres)

thousands of soundings in the South Atlantic, and completed the first detailed survey of an entire ocean.

Meteor found no buried island of Atlantis but did show that the Mid-Atlantic Ridge curved around the Cape of Good Hope toward the Indian Ocean. Future research would establish the existence of a 46,000-mile mountain belt winding through every ocean: the Mid-Ocean Ridge, largest geologic feature on Earth. Geologists continued to wonder why

it was there, but for a closeup look they would have to wait.

Firsthand observation of the deeps was progressing slowly. In the 1930s naturalist William Beebe collaborated with engineer Otis Barton on the bathysphere (Greek for "deep ball"). Fitted with two observation ports, it dangled from a support ship's cable—a throwback to the suspended diving bells of old.

In 1934 Beebe and Barton rode it 3,028 feet down into the seas near

288

Helmeted in wicker to cushion a hard landing, Auguste Piccard (opposite, at right) pauses during preparations for a balloon ascent to the stratosphere in 1931. This Swiss physicist probed the upper atmosphere and then invented the bathyscaph called Trieste, a kind of underwater balloon, to explore the ocean depths with his son Jacques (in sagging knee socks). In 1953, father and son filled the huge metal bathyscaph with lighter-than-water gasoline off Naples, crawled into the vessel's round cabin, and dived to 10,392 feet, deeper than anyone had gone before.

Less than a decade later, Jacques (below, far right) repairs the lurching Trieste. On this 1960 dive for the U. S. Navy, Jacques rode the submersible on an 8½-hour journey down into the 35,800-foot Mariana Trench. Trieste dumped 11 tons of steel shot at intervals to control her descent and ascent.

"Neither sun, nor moon, nor stars," wrote Auguste after one such dive, "nothing but opaque gloom."

Bermuda, observing new species as they went. Had Beebe's ball, tethered to its mother ship, approached the bottom, it might have been dashed against the seafloor as the tender bobbed on the surface.

Auguste Piccard, a Swiss physicist famed for his balloon designs, and his son Jacques overcame that problem with an untethered submersible. They called it a bathyscaph ("deep boat"), a thin-walled hollow float supporting a small, pressure-resistant cabin. It worked on the same principle as the high-altitude balloon Auguste Piccard took into the stratosphere in 1931. Employing the buoyancy principle, each vehicle rose and sank in the surrounding medium, whether air or water, by changing the mass within its suspending floats. Piccard's most ambitious bathyscaph, *Trieste*, had a float filled with lighter-than-water gasoline, which cold water compressed, causing the craft to descend. Free of fragile links to a tender, the *Trieste* could land on the seafloor; she rose as his balloon had: by dumping ballast.

In January 1960 Jacques Piccard and U. S. Navy Lt. Don Walsh voyaged down 35,800 feet in *Trieste* to the floor of the Mariana Trench, a depth no one has reached since. From their vessel, squeezed by eight tons of pressure per square inch, Piccard and Walsh saw what many scientists had thought impossible at such depths—complex life. "A flat-

A polka-dot starfish in fluorescent camouflage spreads suction-cupped arms on coral 30 feet down in the Red Sea. Such sights reward sport divers, first ushered into the depths by Jacques-Yves Cousteau (below) and the Aqua-Lung. With underwater cameras, Cousteau brought millions of armchair aquanauts into his undersea world. In 1959 his "diving saucer" (right) lowered two divers to 1,000 feet, protected by a shell of pressure-resistant forged steel ³/₄ inch thick.

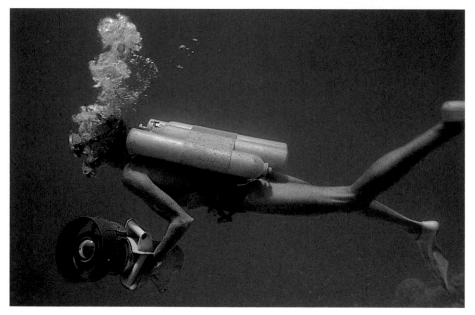

fish at the very nadir of the earth," Piccard wrote after seeing a fish briefly lit by *Trieste*'s lights. But this fish had eyes! Of what use were they in that blackness, he wondered? *Trieste* had no way to collect specimens, so the question remained.

About the same time that Auguste Piccard was working to free the bathysphere from its tether, Jacques-Yves Cousteau was freeing helmeted divers from theirs. In 1943 Cousteau developed the most liberating undersea invention of all, the portable Aqua-Lung. Why? Because, Cousteau said, "I needed it. All the things tested before were junk!"

For decades, divers had been trying breathing gadgets, all awkward, dangerous, or inefficient. One spewed air from bottles nonstop; others required the swimmer to squeeze a rubber bulb with his hand. Cousteau wanted "an automatic device that would release air to the diver without his thinking about it."

He explained it to Emile Gagnan, an engineer in wartime Paris who was making valves that allowed automobiles to run on cooking gas. Gagnan devised a regulator, a one-way valve the size of a man's wallet, connected to a mouthpiece. Each time a diver inhaled, it brought a supply of compressed air from a tank on his back, while another hose delivered exhaled air to exhaust ports. The valve supplied air at the right pressure at any depth. At last, divers could move with total freedom,

swim, and even turn somersaults.

Today, Cousteau says "devouring curiosity and obstinacy" drove him to find the right tools. In later years his team invented new devices, including battery-powered undersea scooters to extend the diver's range, and a "diving saucer" no bigger than a compact car for deeper work.

Cousteau considers himself an explorer more than a scientist. His films pay for further exploration and, he hopes, feed a love of the water world as deep as his: "I like to have guests at my table . . . and serve a meal of visions."

Equipped with what is now called scuba (self-contained underwater breathing apparatus), scientists began exploring Cousteau's world. Fishery experts discovered how conventional trawls damaged the fishes' habitat. Archaeologists found shipwrecks: undersea time capsules that preserved relics of ancient cultures. Diving surveys showed that pollution had alarmingly reduced natural flora and fauna in the upper Mediterranean. Biologists could at last observe marine organisms in their habitats, and put many myths to rest, such as the notion that sharks constantly cruised in order to breathe.

Perhaps the most surprising discovery about ocean life, however, was to come as scientists prepared to explore the Mid-Ocean Ridge. By the 1960s, magnetic readings of the ocean floor had helped gain general acceptance for the theory of plate tectonics: that all of the Earth's sur-

face rode on moving crustal plates. Where an ocean plate met a continental plate, the ocean floor slid beneath, forming trenches like the Mariana. Plates appeared to spread apart at the Mid-Ocean Ridge.

A firsthand look could confirm the theory, and new kinds of submersibles, smaller and less cumbersome than bathyscaphs, were now available. *Alvin,* an American minisub only 25 feet long, was easy to ship from place to place. Its robot arms could pick objects off the seafloor.

In 1974 *Alvin* investigated the Mid-Atlantic Ridge during Project FAMOUS (French-American Mid-Ocean Undersea Study). The trip down to the ridge took one and a half hours at a hundred feet a minute. There *Alvin's* floodlights lit up treasures more precious than gold for explorer-geologist Robert D. Ballard: young pillow lava amid the mountainous terrain of the deep.

"We had to prove our contentions" that Earth was always being recreated, Ballard recalled. "When we first laid eyes on the obviously fresh lava, it was as if there lay the true birthplace of the Earth's crust."

The pillow-shaped rock had solidified when molten magma from the mantle, the layer below Earth's crust, came in contact with cold water. This recent volcanism meant crustal plates were indeed moving apart at the ridge. As new rock formed, it piled higher, building hills on the ocean floor. These were later pulled apart as the Earth's plates

wedged slowly away from each other, making room for newer lava to come billowing through.

Ballard dived again aboard *Alvin* in 1977 to the Galápagos Rift in the Pacific portion of the Mid-Ocean Ridge, where he and his colleagues suspected there were hydrothermal vents. They found the vents, which were fueling undreamed-of habitats.

Until then scientists had assumed that all food chains depended on sunlight, which could be converted

*Oasis in a midnight desert (opposite):
A fish and 18-inch tube worms flourish
near a hydrothermal vent far under the
Pacific's surface. Minisub divers using
a temperature gauge found a "black
smoker" (right, lower) of mineral-rich
water at more than 662°F (350°C).
Craft like Alvin (right) take explorers
to the deeps to retrieve samples, study
life, and even snap a self-portrait with
a camera positioned by a flexible arm.*

to food by plants through photosynthesis. They theorized that even creatures of the abyss relied on food filtering down from the sunlit layers above. (Perhaps Piccard's fish used its eyes to hunt small bioluminescent creatures that fed on this organic "snow.") Yet here in the pitch black was an ecosystem based not on photosynthesis but on chemosynthesis.

From their portholes *Alvin's* passengers saw vents spouting milky blue water. Seawater that had seeped down toward the mantle was returning in superheated springs, rich in dissolved minerals like manganese and sulfur compounds. Bacteria absorbed the hydrogen sulfide and converted it into the organic products necessary for life, thus beginning the food chain for a surprising community of deep-sea animals: blind crabs, giant clams, and scarlet-plumed tube worms twelve feet tall.

Ballard plans each of his dives as an exploration—to a place never seen before. He caught the world's imagination in 1985 when, using a million-dollar camera sled named *Argo*, he found the *Titanic*, 12,500 feet deep, in an Atlantic canyon. In 1986 he took *Alvin* to visit and photograph the noble wreck.

Ballard points out that since 70 percent of what he calls Planet Ocean is submerged, "most of Earth has not been explored. We know less about the ocean's bottom than the moon's backside. Clearly the Lewis and Clark period of exploration in the deep sea is still underway."

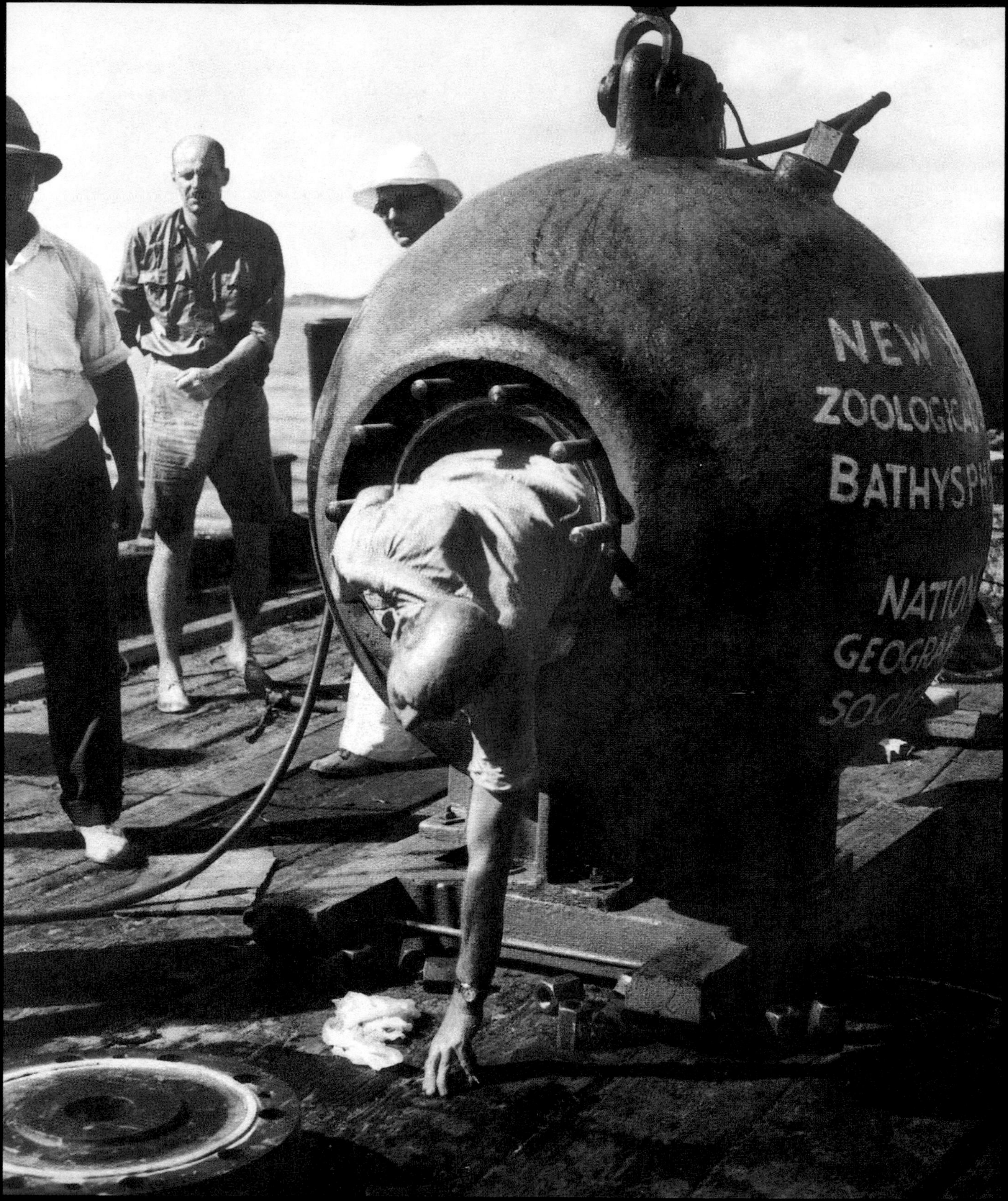
NEW
ZOOLOGICA
BATHYSPH
NATIO
GEOGRA
SOCI

By Thomas B. Allen

Most afternoons, the Beebe boy disappeared. To watch the sunset and write about it, he said. An odd little boy. He began keeping a journal in 1889, when he was 12 years old. Already a naturalist, he wrote one of his earliest entries on an August day that year: "Today, I saw two Monarch Butterflies, *Danais archippus,* flying south."

And then there was the day he came running home, breathless and frightened. What had upset him so? Something about a kite, about the awful loneliness of a kite. No one in his little New Jersey town really knew him. He walked not in a world of childhood but in another world, a place full of mystery and discovery that he desperately tried to describe. He would rarely share his journal with anyone, or tell anyone about his fears. But, many years later, he wrote about the kite: "I remember pulling in a kite with all my might, trembling with terror, for I had sensed the ghastly isolation of that bit of paper aloft in sheer space, and the tug of the string appalled me with the thought of being myself drawn up and up, away from the solid earth."

When William Beebe wrote that, he was no longer a boy and he had already been like that kite. He had been drawn away from the solid Earth, not by going up and up but by going down and down . . . beneath the sea. There he found fame as a writer about the wonders of the undersea world, a new world he introduced to generations of readers. William Beebe, the man, had tethered himself to fame, but even as he soared into the glittery realm of the celebrity, he felt that he was losing touch with the world of the scientist, where people were expected to keep their feet on the ground. "Notorious," he jokingly called himself.

Beebe's underwater career began in 1925, when he donned a crude copper diving helmet and in the waters of the Galápagos discovered sea-

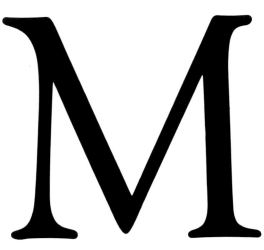

William Beebe wriggling into the sunlight after a three-hour dive; the inventor of the bathysphere, Otis Barton (in shorts), looks on.

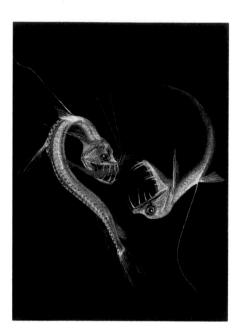

Saber-toothed Viperfish and shrimp at 1,700 feet, as rendered by an artist from Beebe's descriptions and notes.

scapes and creatures that rivaled in mystery and beauty what he had seen on land. He found a watery realm of towering ebony cliffs and jet black sand, scarlet crabs and a "great dusky octopus" that "slides out of its cave, perceives me, and, with a change of emotion, shifts its color to brick red and then to mottled red and gray."

He recorded sights never before seen, and he wrote about them with a sense of enchantment, not scientific detachment. And what enchanted readers often infuriated the scientists Beebe still considered his peers. Beebe did indeed have scientific credentials. He was head of the New York Zoological Society's Department of Tropical Research. He wrote for scientific journals. His four-volume monograph on pheasants of the world still stands as an important work. But a scientist did not write for the public or become the subject of a *New Yorker* cartoon. A scientist did not get divorced with messy publicity, as Beebe had, early in his career. A scientist did not go dancing in Manhattan jazz joints or employ comely young women as expedition members. A scientist did not become a celebrity, especially in an age that made celebrities of a flagpole sitter or a fan dancer.

On the printed page, he exuded humor, warmth, and a conspiratorial charm that invited readers to explore nature's wonders. Through 23 books and hundreds of articles, his army of faithful readers followed. But in person, Beebe could be aloof, sensitive to criticism, tough on assistants who did not work as hard as he did, and disdainful of some scientific peers. One day Beebe walked into a New York club where a friend was talking to Ivan T. Sanderson, a former British Museum scientist turned popular science writer. Since Beebe's own popular books about trekking through jungles had made him a celebrity, the friend, thinking that Beebe and Sanderson had something in common, said, "I don't believe you have met Ivan Sanderson, Will." Beebe looked coldly at Sanderson, the comfortable celebrity, and said, "No. And I never shall." Beebe turned and walked out of the room. A scientist should not associate with popularizers whom he considered reckless.

Beebe was a superb—and popular—interpreter of science. He had the instincts of a showman, though he denied that role as he grandly played it. What scientist would allow a radio announcer on a scientific expedition? Beebe did. In an era of hoopla and quests for frivolous firsts, scientists were not supposed to break records, but Beebe broke them. It was one way to get attention—and money—for other expeditions.

His vehicle was the bathysphere, the steel diving chamber that enabled Beebe to plunge to depths that humans had never seen. The bathysphere weighed 5,000 pounds and was more than four and a half feet in diameter. Its oxygen tanks provided about a six-hour air supply. Trays of soda lime absorbed carbon dioxide, while calcium chloride absorbed moisture. More than half a mile of $7/8$-inch, nontwisting steel cable connected the bathysphere to a steam-driven winch on the deck of a tender. Tied to the cable at intervals were rubber-sheathed wires that sent electric power to the searchlights in the bathysphere and linked its telephone to one on the deck.

Beebe in the 20-pound copper diving helmet used on some of his earliest dives, off Bermuda.

Otis Barton had invented the bathysphere, financed its construction, and accompanied Beebe on every major dive. But Barton earned scant fame. Beebe in fact claimed that the inspiration for the bathysphere came from Teddy Roosevelt. And proof? "There remains," Beebe said, "only a smudged bit of paper with a cylinder drawn by myself and a sphere outlined by Colonel Roosevelt. . . ."

In a 1930 dive the bathysphere had taken Beebe down to 1,426 feet, a new record. At 600 feet, Beebe's disembodied voice crackled on the ship's telephone wire: "Only dead men have sunk below this." He wrote about the experience, in his now distinctive popular style, for the NATIONAL GEOGRAPHIC magazine: "Long strings of salpa drifted past, lovely as the finest lace, and schools of jellyfish throbbed on their directionless but energetic road through life."

Two years later, while preparing for a deeper dive, he sent the bathysphere down empty to 3,000 feet. When he hauled it up, it was almost full of water. As he and an assistant began to open the hatch, the water shot out under tremendous pressure. He concluded a dramatic account of the event with a dire note: If he had been in the bathysphere that day, "in the inky blackness we should have been crushed into shapeless tissues by nothing more substantial than air and water."

Thus adding death-defying daredevil to his showman role, in 1933 he asked the National Geographic Society to sponsor an expedition to explore the ocean deeps off the Bermuda island of Nonsuch, his usual diving site. He did not openly promise to break his own deep-diving record. But he accepted—along with a $10,000 grant—the Geographic's stipulation that the expedition would include "three descents in the bathysphere to approximately one-half mile depth. . . ."

Beebe readied the bathysphere, then on display at the Century of Progress Exposition in Chicago. On August 15, 1934, Beebe and Barton curled into the cold sphere and took up their stations at round quartz windows three inches thick.

The moment the bathysphere was hoisted to a boom and swung over the sea, Gloria Hollister, Beebe's beautiful young research associate, began speaking and listening on the deck-to-depths telephone. Beebe kept up his end of the conversation as he descended. They had agreed that five seconds of silence from the bathysphere signaled danger. So not all of the dialogue was scientific. "Gosh, it's cold," Beebe said. "Wear your red flannels next time," Hollister replied.

Beebe depended on Hollister to write down what he saw. And if he did not adequately describe what he saw, she would ask questions. "I willfully shut my eyes," Beebe wrote, "or turned them into the bathysphere to avoid whatever bewilderment might come while I was searching my memory for details of what had barely faded from my eye."

He now lived for these dives, when he knew no fear of the unknown sea or his unknown self, when, "forehead pressed close to the cold glass," he felt "a tremendous wave of emotion, a real appreciation of what was momentarily almost superhuman, cosmic . . . two conscious

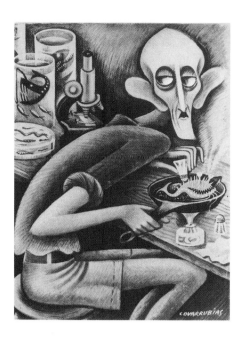

Vanity Fair, *1933: "Professor William Beebe, gourmet and ichthyologist, secretly fries his new discovery, instead of pickling it for posterity."*

human beings sat and peered into the abyssal darkness as we dangled in mid-water, isolated as a lost planet in outermost space."

"Surprises came at every few feet, and again the mass of life was totally unexpected, the total of creatures seen unbelievable. . . . At 2,100 feet two large fish . . . lighted up and then became one with the darkness about them. . . ." At 2,500 feet, he saw a "marine monster" about 20 feet long—"the supreme sight of the expedition."

Beebe ordered the dive ended with only a few turns of cable still left on the winch's drum. "Before we began to ascend, I had to stop making notes of my own, so numb were my fingers from the cold steel of the window sill. To change from my cushion to the metal floor was like shifting to a seat on a cake of ice," he wrote. The bathysphere had reached 3,028 feet—a record that stood for 15 years.

Beebe the showman liked the idea of breaking a record, but not Beebe the scientist. He later claimed that Gilbert Hovey Grosvenor, President of the National Geographic Society, had "demanded no condition of a new record, which is why I gave it to him." Beebe vowed that never again would he attempt record-breaking dives, "which really have no scientific value." He knew his dives for records had made him more vulnerable to the barbs of scientists. But wonder filled the man as it had filled the lonely child, and he had to rhapsodize about it:

"As fish after fish swam into my restricted line of vision—fish, which, heretofore, I had seen only dead and in my nets—as I saw their colors and . . . their activities and modes of swimming and clear evidence of their sociability or solitary habits, I felt that all the trouble and cost and risk were repaid many fold. . . . After these dives were past, when I came again to examine the deep-sea treasures in my nets, I would feel as an astronomer might who looks through his telescope after having rocketed to Mars and back. . . ."

On his dives Beebe marvelously, if unscientifically, described fish that he recognized, along with several he claimed as new species. His Pallid Sailfin was two feet long with "an unpleasant pale, olive drab" color, "the hue of water-soaked flesh," its body "bathed in a strange luminosity." His big-eyed Five-lined Constellation Fish glowed with strange yellow and purple lights. The six-foot-long Untouchable Bathysphere Fish, *Bathysphaera intacta,* had fangs in its large jaw and a "single line of strong lights, pale bluish," strung along its body.

Copeia, the journal of ichthyology and herpetology, scoffed at Beebe's fish stories. The reviewer especially mocked the Five-lined Constellation Fish: "I am forced to suggest that what the author saw might have been a phosphorescent coelenterate whose lights were beautified by halation in passing through a misty film breathed onto the quartz window by Mr. Beebe's eagerly appressed face."

No one ever reported seeing *Bathysphaera intacta* or the Five-lined Constellation Fish again. But not until 1986 did anyone hover off Bermuda as Beebe had, unobtrusive in his bathysphere. In a way, that zone of the sea remains Beebe's memorial. Perhaps someday others will see the wonders he saw, and science will accept his discoveries.

The New Yorker, *1934: "But Dr. Beebe? Where is he?"*

As long and lank and brown as the Ancient Mariner . . . as bold and dictatorial and ambitious as Julius Caesar . . . as hungry to extend the frontiers of experience as Faust.

A CONTEMPORARY DESCRIBING BEEBE

The half-mile dive climaxed Beebe's already long career, but for the rest of his life he would continue to look and wonder. In 1961 at the age of 84, on a walk at the New York Zoological Society's tropical field station in Trinidad, he saw six monarch butterflies going to roost together. Referring to his childhood journal entry of 71 years earlier, he now made a new observation about monarch butterflies: "The northern form is noted for its migrations, whereas the Trinidad insect is prone to roost in company but does not migrate."

William Beebe died in Trinidad the year after he saw those six butterflies. In a final gesture toward the curse of fame, he willed his journals to an associate and asked that no one write his biography too soon after his death. The man who had made a log of his life had closed the book.

This story is based on correspondence between William Beebe and the National Geographic Society and on the explorer's published works, particularly his book Half Mile Down. *More than 25 years after Beebe's death, his private journals remain in the hands of a friend, the contents undisclosed.*

301

Out of the Cradle

By Jonathan B. Tourtellot

At ease in the void, Bruce McCandless becomes history's first human satellite in 1984, orbiting untethered near his space shuttle. The jet backpack gives astronauts maneuvering ability needed for such tasks as repairing satellites and building a space station. Soviet stations Salyut and Mir have become the first permanent footholds in a realm opened to humankind in 1961, when Russian Yuri Gagarin made a single orbit of Earth.

I*t is 1986. The team is worried. It has taken years to prepare for this flyby of Uranus, and now a balky wheel on the Voyager 2 spacecraft is threatening to fail. Dr. Lonne Lane and his Photopolarimetry team, one of eleven Voyager science groups, wait in anxious expectation at the Jet Propulsion Laboratory in Pasadena. Except for TV monitors and computer printers, their fluorescent-lit workroom at JPL could pass for any modern office. But their thoughts are two billion miles away, at Uranus. Radio signals from Earth take 5$\frac{1}{2}$ hours for a round trip, too long to test the repair command sent to Voyager. If it hasn't worked, the wheel will block part of the photopolarimeter sensor. Near one monitor a bottle of champagne waits, unopened.*

It was 1957. President Dwight D. Eisenhower was playing lots of golf; Ford had introduced its new Edsel; "A White Sport Coat—and a Pink Carnation" was high on the charts. America was on top of the world.

October 4. Scientists from around the globe had gathered in Washington, D. C., to discuss the progress of the International Geophysical Year. Many were attending a Soviet Embassy reception when an American geophysicist left the room, returned, and tapped his glass for attention.

"I am informed by the *New York Times*," he announced as the guests fell silent, "that a satellite is in orbit at an elevation of 900 kilometers. I wish to congratulate our Soviet colleagues on their achievement."

Sputnik! From Western newspapers and airwaves a hubbub arose. How powerful was the rocket that could do this? That Sputnik signified the dawn of space exploration received little note; Americans had missiles on their minds. From backyards they could watch the spark of Soviet might sailing their evening skies, and its wake rocked the nation. DEMOCRATS CHARGE ADMINISTRATION WITH FAILURE TO EQUAL SOVIET, read a *Times* headline. A political cartoon portrayed a Sputnik hurtling past a soaring golf ball. An Eisenhower official hit back, belittling the "bauble in the sky."

Amid some embarrassingly fiery launch failures, the U. S., aided by German rocketry genius Wernher von Braun, managed to hoist Explorer 1 into orbit on January 31, 1958. Post-Sputnik American industry began tooling up for rocketry, post-Sputnik schools for science and math. Displeased with military control of the space effort, Eisenhower established the civilian National Aeronautics and Space Administration: NASA. The space race was on.

Why explore space? The answers lie as much in history as in the future. In 1957 the answer was national security. America went into space to counter Russia—as England sent Drake into the Pacific to counter Spain. And where satellites went, people would follow.

But no one knew whether space travel was even survivable. Would

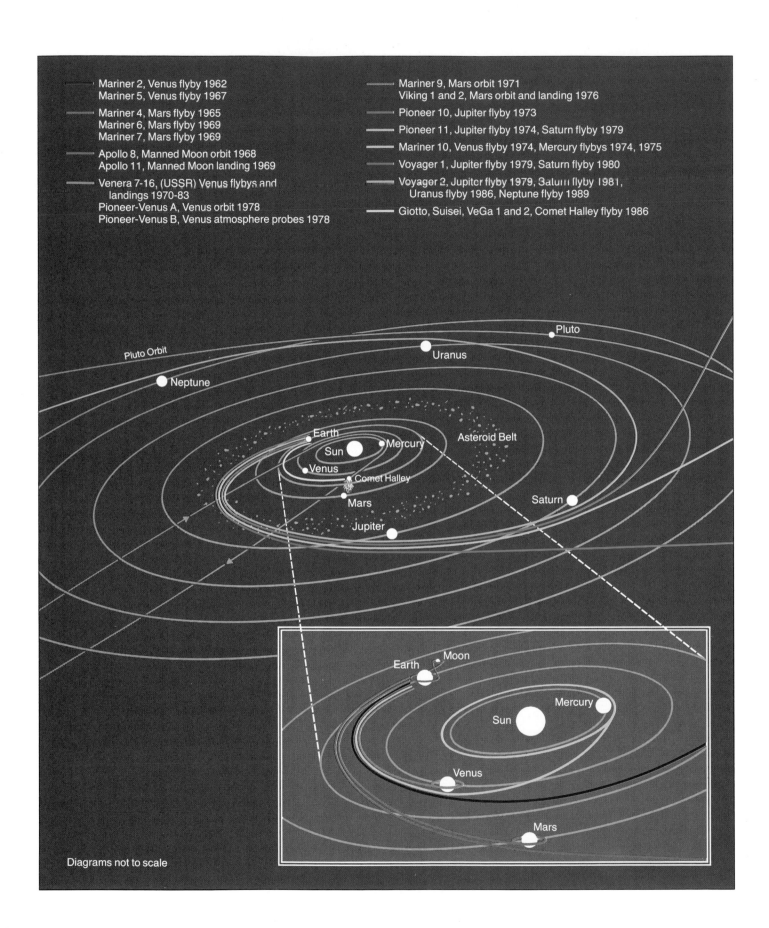

Mariner 2, Venus flyby 1962
Mariner 5, Venus flyby 1967

Mariner 4, Mars flyby 1965
Mariner 6, Mars flyby 1969
Mariner 7, Mars flyby 1969

Apollo 8, Manned Moon orbit 1968
Apollo 11, Manned Moon landing 1969

Venera 7-16, (USSR) Venus flybys and
   landings 1970-83
Pioneer-Venus A, Venus orbit 1978
Pioneer-Venus B, Venus atmosphere probes 1978

Mariner 9, Mars orbit 1971
Viking 1 and 2, Mars orbit and landing 1976

Pioneer 10, Jupiter flyby 1973

Pioneer 11, Jupiter flyby 1974, Saturn flyby 1979

Mariner 10, Venus flyby 1974, Mercury flybys 1974, 1975

Voyager 1, Jupiter flyby 1979, Saturn flyby 1980

Voyager 2, Jupiter flyby 1979, Saturn flyby 1981,
   Uranus flyby 1986, Neptune flyby 1989

Giotto, Suisei, VeGa 1 and 2, Comet Halley flyby 1986

Pluto

Pluto Orbit

Uranus

Neptune

Earth

Sun

Mercury

Asteroid Belt

Venus

Comet Halley

Mars

Saturn

Jupiter

Earth

Moon

Mercury

Sun

Venus

Mars

Diagrams not to scale

Robot spacecraft have spiraled out from Earth to explore the solar system since the early 1960s: U. S. Mariner and Soviet Venera probes to the inner planets; two U. S. Viking landers on Mars; and European, Japanese, and Russian probes to Comet Halley. Apollo 8 made the first manned trip out of Earth orbit in 1968. In the 1970s, the gas-giant planets of the outer solar system were so arrayed that each could act

as a gravitational sling, speeding spacecraft from one world on to the next—four planets in all for Voyager 2.

A replica of Russia's trailblazing satellite, Sputnik 1, draws stares in Moscow. Satellites and space shuttles in low orbits circle the Earth every 90 minutes or so. Much farther out, communications and weather satellites can take 24 hours per orbit, and so seem to hang motionless over the Equator.

Sputnik 1
Launched 10/4/57

Mercury-Atlas 6 (John Glenn)
Launched 2/20/62

Space Shuttle
First launched 4/12/81

Communications Satellite
(geosynchronous orbit)

Military Satellite
(polar orbit)

g forces after lift-off crush the astronaut? Would cosmic rays fry him? Would weightlessness kill him? The Russians, aided by their own rocketry genius, Sergei Korolev, proved otherwise in April 1961. Yuri Gagarin, first man in space, made one full orbit and landed safely—and did it a month before the U. S. sent Alan Shepard on his short suborbital hop.

In May 1961, John F. Kennedy—launched into the presidency himself partly by Sputnik—spoke before Congress, calling on America to "commit itself to achieving the goal, before this decade is out, of landing a man on the Moon and returning him safely to the Earth." When, within a year, John Glenn made his three-orbit flight in a Mercury capsule, the goal began to look less improbable.

But Soviet firsts did not end with Sputnik or Gagarin. They kept coming: First probe to reach the Moon, 1959; first probe to see the back side of the Moon, a month later; first two spacecraft to meet in orbit, 1962; first woman in space—Valentina Tereshkova—1963; first multiple crew, 1964; first walk in space, 1965.

U. S. feats were less spectacular, but methodical. The Mercury program launched six lone astronauts. By 1965 pairs of astronauts in Gemini craft were practicing docking and space walks. A three-man Apollo would go to the Moon.

But in 1967 a fire inside Apollo 1 killed three astronauts during a launchpad test. Almost two years passed before a redesigned Apollo

made its first manned flight in Earth orbit. Russia, too, lost momentum when a cosmonaut died on landing, only months after the Apollo fire.

And suddenly it all changed.

On December 21, 1968, a Saturn V, largest rocket ever built, thundered up from Cape Kennedy, Florida. To make up for lost time, NASA had decided to send Apollo 8 to circle the Moon ten times and return. By December 24, Frank Borman, James Lovell, and William Anders, the first men to leave Earth for another world, were in lunar orbit.

There they pointed their TV camera at the window and made a Christmas Eve broadcast. As the ancient, alien craters slid by beneath them and across the television screens of Earth, their thin radio-borne voices began to read: *In the beginning God created the heaven and the earth. . . .* And people listened to the words once spoken in a language of shepherds, 3,000 years earlier, and stared at their TV sets, some shaking their heads and saying "I don't believe it, I just don't believe it," but believing it.

The team has a new worry. Their photopolarimeter, which detects the way things reflect light, is to record a star's light as it passes through Uranus's rings. As Voyager's motion aligns the star behind the rings, the touchy wheel must work. If it does, Voyager will radio back data on the rings. Now comes news that rain may keep an antenna in Spain from picking up those faint signals.

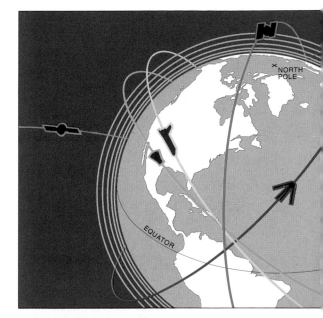

Thundering aloft in 1962, a Mercury-Atlas rocket blasts astronaut John Glenn into history as the first American to orbit the Earth. Project Mercury's six flights in the early 1960s launched the U. S. effort to reach the Moon. Astronauts rode atop liquid-fuel rockets invented in 1926, when space pioneer Robert Goddard sent his first crude prototype soaring 41 feet over a field in Auburn, Massachusetts.

It was July 21, 1969. Once again the thin radio-borne words reach Earth from the Moon, now from the lunar surface. "That's one small step for [a] man"—history has filled in the "a" Neil Armstrong's voice-activated mike may have lost—"one giant leap for mankind." Apollo 11 had won the never declared race to the Moon.

Fears of Russia forgotten, newspapers bannered the sheer triumph of exploration, a fantasy of the ages at last fulfilled. MEN WALK ON MOON roared the usually restrained *New York Times* in 72-point type, the largest in its history. A front-page poem by Archibald MacLeish honored the first footfall upon the "beaches" of the Moon. On inside pages the doubters still doubted, but now they questioned not America's lack of initiative, but its direction. Was this worth the cost? they asked.

Why explore the Moon? In 1969 it was for national prestige, just as when a young republic with 26 stars on its flag sent the Wilkes expedition off into the Pacific, for science, yes, but also for pride, to take a place among the questing nations of the world. Now that flag, with 50 stars, stood stiff on the windless Moon.

But there was something more this time: unexpected perspectives, brought by space travel itself. When Kennedy issued his challenge, no orbiting camera had yet revealed an Earth new to human eyes—fragile, dynamic, whole; Telstar had not yet linked televisions oceans apart; Apollo 8 had not filled those TV

A helicopter winches astronaut Alan Shepard from the sea just four minutes after his splashdown in the Atlantic. The smooth recovery capped his 302-mile suborbital flight in 1961, America's first manned space mission.

Requiring "more alterations than a bridal gown," pressurized flight suits (right) were tested against submersion, heat, and g forces. Astronauts wore vented long johns beneath to keep cool.

screens with its Christmas card of a living world rising over a lifeless one.

"O, a meaning!" wrote MacLeish: "over us on these silent beaches the bright earth, presence among us."

In every building on the campuslike grounds of JPL, even in the cafeteria, TV monitors display each new image coming from Voyager—the rings, a moon, the Uranian atmosphere—every picture new to history. The Imaging team's pictures attract throngs of reporters. The Photopolarimetry team can claim no such glamor; they hope only for strings of numbers. Yet such prosaic data are the brick and mortar of scientific exploration, building a foundation of knowledge for uses yet unknown.

It was 1976. Viking 1 landed on Mars. Cameras panned; sensors tasted the thin carbon dioxide atmosphere; and a tiny shovel extended itself to sample soil for a test, *the* test: Was there life on another planet?

Planetary exploration had begun only six months after John Glenn's three orbits. The U. S. Mariner 2, launched in 1962, made the first successful flyby of Venus, sending back hints of the ferocious heat trapped inside its thick atmosphere. Soviet Venera probes survived the 800°F climate long enough to radio back pictures of a rocky, baked surface.

More U. S. Mariner probes flew by Venus, and one went on to Mercury. Many others mapped Mars, in preparation for the Viking program.

Viking involved two orbiters, two

Making a rendezvous 185 miles high, Gemini 6 looks down on the Pacific and on Gemini 7, launched 11 days earlier. The two spacecraft sometimes flew only one foot apart. From 1964 to 1966, astronauts on ten manned Gemini missions honed skills such as rendezvous and docking—the kind of multiple-craft maneuvers needed to land men on the Moon and bring them home again.

June 1965: Edward White enjoys the first U. S. space walk—"extra-vehicular activity" in the poetry of NASA. A similar feat by Russian Alexei Leonov, three months earlier, persuaded NASA to let White leave his two-man Gemini 4 capsule, instead of simply standing in the hatchway. Tethered by a 25-foot lifeline, White cavorted outside for 20 minutes, propelling himself with a hand-held jet gun.

landers, and an army of 10,000 people. Deployed by program chief James Martin, a John-Wayne-like figure with a head for tactics, squadrons of technicians and subcontractors readied the invasion of Mars by remote control—the most complex exploration of another planet ever.

Why explore the planets? In 1976 it was for science, just as when an eager Alexander von Humboldt leaped off his ship and onto a Venezuelan beach—landfall on South America, his new planet—and plunged a thermometer into the sand.

Inside Viking 1, a pocket-size laboratory analyzed its shovelful of soil, and found ambiguous results, more typical of chemical reactions than biological ones. Partway around the martian globe, Viking 2 found the same. Life? Question unresolved.

And staying that way for a while. In the late 1970s something else took precedence: A rare alignment of the planets that would enable a probe to make a "grand tour" of the outer solar system—a once-in-180-year opportunity, not to be missed.

It almost was. The heroes of this exploration faced not stormy seas but the vexing halls of government. Months of argument and negotiation yielded funds, but only to explore Jupiter and Saturn—first by two simple Pioneer scouting probes, then by a pair of more complex Voyagers. So engineers performed their own heroics: They jury-rigged and reprogrammed and improvised so that Voyager 2 could continue on past

Saturn to Uranus and then Neptune.

The Voyagers were to make the most sweeping exploration in history. The probes were to reconnoiter ten new worlds—four giant planets and their six major moons—not to mention dozens of smaller satellites.
· Somehow it worked. At Jupiter, Voyager discovered a ring girding the equator, centuries-old storms churning the atmosphere, volcanoes fountaining from the moon Io, and an iced-over ocean sheathing the moon Europa; at Saturn, it found rings—not the three that telescopes saw, but hundreds, shepherded by dark moonlets—and on the giant moon Titan an atmosphere like that of primordial Earth. From Saturn, Voyager 1, having inspected Titan rather than aiming for Uranus, sailed off toward interstellar space; Voyager 2 sped on to Uranus.

Voyager's discoveries inspired a trick question around NASA: Which planet have we learned the most about from space? Answer: Earth.

Much of that knowledge comes from low Earth orbit, of course— from manned laboratories, shuttle missions, and satellites. Satellites for oceanography, for geology, for climate, for radar-mapping, for agriculture, and satellites that guide explorers below. An orbiting navigation system helped Robert Ballard's team find the *Titanic*. Satellite radar has discovered Maya ruins and ancient riverbeds in the Sahara.

But the other planets teach us of Earth, too, placing it in the scheme of things. On Venus we see a runaway greenhouse effect, on Mars a runaway ice age. Io's surface is more volcanic; Titan's atmosphere more pristine. The ice of Comet Halley is older than life itself on Earth.

And not by chance, it seems. When European, Soviet, and Japanese probes looked at Halley, they found the same dark material Voyager was seeing a lot of in the moons and rings of the outer solar system: organic, carbonaceous matter—the stuff of life. Comets carried it inward to the sun-warmed Earth. Life born of comet dust! Some experts now ask if life might even exist in the carbon-rich outer worlds, too, far from the sun. If deep-ocean vent colonies that explorers found on Earth don't need sunlight, then how about a place like Europa, under the ice?

At JPL, Lane's team stares at the monitors. The rain has held off in Spain. Voyager's signals are now winging toward Earth at 186,000 miles per second. The 2-hour, 45-minute trip should be about to end. A timekeeper studies his watch. "The data should be on the ground—" he swings his arm down, "NOW!" As the screens fill with numbers, cheers fill the room.

It was 1986. Six months after the shuttle *Challenger* exploded, the Smithsonian's air and space museum was still the most popular museum in the world. In front of a Mars display a mother and her teenage daughter were reading about Mars' deep cold,

Apollo 17 astronaut Harrison Schmitt revels in a geologist's paradise as he investigates a 50-foot boulder in the Moon's Taurus-Littrow Valley. Like Apollo 15 and 16, this last U. S. lunar expedition, in 1972, brought a lunar rover (below, at right). Explorers covered 22.5 miles in it, studying terrain, collecting samples, and deploying scientific instruments.

The Victorian baby buggy (opposite) is actually Lunokhod 1, a robot vehicle landed by the Russians in 1970. Di-rected by earthbound controllers, it crawled for 6.5 miles, sampling rocks and soil and sending information home.

Lunar dust scooped up by Apollo explorers proved to be capable of making concrete stronger than terrestrial types—good news for future lunar-base builders. Apollo's rocks failed to verify any single pre-existing theory about how the Moon formed, and led to a new one: that a huge object hit the Earth over 4 billion years ago, ejecting debris that coalesced into the Moon.

OVERLEAF: *High above Baja California in 1984, the space shuttle Challenger launches the first satellite ever built for recovery, LDEF-1. Challenger exploded after launch in January 1986, leaving it to other shuttles to retrieve the LDEF, a unit for testing how lengthy periods in space affect various materials. Shuttles may someday service a permanent space station made from substances that prove most durable.*

Scene from the IMAX/OMNIMAX film, The Dream is Alive
Smithsonian Institution and Lockheed Corporation 1985

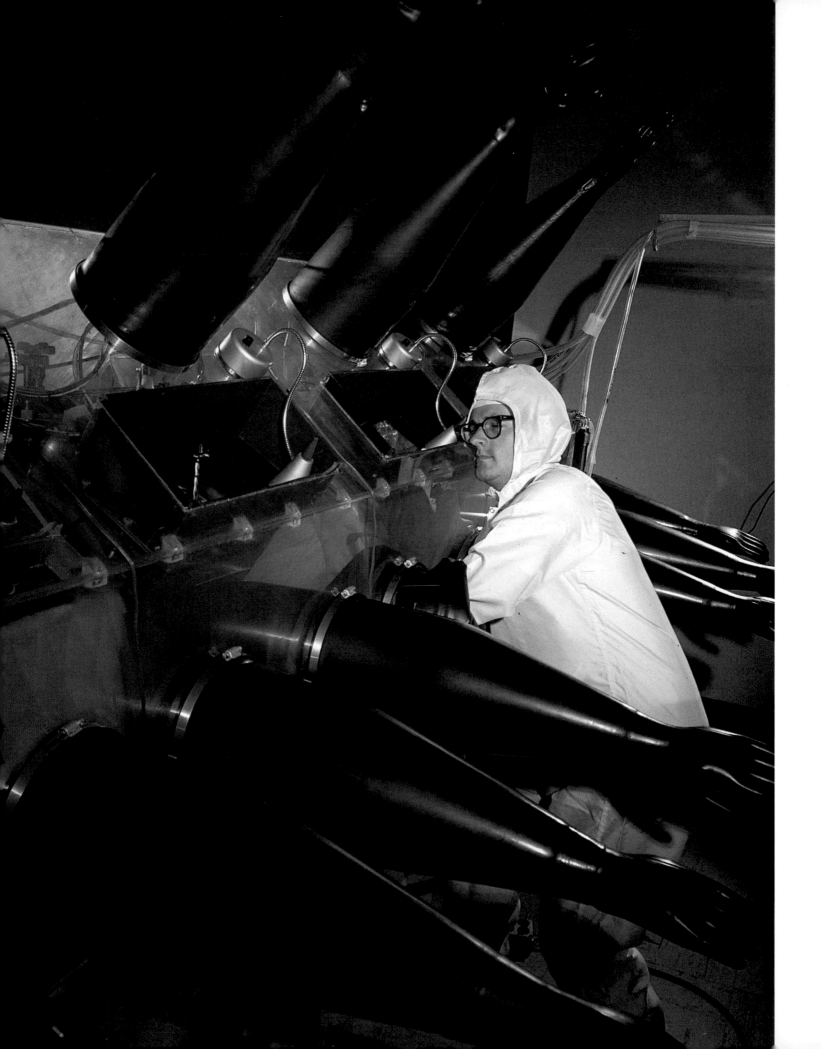

wisp-thin atmosphere, and apparent lifelessness.

"Not a very good place for a vacation," remarked the mother.

"Not yet," said the daughter.

Why explore space? In 1986, it was for all the reasons since Sputnik, but also for dreams. For the dreamers the roots of space exploration reach deep into time. Not since early humans left the Rift Valley in Africa has such an uninhabited vastness called. And just in time, say thinkers like Freeman Dyson, a physicist who argues that Earth, with no white spots left on its map, is "getting too homogenized. It's very hard for cultural minorities to survive. We're just too close together, whereas there's a lot of room out there."

Setbacks do not daunt visionaries. If a shuttle explodes, if discovery transforms the once-imagined jungles of Venus into an oven, or the canals of Mars to dust, the dreams live on. As Frémont went West with Manifest Destiny singing in his soul, or Livingstone to Africa with Christ singing in his, so the space dreamers seek the stars, singing of hope.

Their songs count, too. Inspired by the stories of Jules Verne, Konstantin Tsiolkovsky wrote, "Earth is the cradle of humanity, but humanity cannot remain in the cradle forever," and he wrote it in tsarist Russia in 1899. Tsiolkovsky was the first man to realize that rockets were the way into space. His research helped Korolev put Sputnik into orbit. And Korolev's rival, von Braun,

was inspired to seek the Moon by another visionary—H. G. Wells.

Between sips of champagne, team members laugh and chatter about what the data may hold. Relief and triumph under the fluorescents. Time will publish no pictures of their graphs, KCBS will air no film at 11. It doesn't matter. They have been to Uranus.

Each morning during the Uranus encounter, the science teams at JPL gathered in private to discuss what new data Voyager had transmitted, what it meant, what to tell the eager press. "Instant science," the methodical scientists complained—but not too much. This was their hour.

They jammed into a conference room under TV monitors now revealing the moon Miranda. The Imaging team reported first: "One new satellite and one new ring, about half way between the Epsilon and Delta rings." Ultraviolet Spectroscopy

Ear to the sky, a Deep Space Network antenna in the Mojave desert picks up signals from Voyager 2 at Uranus, 2 billion miles away—a feat comparable to seeing a 20-watt light bulb from across the Atlantic. The signals carry encoded images such as this nightside view of the huge seventh planet. Voyager discovered that Uranus's smooth clouds may conceal a great ocean of searingly hot water.

threw graphs on a screen: atmospheric density as expected. Photopolarimetry—and Lonne Lane rose to report among first findings that the Gamma Ring was only 0.6 kilometers wide, "much, much smaller than ground data indicated." "Does that mean it's denser, since it's much narrower than people thought?" "Possibly." Another brick, mortar to come. Reporting moved on.

Today the two Pioneers and two Voyagers continue outward, heading for the stars. The relic craft are expected to survive for a billion years, long enough to circle the Milky Way galaxy four times. They are the first artifacts ever to leave our home star, bottled messages cast into the widest ocean of all. The dreamers made sure they carried diagrams, photographs, even an LP record of earthly sounds —all to greet any alien race, perhaps unborn, that finds them.

From here the story of exploration moves into science fiction's realm, where Yuri Gagarin was only a generation ago. Will people someday follow Voyager to the stars? They would measure their journeys, longer than any Captain Cook dreamed of, not in years and leagues, but in decades and light-years. Yet for every island Cook charted, the dreamers argue, there waits a galaxy; for every grain of sand he saw, a world.

Such starfarers would still share one thing with Cook—that same thrilling and frightening and hopeful question known to all explorers:

What's out there?

317

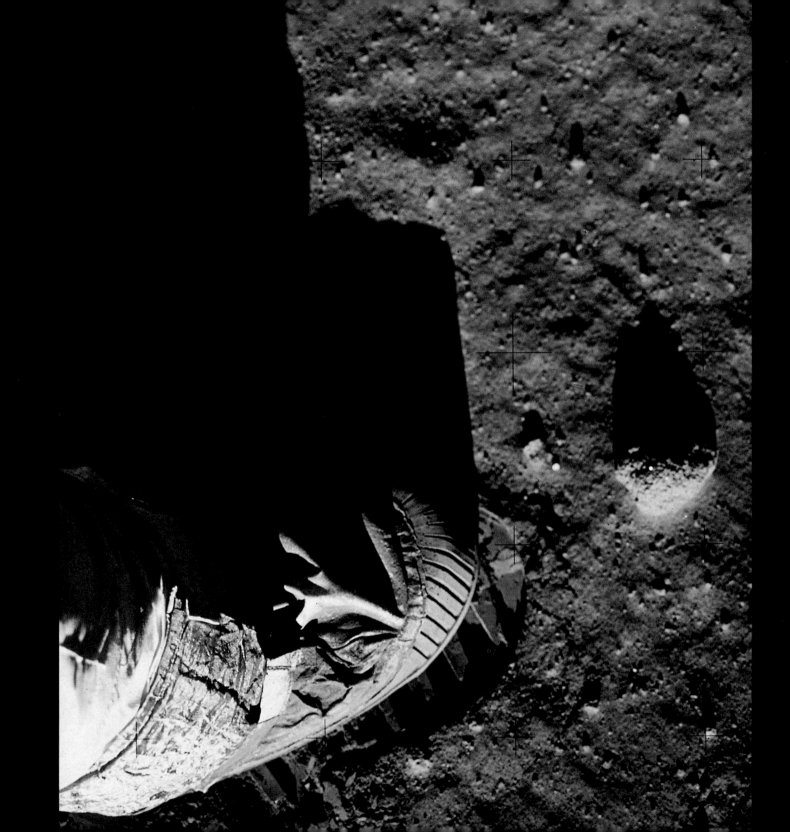

Neil Armstrong
Edwin Aldrin, Jr.
Michael Collins

By Michael Collins

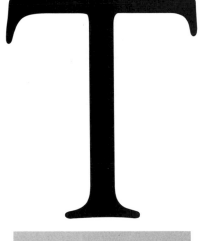

A dream fulfilled by Apollo 11: Neil Armstrong's photograph of his foot on the Moon, July 20, 1969.

The big rocket engine used to wake my wife and me in the middle of the night. Its test stand was 17 miles away, across the dry lake bed at Edwards Air Force Base, California, but what's 17 miles to a Saturn V engine? Its deep roar rumbled right through our bedroom windows and rattled every teacup in our kitchen cabinet.

At that time, in the early sixties, I was just a test pilot and had no idea that before the end of the decade I'd be strapped atop a cluster of five of these monsters, ready to escape Earth's gravity and begin a three-day coast to the Moon.

A voyage of a quarter of a million miles begins with a thousand different steps. As with any complicated expedition, success depends on the details—all of them. In addition to the gigantic Saturn V, tall as a 35-story building, smaller but more densely packed machines had to be designed, tested, built, and filled with hundreds of items of complex equipment and a highly trained crew. This process took the better part of a decade, and at its height employed over 400,000 Americans.

Two of them would go with me: Edwin ("Buzz") Aldrin, our most learned pilot, and Neil Armstrong, the premier test pilot in the Apollo program, who would be first to step on the Moon. A good choice—Neil made decisions slowly and well, rolling them around in his mouth like fine wine and swallowing at the last minute.

By July 1969, six months before John F. Kennedy's deadline of "landing a man on the Moon," we were ready to give it a try. Personally I figured our chance of success was not much better than 50-50. Our trip would be complicated, and therefore fragile. I thought of it as a long daisy chain in which any severed link could result in failure, and perhaps death. Probably not my own, because I wasn't going all the way to the Moon's surface. As pilot of the command module, I would remain in lunar orbit while Neil and Buzz descended to the surface in the lunar

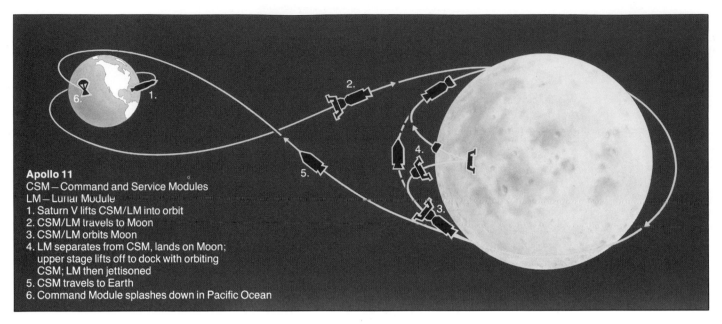

Apollo 11
CSM — Command and Service Modules
LM — Lunar Module
1. Saturn V lifts CSM/LM into orbit
2. CSM/LM travels to Moon
3. CSM/LM orbits Moon
4. LM separates from CSM, lands on Moon; upper stage lifts off to dock with orbiting CSM; LM then jettisoned
5. CSM travels to Earth
6. Command Module splashes down in Pacific Ocean

Not since Adam has a human known such solitude as Mike Collins is experiencing. . . .
<small>NASA OFFICIAL</small>

module. At our preflight press conference reporters kept asking whether I would feel terribly alone or frightened while orbiting the Moon by myself. I didn't know yet. I did have a secret fear, but not about that.

We had plenty enough to worry about. We were utterly dependent on the proper functioning of a frightening series of machines: the Saturn V, to reach Earth orbit and then escape velocity; the service module, for course corrections and braking into lunar orbit; the lunar module descent stage, to decelerate to a landing; the pressure suit and backpack, for extravehicular forays; the lunar module ascent stage, to blast off and rendezvous with the command module; the service module again, to escape the Moon and correct the trajectory to Earth; and parachutes, to bring our command module safely to splashdown.

Of all these links, the weakest, I thought, was Neil and Buzz's ascent and return to me in the command module. We had practiced this rendezvous over and over in the simulator, and it was a piece of cake as long as everything took place precisely on schedule, but it was terribly unforgiving of small deviations. Ideally, I would be in a circular orbit 69 miles over their heads when they lifted off. They would shoot for a lower, 52-mile orbit, calculated to give them a leisurely catch-up rate—but not too leisurely, because their oxygen was limited. A piece of cake. But suppose, for a host of possible reasons, Neil and Buzz were late taking off. Then we would have to try some new, untested orbit, in hopes of linking up before their oxygen ran out—the stuff of nightmares.

By launch day I am more than a little tense about rendezvous and a hundred other things, but eager to abandon the simulator and reenter the real world of spaceflight—nearly three years after my Earth-orbiting Gemini flight. I am everlastingly grateful that I have flown in space before. Still, Gemini 10 was a local affair. This Apollo 11, on the other hand, is serious business, with the ghost of John F. Kennedy riding with us in full view of a watchful world. Superimposed on the normal pres-

Edwin Aldrin, Jr., deploying foil for sampling solar-wind particles.

sure—the nagging worry of "What have I overlooked?"—is the imperative *not* to fail, to distill American expertise into eight flawless days, to drape that daisy chain around the Moon and return it to Earth.

A spaceflight begins when your helmet locks in place. From that moment on, no air will be breathed, only pure oxygen; no human voice heard, unless electronically piped in. The world can still be seen, but not smelled, or heard, or felt, or tasted. As Neil, Buzz, and I get out of a small van at the base of the launch tower, we can see it's a clear day, and we are told it's hot already, even at 6:45 a.m., a scorcher in the making. Usually this place is a beehive of activity, but now only a handful of us are left with our steaming tanks of liquid hydrogen and oxygen. A small elevator takes us 320 feet up to our command module, *Columbia*. I pause on the narrow walkway there to savor the view and consider the moment. If I cover my right eye I can see only the unsullied beach, the Florida of Ponce de León, and beyond it the ocean. If I cover my left I see the United States of America embodied in the most colossal pile of machinery ever assembled. I have to confess that the explorer in me pulls me toward the beach, but I have made my commitment to the machine. There will be time for beaches after the Moon, I hope.

At ignition the Saturn V gives us a little surprise. Instead of the hideous din one would expect, it is merely noisy inside. But the motion! As we leave the ground I feel our engines swiveling left and right, keeping us poised in delicate balance against crosswinds and sloshing fuel tanks. It is like a nervous novice driving a wide car down a narrow alley and jerking the wheel spasmodically back and forth. Still, the Saturn V is a gentle giant and pushes us back in our couches with an acceleration only slightly over four times that of gravity. Its first stage empties and separates at an altitude of 52 miles. Five more engines in the second stage take over. High above atmospheric disturbances now, our climb is smooth as glass. At 115 miles, the single third stage engine ignites and drives us down range, increasing our speed to the 17,500 miles per hour needed for orbit. The third stage is rough, buzzing and rattling, and I'm relieved when it shuts down. It is less than 12 minutes from launch.

Now we have an orbit and a half to make sure everything is operating properly before we reignite the third stage engine and commit ourselves to leaving the Earth's gravitational field. It all checks out, and Mission Control gives us their blessing in the esoteric patois of spaceflight: "Apollo 11, this is Houston. You are go for TLI"—translunar injection.

The burn is over in six minutes. We are 1,400 miles out now, climbing like a dingbat—six miles a second, far faster than a rifle bullet. Yet it is hard to tell that by looking out the window. We are entering a slow-motion domain where time and distance seem to mean more than speed. Distance from home especially. For the first time I know what "outward bound" means. We cannot watch the slowly shrinking Earth for long, because we must distribute the sun's heat by turning our craft broadside to it and rotating slowly, like a chicken on a barbecue spit.

Things are quiet on board *Columbia.* Neil and Buzz spend a lot of time studying their lunar module checklists, while I keep house. For three days between Earth and Moon we are in continual sunshine, but I notice that if I look downsun, and shield my eyes from all light, I can see stars. In this strange cislunar region we keep our watches and our circadian rhythm on Houston time. When sleeping, we use light nylon bags below our couches. It is pleasant to doze off with no pressure anywhere on the body—just floating and falling all the way to the Moon.

As we approach our destination we stop our barbecuing motion and swing around for our first closeup look at the Moon. The Moon I have known all my life, that flat, small yellow disk in the sky, has gone, replaced by the most awesome sphere I have ever seen. It is huge. It fills our windows, its belly bulging out toward us so that I feel I can almost reach out and touch it. The Sun, eclipsed behind it, sends light cascading around the lunar rim. Part of the Moon's face below us is in deep shadow, but another region basks in whitish light reflected from the Earth. This earthshine, as it's called, is considerably brighter than moonlight on Earth. The reddish yellow of the sun's corona, the blanched white of earthshine, and the pure black of the star-studded sky all combine to cast a bluish glow over the Moon. This cool, magnificent sphere hangs there ominously, a formidable presence without sound or motion, and issues us no invitation to invade its domain.

We brake into lunar orbit, from which we can examine the far side of the Moon, never visible from Earth. Unlike the front, it has no flat maria, or seas. It is all highlands, densely pocked by 4.6 billion years of meteoroid bombardment. Back over the near side it is just past dawn in the Sea of Tranquillity, and the sun's rays strike the landing site at such a shallow angle that craters cast long, jagged shadows. I don't see any place smooth enough to park a baby buggy, much less a lunar module.

Despite years of studying photographs of the Moon, I nevertheless find it a shock actually to be here and see the vivid contrast between Earth and Moon. One has to see the second world up close to truly appreciate the first. This withered, sun-seared peach pit out my window offers no competition to Earth's verdant valleys and misty waterfalls.

Neil and Buzz board their landing craft and undock. They have named it *Eagle,* but it doesn't look like one. The creature now suspended upside down outside my window is spindly and ungainly, with four legs jutting out above a body that has neither symmetry nor grace. Designed only for the vacuum of space, its shape ignores all streamlining rules, with antennas and other accessories stuck on at odd angles.

When *Eagle* begins its descent I am left alone with my thoughts in *Columbia.* Two hours per orbit, 48 minutes of which I am behind the Moon and unable to communicate with anyone. A census would count three billion plus two humans on one side of the Moon and one plus God only knows what on the other. Recalling reporters' questions about feeling lonely, though, I now know the answer is "absolutely

322

Lunar module returning to link up with author Collins in the command module.

not." I am accustomed to being alone in a flying machine and I like it—the more unusual the surroundings, the better. This is the ultimate solo flight. Far from fear, I feel satisfaction, confidence, almost exultation, as if I had a superhuman ability to cope with whatever might arise.

I am over the near side as the landing begins, so I can hear Buzz calling out altitude and velocity to Neil, whose eyes are glued to the window. "Forty feet" says Buzz. "Thirty seconds" says Houston—the fuel remaining. Better get it down, Neil. "Contact light!" calls out Buzz. "We copy you down, *Eagle*," says Houston, half statement and half question. Neil will later explain he was overflying a boulder field, trying to find the best place to land. Savoring the wine. Now he confirms, "Tranquillity Base here. The *Eagle* has landed." I am over the far side hours later when Neil speaks his historic first words on the Moon, but in radio range again as Buzz hops around like a kangaroo and Neil chats with President Nixon. They also gather a precious cargo of Moon rocks.

It is morning again and this, as far as I'm concerned, is the day of reckoning. As the moment of lift-off nears, I become more and more nervous. *Columbia* has no landing gear; I cannot rescue them from the surface. If they limp up into a lopsided orbit, I may not be able to catch them. For the past six months *that* has been my secret terror: to have to leave them here and return to Earth alone. If I must, I will, but. . . . It would almost be better not to have that option.

Buzz counts down, and now they are off! For the seven minutes of their powered ascent, I barely breathe. There is no backup for their engine; it must work. After much fiddling with my sextant, I finally see *Eagle*, first as a tiny blinking light in the darkness, and then as a golden bug in the light of sunrise, gliding through the crater fields below. Reassuringly they grow in my window, easing to a stop just 50 feet away.

As the Earth pops up over the horizon I snap a couple of pictures. I can't see Neil or Buzz, or the three billion on the small blue blob just behind them, but I know they are there—every human being in the entire universe, framed in my window. Now my rendezvous worries are over. I can throw away the book I have clipped to the front of my pressure suit, the book with 18 emergency variations on our rendezvous scheme. God knows we are still a long way from home. There are still fragile links in the quarter million miles of daisy chain ahead of us. I must dock with *Eagle*, and Neil and Buzz must transfer themselves and their two boxes of rocks back into *Columbia*. The service module engine behind me must ignite when I ask it, or we will become a permanent satellite of the Moon. A couple of days from now we must jettison the service module and slice into Earth's atmosphere at precisely the correct angle. Our parachutes must open. Yet despite all that, for the first time I feel we are going to carry it off. I can see it all out my window now, our beautiful home planet and my two compatriots, successfully returned to me. From now on it will be all downhill—for there they are!

Michael Collins continues to promote exploration, as a trustee of the National Geographic Society. His book Carrying the Fire *tells of Apollo 11's trip.*

Welcome home: Armstrong, Collins, and Aldrin waving to fans amid the blizzard of a ticker-tape parade, one of the largest in New York history.

"Aiming at the stars"... is a problem to occupy generations, so that no matter how much progress one makes, there is always the thrill of just beginning.
ROBERT GODDARD, 1932

Explorers by the Ages

This list presents a selection of significant explorers, with their life dates, listed alphabetically for each of four major eras of exploration.

In the entries, you will find the regions in which they explored, their nationalities, what they did, and the years during which they did it. Explorer teams like Lewis and Clark are listed together.

Early Quests (3000 B.C.-A.D. 1000)

Alexander the Great (356-323 B.C.)
Asia: Greek; pushed into Egypt, Syria, Persia, and eastward to Indus River (334-323 B.C.).

Saint Brendan (ca A.D. 484-578)
Atlantic: Irish; sailed to Hebrides, Wales, and Brittany (A.D. 565-573). Legends say he reached North America.

Chang Ch'ien (?-114 B.C.)
Asia: Chinese; explored China's hinterlands and opened trade along Silk Road, primary means of East-West exchange for centuries.

Erik the Red (10th century A.D.)
Atlantic: Norwegian; explored Greenland (A.D. 982-85); established colony there (A.D. 986).

Leif Eriksson (ca A.D. 970-1020)
Atlantic: Norse; sailed from Greenland to Labrador, Newfoundland or Nova Scotia, and perhaps farther south (ca A.D. 1000).

Eudoxus (2nd century B.C.)
Asia: Greek; explored Arabian Sea and made two voyages to India; disappeared while attempting to circumnavigate Africa.

Hanno (5th century B.C.)
Africa: Carthaginian; explored from Carthage, colonizing down west African coast to Gambia, Sierra Leone, maybe Cameroon (ca 450 B.C.).

Pytheas (4th century B.C.)
Atlantic: Greek; sailed to Britain, Orkney Islands, and perhaps Iceland or Norway (325 B.C.).

Scylax (6th century B.C.)
Asia: Greek; followed Indus River to Indian Ocean, and home via Red Sea (ca 510 B.C.).

The World Discovered (1000-1600)

Diego de Almagro (1475-1538)
South America: Spanish; joined Pizarro in conquest of Peru (1532-35); explored Andes Mountains of northern Chile (1535-37).

Vasco Núñez de Balboa (1475-1519)
Central America: Spanish; explored Panama; first European to see Pacific Ocean (1513).

Álvar Núñez Cabeza de Vaca (ca 1490-1560)
Americas: Spanish; wandered Southwest in North America (1528-1536); explored southern Brazil and discovered Iguazú Falls (1541-44).

John Cabot (ca 1450-1499)
Canada: Italian sailing for British; searched for North American route to Asia, landed on Canada's east coast, claimed it for Britain (1497).

Pedro Álvares Cabral (1467-1520)
South America: Portuguese; en route to India, sailed down west coast of Africa, swung southwestward and discovered Brazil (1500-1501).

Jacques Cartier (1491-1557)
Canada: French; penetrated Gulf of St. Lawrence in search of Northwest Passage (1534-35).

Cheng Ho (15th century)
Asia, Africa: Chinese; sailed to Japan, India, and eastern Africa (1405-1433).

Christopher Columbus (1451-1506)
Americas: Italian sailing for Spanish; possibly landed at Samana Cay, Bahamas (1492-93); also discovered Dominica, Trinidad, and other Caribbean islands before return to Spain (1493-1500); then discovered Martinique, Honduras, and explored Panama's Caribbean coast (1502-04).

Francisco Vásquez de Coronado (ca 1510-1554)
Americas: Spanish; explored the Southwest; his patrol discovered Grand Canyon (1540-42).

Hernán Cortés (1485-1547)
Central America: Spanish; conquered Mexico (1518-1521); laid siege to Tenochtitlán (1521); explored southeast to Honduras (1524-26).

Vasco da Gama (1460-1524)
Asia, Africa: Portuguese; made first recorded voyage from Europe to India (1497-99).

John Davis (ca 1550-1605)
Arctic, Americas: English; searched for Northwest Passage on three voyages; sailed into Baffin Bay from Davis Strait (1585-87).

Hernando de Soto (ca 1496-1542)
North America: Spanish; explored Southeast; discovered Mississippi River (1539-1542).

Bartholomeu Dias (ca 1450-1500)
Asia: Portuguese; first European to make confirmed passage around Africa's Cape of Good Hope, opening sea route to India (1487-88).

Martin Frobisher (ca 1535-1594)
Arctic: English; searched for Northwest Passage and discovered Frobisher Bay (1576); returned there to search for gold (1577-78).

Ibn Battutah (ca 1304-1368)
Africa, Asia: Moroccan; ranged over 75,000 miles, as far as China and Sumatra, to visit and write about Muslim world (1325-1353).

Ferdinand Magellan (ca 1480-1521)
Pacific: Portuguese sailing for Spanish; led first expedition to sail around globe (1519-1521).

Francisco de Orellana (ca 1490-1546)
South America: Spanish; first European to explore Amazon River (1541-42).

Francisco Pizarro (ca 1475-1541)
South America: Spanish; with Balboa at discovery of Pacific (1513); conquered Incas (1532-35).

John of Plano Carpini (ca 1180-1252)
Asia: Italian; first European known to visit Mongol capital of Karakorum (1245-47).

Marco Polo (1254-1324)
Asia: Italian; with father and uncle, **Niccolò** and **Maffeo Polo,** opened overland route to China from Europe (1271-1295).

Juan Ponce de León (1460-1521)
North America: Spanish; discovered and explored Florida (1513).

Giovanni da Verrazano (ca 1485-1528)
North America: Italian; explored Atlantic coast from Cape Fear, probably to Cape Breton; discovered New York Bay and Narragansett Bay (1524).

Saint Francis Xavier (1506-1552)
Asia: Spanish; missionary who traveled to India and Japan to spread Christianity (1540-1552).

Yermak Timofeyevich (?-1585)
Asia: Russian; Cossack who crossed Urals, battled Tatars, and paved way for Russian conquest of Siberia (1581-85).

The World Explored (1600-1900)

Karell Johan Andersson (1827-1867)
Africa: Swedish; explored southwestern Africa and discovered Okavango River (1851-59).

Samuel W. Baker (1821-1893)
Africa: English; explored Nile tributaries in Ethiopia (1861-62); discovered Lake Albert (1864).

Heinrich Barth (1821-1865)
Africa: German; traveled through Sahara and West Africa, gathering detailed information about interior (1850-55).

Vitus Jonassen Bering (1681-1741)
North America: Danish; sailed through Bering Strait (1728); explored Alaskan coast and discovered Aleutian Islands (1741).

Louis-Antoine de Bougainville (1729-1811)
Pacific: French; circumnavigated globe; explored Tahiti, Samoa, New Hebrides, and other islands (1766-69).

James Bruce (1730-1794)
Africa: Scottish; explored Ethiopia; located source of Blue Nile (1768-1773).

Robert O'Hara Burke (1820-1861)
Australia: Irish-born, settled in Australia; with assistant **William John Wills,** led first expedition across continent, south to north (1860-61).

Richard Francis Burton (1821-1890)
Africa: British; with John Speke, explored Somali and Lake Tanganyika regions (1854).

René-Auguste Caillié (1799-1838)
Africa: French; disguised as Arab, he was first European to reach Timbuktu and return (1827-28).

Samuel de Champlain (ca 1567-1635)
North America: French; founded Quebec Colony (1608); discovered Lake Champlain (1609), Ottawa River (1613), and Great Lakes (1615).

Hugh Clapperton (1788-1827)
Africa: Scottish; with **Dixon Denham** and **Walter Oudney,** crossed Sahara from north; Denham explored Lake Chad region (1823); Oudney died; Clapperton reached Hausa region of Nigeria (1824), returned to Africa (1825-27) where he found and crossed Niger.

James Cook (1728-1779)
Pacific: English; explored most of world's largest ocean; disproved myth of a great Southern Continent; charted New Zealand, Bering Strait, and Canada's west coast; discovered Hawaiian Islands (1768-1779).

Charles R. Darwin (1809-1882)
South America, Australasia: English; naturalist on *Beagle's* worldwide voyage (1831-36), which provided basis for his theory of evolution.

Benito de Goes (1562-1607)
Asia: Portuguese; Jesuit who went overland to China via Pamirs; confirmed that China and Cathay were same place (1602-07).

Charles Montagu Doughty (1843-1926)
Arabia: English; traveled undisguised through west and central Arabia and wrote about geography and culture (1876-78).

J.S.C. Dumont d'Urville (1790-1842)
Antarctic: French; first to Adélie Land (1840).

John Franklin (1786-1847)
Arctic: English; headed three Arctic expeditions (1818-1827). Perished with his men in Canada while seeking Northwest Passage.

Simon Fraser (1776-1862)
Canada: Canadian; explored westward from Rockies, through British Columbia to Pacific at Vancouver (1805-08).

John Charles Frémont (1813-1890)
North America: American; mapped Oregon Trail (1842); crossed Rockies to California (1845).

Henry Hudson (ca 1550-1611)
Arctic, North America: English; searched for Northwest Passage; discovered Hudson River and sailed upstream to Albany (1609); found Hudson Bay and died there after mutiny (1610-11).

Alexander von Humboldt (1769-1859)
Americas: German; naturalist who explored South America, Cuba, and Mexico; collected extensive scientific data (1799-1804).

Mary H. Kingsley (1862-1900)
Africa: English; explored Gabon, Congo, and Cameroon to study Fang and other tribes (1895).

Alexander Gordon Laing (1793-1826)
Africa: Scottish; first European to reach Timbuktu; killed as he left.

Richard Lemon Lander (1804-1834)
Africa: English; completed Clapperton's mission by finding mouth of Niger River (1830).

René-Robert Cavelier de La Salle (1643-1687)
North America: French; traveled through Mississippi Valley, claimed it for France (1682).

Meriwether Lewis (1774-1809)
North America: American; with **William Clark** led first crossing of continent to Pacific via Missouri and Columbia Rivers (1804-06).

David Livingstone (1813-1873)
Africa: Scottish; missionary and explorer of interior. Discovered Lake Ngami (1849), Zambezi River (1851), Victoria Falls (1855), and Lake Malawi (1859).

Alexander Mackenzie (1764-1820)
Canada: Scottish; charted Mackenzie River (1789); became first European to cross North America to Pacific, via Peace River (1793).

Jacques Marquette (1637-1675)
North America: French; missionary who, with **Louis Jolliet,** explored from Michigan down Mississippi River (1673).

Matthew Fontaine Maury (1806-1873)
Oceans: American; directed history's first major deep-sea survey, in Atlantic (1849).

Fridtjof Nansen (1861-1930)
Arctic: Norwegian; led first expedition across Greenland's ice cap (1888-89). Tried to drift across North Pole by ship, forced by ice to continue on foot, setting new latitude record (1895).

Mungo Park (1771-1806)
Africa: Scottish; probed West African interior (1795-96); explored Niger River to Bussa (1805-06).

Zebulon Montgomery Pike (1779-1813)
North America: American; mapped territory westward from St. Louis to Colorado (1806).

Nikolay Mikhaylovich Przhevalsky (1839-1888)
Asia: Russian; explored much of central Asia, bringing back extensive scientific data, such as route surveys, botanical collections (1870-1888).

Matteo Ricci (1552-1610)
Asia: Italian; Jesuit missionary who settled in China to spread Christianity and encourage

exchange of cultural and scientific information between East and West (1578-1610).

James Clark Ross (1800-1862)
Poles: Scottish; with his uncle, **John Ross,** located North Magnetic Pole (1831); commanded Antarctic expedition for geographical discovery (1840-43); searched Baffin Bay area for John Franklin (1848-49).

Jedediah Strong Smith (1799-1831)
North America: American; first to cross Great Basin into California (1826).

John Hanning Speke (1827-1864)
Africa: English; explored eastern Africa with Richard Burton; found primary source of White Nile at Lake Victoria (1857-59).

Henry Morton Stanley (1841-1904)
Africa: Welsh-born, settled in U.S.; commissioned by *New York Herald* to find David Livingstone in Africa (1871); circumnavigated Lake Victoria; discovered Lake Edward; descended Congo (Zaire) River (1874-77).

Abel Janszoon Tasman (1603-1659)
Pacific: Dutch; discovered Tasmania, New Zealand, and Fiji (1642-43); circumnavigated Australia without knowing it (1644).

Alfred R. Wallace (1823-1913)
South America: English; naturalist who made extensive collections in Amazonia with **Henry W. Bates** (1848-1852) and originated a theory of natural selection similar to Charles Darwin's (1858).

Samuel Wallis (1728-1795)
Pacific: English; discovered Tahiti during search for the mythical Southern Continent (1766-68).

Charles Wilkes (1798-1877)
Pacific: American; confirmed existence of Antarctica; charted Melanesian regions of Pacific (1838-1842).

Francis E. Younghusband (1863-1942)
Asia: British; crossed China from Peking to India (1886); probed Pamirs and Karakoram Range; led an army into forbidden city of Lhasa (1903-04).

To Worlds Beyond (1900-present)

Roald Amundsen (1872-1928)
Poles: Norwegian; first to sail through Northwest Passage (1903-06); first at South Pole (1911).

Roy Chapman Andrews (1884-1960)
Asia: American; led teams of specialists on five expeditions to Gobi Desert, where he uncovered dinosaur eggs and fossil evidence of Earth's largest land mammals (1922-1930).

Neil A. Armstrong (1930-)
Space: American; first to walk on Moon (1969), after first lunar landing with **Edwin E. Aldrin, Jr.,** on Apollo 11 mission with **Michael Collins.**

Robert D. Ballard (1942-)
Oceans: American; explored Mid-Atlantic Ridge (1973-74); found deep-sea life at hydrothermal vents in Pacific (1977); found *Titanic* (1985).

C. William Beebe (1877-1962)
Oceans: American; dived to record 3,028 feet in bathysphere (1934).

Frank Borman (1928-)
Space: American; commander of Apollo 8, which first orbited Moon; accompanied by **James A. Lovell, Jr.,** and **William A. Anders** (1968).

Richard E. Byrd (1888-1957)
Poles: American; first to fly over North Pole (1926); first to fly over South Pole (1929); established American base in Antarctica (1929).

Jacques-Yves Cousteau (1910-)
Oceans: French; developed Aqua-Lung with **Emile Gagnan** (1943); began worldwide ocean surveys on research ship *Calypso* (1950).

Alexandra David-Néel (1868-1969)
Asia: French; reached Lhasa by traveling in disguise as a poor Tibetan pilgrim (1923-24).

Ranulph Fiennes (1943-)
World: British; led first Pole-to-Pole circumnavigation of globe (1979-1982).

Yuri Alekseyevich Gagarin (1934-1968)
Space: Russian; first man in space (1961).

John H. Glenn, Jr. (1921-)
Space: American; first American to orbit Earth, in Mercury capsule *Friendship 7* (1962).

Sven Anders Hedin (1865-1952)
Asia: Swedish; explored and mapped central Asian highlands (1905-08).

Wally Herbert (1934-)
Arctic: British; first to cross surface of Arctic Ocean via North Pole, by dogsled (1968-69).

Robert E. Peary (1856-1920)
Arctic: American; might have reached North Pole on fourth attempt (1909).

Auguste Piccard (1884-1962)
Oceans, skies: Swiss; designed balloon and made first manned ascent into stratosphere in it (1931); dived to record 10,392 feet in bathyscaph built

with son **Jacques** (1953). Jacques dived to ocean's deepest point, Mariana Trench, 35,800 feet (1960).

Ralph Plaisted (1927-)
Arctic: American; first confirmed arrival at North Pole (1968).

Joseph F. Rock (1884-1962)
Asia: American; explored central China and unmapped borderlands of China's southwest (1922-1949).

Robert Falcon Scott (1868-1912)
Poles: English; reached South Pole one month after Amundsen (1912) and died on return trip.

Ernest H. Shackleton (1874-1922)
Antarctic: British; went farther south than anyone before him—111 miles from South Pole (1908-09).

Alan B. Shepard, Jr. (1923-)
Space: American; first American in space (1961).

Vilhjalmur Stefansson (1879-1962)
Arctic: Canadian; explored Alaskan and Canadian Arctic (1913-18).

Claudio Villas Boas (ca 1916-)
South America: Brazilian; explored southern Amazon basin with brothers **Orlando** and **Leonardo;** all studied Amazonian Indians and worked to preserve Indian cultures (1961).

About the Authors

Thomas B. Allen is a novelist, journalist, and former National Geographic book editor.

Elisabeth B. Booz lived in several Asian countries for 16 years. Her books include a novel set in India and the first comprehensive guidebook to Tibet.

Ian Cameron's name appears on many popular British books about adventure, including four published by the Royal Geographical Society.

Douglas H. Chadwick, writer and wildlife biologist, covers ecological topics on assignment from his home in Montana.

Michael Collins, pilot of the Apollo 11 command module, is an aerospace consultant and continues to write and speak about space.

James A. Cox, former National Geographic staffer, writes about many historical topics from his home in Nutley, New Jersey.

Ernest B. "Pat" Furgurson, a national columnist and chief of the Baltimore *Sun*'s Washington bureau, makes a specialty of seeking out-of-the-way datelines and offbeat Americana from Meddybemps, Maine, and West Frostproof, Florida, to Honolulu, Alaska.

Denis Hills, a British author and journalist who lived in Africa for many years, has written several books about the continent. In 1975 Ugandan president Idi Amin arrested him and sentenced him to death, sparking an international incident; the British Foreign Secretary successfully negotiated his release.

Philip Kopper, a Washington, D. C., author, journalist, and occasional scuba diver, writes about many topics, including seacoasts and history.

Loren McIntyre, writer, photographer, and seasoned expert on South America, has traveled most of the routes followed by the conquistadores.

Elizabeth L. Newhouse, National Geographic writer and book editor, grew up in Hernán Cortés's first New World conquest, Cuba.

Michael Parfit has lived for part of each season in Antarctica and written about it extensively.

Edwards Park, former National Geographic staffer, lived for years in Australia after World War II and returns there from time to time. He writes for *Smithsonian* and other publications, most often about matters historical.

Robert M. Poole, National Geographic writer and book editor, traced James Cook's routes through the Pacific from Tahiti to New Zealand, Australia, and Hawaii.

David F. Robinson, National Geographic writer and book editor, crews aboard the square-rigged *Maryland Dove* (pages 36-7), and has sailed the open ocean on the brigantine *Sheila Yeates*.

Margaret Sedeen, National Geographic writer and book editor, researches original documents to write her pieces about social history and scientific biography.

Jonathan B. Tourtellot, National Geographic writer and book editor, has followed space exploration issues for more than 25 years.

Lynn Addison Yorke, National Geographic writer and book editor, flew to 83° N for a brief rendezvous with the Steger International Polar Expedition on the frozen surface of the Arctic Ocean.

Acknowledgments

We gratefully acknowledge the individuals, groups, and institutions who gave us generous help in the preparation of this book: Richard P. Binzel, Planetary Science Institute, Tucson; Jim Brandenburg, Minneapolis; Geoffrey A. Briggs, NASA, Washington, D. C.; James A. Casada, Winthrop College, Rock Hill, SC; John Clune, Public Information Office, Australian Embassy; Michael Cooper, S. J., Sophia University, Tokyo; Bengt Danielsson, Papeete, Tahiti; J. Pieter deVries, Jet Propulsion Laboratory, Pasadena; W. Donald Duckworth, Bernice P. Bishop Museum, Honolulu; Liliana Gagliardi, Naples; James Gasperini, Steger International Polar Expedition, Stillwater, MN; Pericles B. Georges, Harvard University; Gordon D. Gibson, Escondido, CA; William H. Goetzmann, University of Texas; Carmen Gonzáles Sánchez, Madrid; Jocelyn Crane Griffin, Princeton, NJ; Gregory G. Guzman, Bradley University, Peoria; Sam Iftikhar, Library of Congress; Terry and Bezal Jesudason, High Arctic International, Resolute Bay, Canada; Robert McKerrow, Steger International Polar Expedition, Picton, New Zealand; Luis Marden, National Geographic Society; Earl J. Montoya, NASA, Washington, D. C.; Lee Motteler, Bernice P. Bishop Museum, Honolulu; Barbara Perry, National Library of Australia, Canberra; Capt. Geoffrey Pope of the *Sheila Yeates*, Excelsior, MN; Darrell A. Posey, Universidade Federal do Maranhão, São Luís, Brazil; Pierre Rouyer, Paris; Ahutiare Sanford, Office de Promotion et d'Animation Touristiques de Tahiti et ses Îles, Papeete, Tahiti; Denis Sinor, Indiana University; Yosihiko H. Sinoto, Bernice P. Bishop Museum, Honolulu; Capt. Eric Speth and the crew of the *Maryland Dove,* St. Mary's City, MD; Deborah Ward, Bernice P. Bishop Museum, Honolulu; Eric Widmer, Brown University; Diego R. Yuuki, S. J., Martyrs Museum, Nagasaki; and the National Geographic Society Library, Illustrations Library, Administrative Services, Translations Division, and Travel Office.

Illustration Credits

The following abbreviations appear in this list: (t)-top; (c)-center; (b)-bottom; (r)-right; (l)-left; BA-The Bettmann Archive; AA-BPCC Aldus Archive; GC-Granger Collection, New York; LC-Library of Congress; NGP-National Geographic Photographer; NGS-National Geographic Society Staff; NMM-National Maritime Museum, London; RGS-Royal Geographical Society.

Dust jacket and page 2: *Half Moon* model provided by John R. Phillips, Uniondale, New York; compass and hourglass provided by Bob Pryor Antiques, New York, New York; calipers provided by Philip W. Pfeifer Antiques, New York, New York; photography by Kan. Pages 6-7, Ann Bancroft. 8-9, Robert Caputo. 11(lt), Thomas Höpker, Agency Anne Hamann, Munich. 11(rt), Michael Holford. 11(rb), Victor R. Boswell, NGP. 12(t), Culver Pictures. 12-13(b), M. P. Kahl, DRK Photo. 14, Culver Pictures. 15, Michael Holford. 16-17, Kevin Fleming. 18-19, National Gallery, London. 20-21, David Hume Kennerly, Liaison Agency. 22, Michael A. Hampshire. 24, AA. 26-27, Michael A. Hampshire. 28, Gordon W. Gahan. 31(rt), GC. 32-33, George F. Mobley, NGP. 34, Werner Forman Archive, London. 35, AA. 36-37, Kenneth Garrett. 37(c), National Board of Antiquities, Helsinki. 37(rt), NMM. 38(ct), NMM. 38-39, GC. 39(r), Mansell Collection. 40-41, Adam Woolfitt. 42-43, BA. 44-45, Yva Momatiuk and John Eastcott. 45(r), R. W. Board. 46-47, LC. 48, NMM. 49, Bruce Dale, NGP. 50, AA. 53, BA. 54-55, AA. 57, LC. 58, GC. 60, GC. 62-63, GC. 65, Musée des Arts Africains et Océaniens. 66, David Hiser, Photographers Aspen. 69(c), NGS Library Rare Book Collection (J.E. Gottfried and T. DeBry, *Newe Welt und Americanishe Historien*, 1655). 69(lb), Susan Griggs Agency, London. 69(rb), Banco Central de Costa Rica. 70, GC. 71, Danny Lehman. 72, GC. 73, James Blair, NGP. 74-75, Guillermo Aldana Espinoza. 76, Muséo de America, Tor Eigeland. 77, GC. 78-79, Loren McIntyre. 80, AA. 81, Loren

Index

Illustrations and maps appear in **boldface,** picture captions in *italic,* and text references in lightface.

331

Type composition by the Typographic section of National Geographic Production Services, Pre-Press Division. Color separations by Chanticleer Co., Inc., New York, NY; Dai Nippon Printing Company Ltd, Tokyo, Japan; Graphic Color Plate Inc., Stamford, CT; The Lanman Companies, Washington, D. C.; Litho Studios Ltd, Dublin, Ireland. Printed and Bound by Kingsport Press, Kingsport, TN. Paper by Mead Paper Co., New York, NY.

Library of Congress CIP Data

Into the unknown.

Includes index.
1. Discoveries (in geography) I. National Geographic Book Service. II. National Geographic Society (U. S.)
G80.I58 1987   910'.9   87-5525
ISBN 0-87044-694-0 (alk. paper)
ISBN 0-87044-695-9 (deluxe: alk. paper)

You are invited to join the National Geographic Society or to send gift memberships to others. (Membership includes a subscription to the NATIONAL GEOGRAPHIC magazine.) For information call 800-638-4077 toll free, or write to the National Geographic Society, Washington, D. C. 20036.